This is a timely and thoughtful collection, which addresses an important gap: digital journalism in Latin America. The contributions go beyond the contemporary concerns of the Global North about fake news, misinformation and disinformation. Instead, they broaden the debate by examining case studies from Brazil, Chile, Costa Rica and the whole region, as well as by – crucially – highlighting other pressing and equally important discussions. The collection is aimed not only at those who look at Latin America: it should be read by everyone interested in digital journalism and everyone wanting to subvert the global hierarchies of knowledge that dominate academia.

César Jiménez-Martínez, JOMEC, Cardiff University, Wales

Eugenia Mitchelstein and Pablo J. Boczkowski have not only moved forward Communication Research about Latin America but also inspired authors from our region to do the same. The sparkling set of studies in this volume pays close attention to issues such as the impact of digital technologies on journalism, the opportunities for creating a more diverse media landscape, and the singularities of information sharing in polarized settings. This far-reaching, insightful, and illuminating reading demonstrates the complexities of our societies and how cases beyond Western Europe and the United States can contribute to our broader literature.

Francisco Paulo Jamil Marques, Federal University of Paraná, Brazil

Why are findings that stem from Global North contexts assumed to be universal whilst the South is treated as exotic? How can we deal with the lack of representativeness, reflexivity, decentering, and cosmopolitanism that still – problematically – characterizes our field? This volume asks these and other key questions, challenging the persistence of ethnocentrism in journalism, audiences, and media studies in general. From Chile to Mexico and from TV to WhatsApp, the issue offers a very welcome contribution to a more equitable and multi-centric intellectual field.

Dr Andrea Medrado, University of Westminster, England

Digital Journalism in Latin America

This volume showcases the vibrancy of the study of digital journalism in Latin America. It includes an inquiry into journalists' perceptions of media companies' policies regarding social media use; a survey of investigative reporters; an examination of the interaction between traditional broadcast journalists and online news teams in two television stations in Colombia; research on modes of news consumption on Facebook and WhatsApp in Costa Rica and Chile; and a study of the institutionalization of independent journalism in Brazil. The methods employed by the contributors include surveys, in-depth interviews, eye tracking, and participant observation. These texts reveal differences across and within Latin American media and their audiences. This underscores the importance of abandoning the ethnocentric perspective of most journalism scholarship, which tends to homogenize a supposedly exotic other. In a research field marked by inequality, in which the vast majority of studies, authors, and reviewers are from the Global North, where only 14% of the global population lives, the studies included in this volume illustrate how research about and from the other 86% can increase the representativeness of the scholarly endeavor. It was originally published as a special issue of the journal *Digital Journalism*.

Eugenia Mitchelstein is Associate Professor and Chair of the Social Sciences Department at the University of San Andrés in Buenos Aires, Victoria, Argentina, and Co-Director of the Center for the Study of Media and Society in Argentina (MESO). She has authored two books, one edited volume, and more than thirty journal articles.

Pablo J. Boczkowski is Hamad Bin Khalifa Al-Thani Professor in the Department of Communication Studies at Northwestern University, USA. He is the author of six books, four edited volumes, and more than sixty journal articles. His latest book (forthcoming) is *To Know Is to Compare: Studying Social Media Across Nations, Media, and Platforms* (with Mora Matassi).

Digital Journalism in Latin America

Edited by
Eugenia Mitchelstein and
Pablo J. Boczkowski

Routledge
Taylor & Francis Group
NEW YORK AND LONDON

First published 2023
by Routledge
605 Third Avenue, New York, NY 10158

and by Routledge
4 Park Square, Milton Park, Abingdon, Oxon, OX14 4RN

Routledge is an imprint of the Taylor & Francis Group, an informa business

Chapters 1–7 © 2023 Taylor & Francis

All rights reserved. No part of this book may be reprinted or reproduced or utilised in any form or by any electronic, mechanical, or other means, now known or hereafter invented, including photocopying and recording, or in any information storage or retrieval system, without permission in writing from the publishers.

Trademark notice: Product or corporate names may be trademarks or registered trademarks, and are used only for identification and explanation without intent to infringe.

British Library Cataloguing-in-Publication Data
A catalogue record for this book is available from the British Library

ISBN13: 978-1-032-44087-3 (hbk)
ISBN13: 978-1-032-44090-3 (pbk)
ISBN13: 978-1-003-37038-3 (ebk)

DOI: 10.4324/9781003370383

Typeset in Myriad Pro
by codeMantra

Publisher's Note
The publisher accepts responsibility for any inconsistencies that may have arisen during the conversion of this book from journal articles to book chapters, namely the inclusion of journal terminology.

Disclaimer
Every effort has been made to contact copyright holders for their permission to reprint material in this book. The publishers would be grateful to hear from any copyright holder who is not here acknowledged and will undertake to rectify any errors or omissions in future editions of this book.

Contents

Citation Information viii
Notes on Contributors x

1. Introduction: What a Special Issue on Latin America Teaches Us about Some Key Limitations in the Field of Digital Journalism 1
   Eugenia Mitchelstein and Pablo J. Boczkowski

2. Re-Digitizing Television News: The Relationship between TV, Online Media and Audiences 7
   Víctor García-Perdomo

3. The Personal Is the Political? What Do WhatsApp Users Share and How It Matters for News Knowledge, Polarization and Participation in Chile 26
   Sebastián Valenzuela, Ingrid Bachmann, and Matías Bargsted

4. Protecting News Companies and Their Readers: Exploring Social Media Policies in Latin American Newsrooms 47
   Summer Harlow

5. Stronger and Safer Together: Motivations for and Challenges of (Trans)National Collaboration in Investigative Reporting in Latin America 67
   Lourdes M. Cueva Chacón and Magdalena Saldaña

6. The Mechanisms of "Incidental News Consumption": An Eye Tracking Study of News Interaction on Facebook 86
   Adrián Vergara, Ignacio Siles, Ana Claudia Castro, and Alonso Chaves

7. Between Attack and Resilience: The Ongoing Institutionalization of Independent Digital Journalism in Brazil 106
   Sarah Anne Ganter and Fernando Oliveira Paulino

Index 127

Citation Information

The chapters in this book were originally published in the journal *Digital Journalism*, volume 9, issue 2 (2021). When citing this material, please use the original page numbering for each article, as follows:

Chapter 1
Introduction: What a Special Issue on Latin America Teaches Us about Some Key Limitations in the Field of Digital Journalism
Eugenia Mitchelstein and Pablo J. Boczkowski
Digital Journalism, volume 9, issue 2 (2021) pp. 130–135

Chapter 2
Re-Digitizing Television News: The Relationship between TV, Online Media and Audiences
Víctor García-Perdomo
Digital Journalism, volume 9, issue 2 (2021) pp. 136–154

Chapter 3
The Personal Is the Political? What Do WhatsApp Users Share and How It Matters for News Knowledge, Polarization and Participation in Chile
Sebastián Valenzuela, Ingrid Bachmann, and Matías Bargsted
Digital Journalism, volume 9, issue 2 (2021) pp. 155–175

Chapter 4
Protecting News Companies and Their Readers: Exploring Social Media Policies in Latin American Newsrooms
Summer Harlow
Digital Journalism, volume 9, issue 2 (2021) pp. 176–195

Chapter 5
Stronger and Safer Together: Motivations for and Challenges of (Trans)National Collaboration in Investigative Reporting in Latin America
Lourdes M. Cueva Chacón and Magdalena Saldaña
Digital Journalism, volume 9, issue 2 (2021) pp. 196–214

Chapter 6
The Mechanisms of "Incidental News Consumption": An Eye Tracking Study of News Interaction on Facebook
Adrián Vergara, Ignacio Siles, Ana Claudia Castro, and Alonso Chaves
Digital Journalism, volume 9, issue 2 (2021) pp. 215–234

Chapter 7
Between Attack and Resilience: The Ongoing Institutionalization of Independent Digital Journalism in Brazil
Sarah Anne Ganter and Fernando Oliveira Paulino
Digital Journalism, volume 9, issue 2 (2021) pp. 235–254

For any permission-related enquiries please visit:
http://www.tandfonline.com/page/help/permissions

Notes on Contributors

Ingrid Bachmann, School of Communications, Pontificia Universidad Catolica de Chile, Santiago, Chile.

Matías Bargsted, Institute of Sociology, Pontificia Universidad Catolica de Chile, Santiago, Chile.

Pablo J. Boczkowski, Department of Communication Studies, Northwestern University, Evanston, USA.

Ana Claudia Castro, School of Philology, Linguistics and Literature, Universidad de Costa Rica, San Jose, Costa Rica.

Lourdes M. Cueva Chacón, School of Journalism, University of Texas at Austin, USA; School of Journalism & Media Studies, San Diego State University, USA.

Alonso Chaves, School of Communication, Universidad de Costa Rica, San Jose, Costa Rica.

Sarah Anne Ganter, School of Communication, Simon Fraser University, Burnaby, Canada.

Víctor García-Perdomo, Journalism Department, School of Communication, Universidad de La Sabana, Bogotá, Colombia.

Summer Harlow, Jack J. Valenti School of Communication, University of Houston, USA.

Eugenia Mitchelstein, Department of Social Sciences, Universidad de San Andres, Victoria, Argentina.

Fernando Oliveira Paulino, School of Communication, Universidad de Brasilia, Brazil.

Magdalena Saldaña, School of Communications, Pontificia Universidad Catolica de Chile, Santiago, Chile; Millennium Institute for Foundational Research on Data, Santiago, Chile.

Ignacio Siles, School of Communication, Universidad de Costa Rica, San Jose, Costa Rica.

Sebastián Valenzuela, School of Communications, Research Center for Integrated Disaster Risk Management (CIGIDEN), Millennium Institute for Foundational Research on Data (IMFD), Pontificia Universidad Catolica de Chile, Santiago, Chile.

Adrián Vergara, School of Philology, Linguistics and Literature, Universidad de Costa Rica, San Jose, Costa Rica.

INTRODUCTION

What a Special Issue on Latin America Teaches Us about Some Key Limitations in the Field of Digital Journalism

Eugenia Mitchelstein and Pablo J. Boczkowski

"Solutions to the problem of knowledge are solutions to the problem of social order."

(Shapin and Shaffer 1985, 312)

This special issue showcases research on digital journalism in Latin America. As such, it serves an important mission of contextualization of knowledge in a nascent field of inquiry dominated by Global North papers, perspectives, scholars, and institutional arrangements. Yet, its very existence foregrounds the depth of the inequities between North and South that still mark the production of knowledge about digital journalism—and in journalism studies more generally. These inequities affect disproportionally the regions of the world most disadvantaged in terms of institutional resources, but by implication impoverish the field of inquiry as a whole: since all knowledge is contextual and comparative in essence, knowing less about the other implies also knowing less about the self. Thus, we take advantage of the opportunity to write this introduction to reflect on what the conditions of possibility of putting together this special issue say about dynamics of inclusion and exclusion in scholarship on digital journalism—and in communication and media studies more broadly. More concretely, we identify four problems that characterize these dynamics: lack of representativeness, lack of reflexivity, lack of decentering, and lack of cosmopolitanism. On the basis of this diagnosis about the current state of affairs, we also offer some steps towards a more scholarly robust and politically equitable domain of inquiry. We conclude this introduction by providing an overview of the papers that are featured in this special issue.

First is the problem of lack of representativeness. The countries that constitute the Global North amount in the aggregate to approximately 14% of the global population, but much more than 14% of the published scholarship, the reviewer pool, and the positions of power in the journalism studies field. In statistical terms, the Global North is pretty much an outlier. Yet, this status is never mentioned. On the contrary, the findings are typically assumed to be universal and are rarely contextualized with regards to the statistical norm. When was the last time that you read a paper on, say, the United States, Norway or Germany where the authors contextualized the findings with respect to comparable phenomena in, say, Thailand, Paraguay, and Ghana? If arguments obliterating the issue of lack of representativeness of the findings were made by an undergraduate student in a term paper for a class taught by any of the faculty readers of this journal, there would be points deducted and observations written in the margin; perhaps the reservations would be so high that the term paper would be marked with a failing grade. However, this basic, fundamental argumentative error very seldom constitutes ground for rejection of a manuscript submission. Thus, coupling the lack of representativeness with the editorial failure to keep it in check constitutes a remarkable sociopolitical achievement within a domain of inquiry built around dynamics of inclusion and exclusion that have less to do with epistemic excellence and more to do with the exercise of power that maintains the prevailing social order.

Second is the problem of lack of reflexivity. Not only there are evident majority-minority imbalances that result from these dynamics of inclusion and exclusion, but these imbalances and dynamics are further reinforced by the limited awareness about them. Yes, there are the occasional, well-intended statements noting that things should be more equitable, but they are largely decoupled from the processes that keep the machinery of knowledge production going. This is not just an ethical matter, but also—and primarily—an epistemic one. Take one of the latest topical obsessions of scholarship about digital journalism and other domains of inquiry in communication and media studies: fake news, misinformation, and disinformation. Interest in these topics spiked since 2016 and the vast majority of the scholarship shows a contemporary focus exhibiting a remarkable level of ethnocentrism and historical ignorance. The ethnocentrism is tied to the moral outrage of having domestic politics in countries of the Global North being interfered by foreign powers through various modes of information infiltration in news and social media. Yet, what this ethnocentric view conveniently ignores is a long history of similar attempts undertaken by nations in the North towards their counterparts in the South.

For instance, a particularly salient case in light of the regional focus of this special issue are the well-documented actions pursued by the United States' Central Intelligence Agency to unsuccessfully try to prevent Salvador Allende's victory in the 1970 presidential elections in Chile. As Dorfman (2016) eloquently put it, Allende won "in spite of the United States' spending millions of dollars on psychological warfare and misinformation to prevent its victory (we'd call it 'fake news' today)." This misinformation campaign—partly implemented through subsidies to the country's leading daily, *El Mercurio*—continued after Allende took office until his government "was overthrown and replaced by a vicious dictatorship that lasted nearly 17 years. Years of torture and executions and disappearances and exile" (Dorfman 2016). Ignoring these historical antecedents prevents the field from asking the kind of comparative questions that would shed light on all forms of misinformation by contrasting, for example, those undertaken through print and digital media, and those sponsored by state bureaucracies versus operators not belonging to the state apparatus.

Third is the problem of lack of decentering. It is not only that most scholarship is produced in and about a small number of countries, and also treated as universal by default instead of as a statistical outlier that expresses a peculiar set of historical circumstances. There is also the issue that whatever happens in the Global North is considered to be the norm, and whatever happens everywhere else should aspire to achieve that status if it is to have a positive connotation. The world has a normative center and a deviant—or at least un-developed—periphery; a periphery that is to be redeemed by aspiring to shed its singularities and model itself in the virtuous image of the center. Take for instance the much-touted norm of impartiality, that for decades led journalism scholars, in particular those researching media in the United States, to look down on the occupational culture of practitioners in Latin America, usually more engaged with particular positions and more entangled with the larger institutional environment. Since the beginning of the presidency of Donald Trump, and even more so since the recent wave of protests against centuries-long racial violence, those very scholars have been advocating towards abandoning the pristine perch of impartiality in favor of various forms of advocacy. However, these conversations proceed as if these very practices have not been in existence for decades in Latin America and other parts of the world. This kind of navel-gazing prevents the field from asking comparative questions between past and present, and across different national contexts that could provide heuristically superior accounts of the processes and outcomes than those produced through the currently dominant center-periphery approach. Decentering journalism studies would lead to better scholarship, and by implication, to a more equitable and multi-centric intellectual field.

Fourth is the problem of lack of cosmopolitanism. This is the flip side of the previous problem: the expectation about research on the "other" 86% is that findings will be about the local, particular, and, ultimately, exotic. Those of us who publish studies on both the Global North and the Global South are familiar with typical parochialism of reviewers and editors: while the findings of the former are assumed to be universal, those of the latter are expected to reveal something that make them distinct. But in a world without a center, neither what happens in the North should be assumed to be universal nor what transpires in the South should be expected to be exotic. Similarities and differences need to be uncovered through research, rather than become an implicit a priori of the process of inquiry. For this, we long for the days in which in addition to a special issue on digital journalism in Latin America there will be comparable dossiers about Scandinavia, North America, Continental Europe, and so on, and the guest editors will encourage the manuscript authors to reflect on what is shared and unique about their findings in relation to comparable phenomena in other regions.

Taken together, these problems of lack of representativeness, reflexivity, decentering and cosmopolitanism give an enormous advantage to scholarship on the Global North and a comparatively steeper hill to climb to research on the Global South—as if the asymmetries in resources between the two did not create enough inequalities for knowledge production already. Yet, as we have argued, the issue transcends the domain of power and politics in the academic community, and it becomes eminently epistemic: the combination of these four problems amount to a significant impoverishment of the scholarship on digital journalism—and in the journalism studies field as whole. The ethnocentrism of the Global North not only reproduces and reinforces inequalities, but also results in inferior scholarship. There are no winners in this state of affairs in terms of what we know about the world and the quality of this knowledge; on the contrary, we are all losers. Thus, to help overcome the limitations that the current mindset has generated we propose the following four steps.

First, appoint scholars in the Global South as journal editors. The recent steps undertaken by publications such as *Digital Journalism* to make the boards more representative are positive. Second, require all authors to contextualize findings with respect to other relevant national and regional settings—not only those making submissions about the Global South. Third, in relation to the previous recommendation, encourage authors to elaborate on patterns of what is shared and what is unique about the findings, rather than assume that those from the Global North are universal while results from other settings tend to be locally contingent and therefore unique. Fourth, develop editorial practices that are sensitive to, and accepting of, different genre options as well as business models that can support multi-language editions. The English-language-social-science article—the Ford Model T of scholarly communication—is a well-suited textual option for a non-representative, non-reflexive, self-centered, and parochial regime of knowledge production, and an inequitable social order often tied to it. As the field becomes more representative, reflexive, decentered, and cosmopolitan, and aspires to contribute to a more equitable social order, it is imperative to be mindful that scholars in different parts of the world write in different languages and resort to different argumentative genres. Thus, it is time for the field to switch from universal deployment of the Model T of scholarly publishing into a more pluralistic set of communication options.

This special issue includes papers that showcases vibrancy in the study of digital journalism in Latin America. It includes an inquiry into journalists' perceptions of media companies' policies regarding social media use; a survey of investigative reporters in the region; an examination of the interaction between traditional broadcast journalists and online news teams in two television stations in Colombia; and research on modes of news consumption on Facebook and WhatsApp in Costa Rica and Chile and a study of the institutionalization of independent digital journalism in Brazil. The methods employed by the authors include surveys, in-depth interviews, recordings of ocular movement on the screen, and participant observation. Moreover, these papers underscore the importance of abandoning the ethnocentric perspective which tends to homogenize a supposedly exotic other by revealing differences across and within Latin American media and their audiences. The findings from these five studies exemplify how research from the 86% can both increase the representativeness of the scholarly endeavor while contribute to deeper understanding of the processes and practices of digital journalism in Latin America and beyond.

Summer Harlow (2020) examines the perceptions of 1,094 journalists from Latin America about their policies implemented by their employers regarding social media use, and the consequences of these guidelines—and lack thereof—for their reportorial work. Her research shows that most of the respondents worked in companies with no social media policies, although the proportion of news outlets without such policies varied from 33% in Cuba to 100% in Paraguay. Those companies which had policies in place were more focused on protecting their brand, their audiences and their sources than on either keeping journalists safe or providing them with innovative tools to do their work. Harlow does not propose that "a universal social media policy should be applied in newsrooms throughout the region" given that "tenets of journalism and understandings of professionalism vary by country," but that some commonalities "could underlie social media policies across countries to make them more effective" (176–195).

The differences across countries are also evident in Cueva Chacón and Saldaña's (2020) analysis of participation in collaborative projects among 251 investigative reporters. These scholars find that, although cooperation was high, with 59% of respondents reporting having worked on such a project with colleagues from their own country, and 45% with journalists from other countries, the percentages varied by country and region. Journalists from México were the least likely to embark on a joint investigative project, and the authors propose that this relative lack of engagement is due to the extremely high levels of violence against journalists in the region. Cueva Chacón and Saldaña finish their study by arguing for a "need to analyze Latin American countries separately instead of as a whole, advocated by previous research about journalism in the continent (...) to understand the nuances and specificities of each region" (196–214).

Diversity across journalistic cultures do not cease at the country level. García-Perdomo (2020) looks into the online operations of two major Colombian TV organizations through ethnographic work and in-depth interviews. His research shows that, although the interaction between traditional media and online and social media teams was fraught at both the national broadcasting company Caracol and the local-level Citytv, the orientation towards members of the public on social media differed widely at these two outlets. While Caracol uses social listening and surveillance to capture audiences and strengthen the brand, Citytv aims at maintaining a dialogic relationship with local communities, so that they can serve as sources for local issues. This difference between a national level network and a local television station is not unique to Colombian television stations and contributes to scholarly understanding of the relationship between television, online media and the audience, by unveiling "how multiple networked actors participate in the production and distribution of news, and how their practices become intertwined with platform and other artefacts" (136–154).

The interaction of audiences with news on digital platforms, and particularly on Facebook, is the focus of the research conducted by Vergara et al. (2020). These scholars conduct an eye-tracking study of how college students and recent graduates in Costa Rica consumed news incidentally on social media. Building on a growing corpus of academic literature on incidental news consumption, they focus on the specific procedures and operations that shape user interaction with news on Facebook, rather than on self-reported data. Their research shows that less than a tenth of the content encountered by participants was news, and that the consumption of news was not triggered by the subject matter of the posts, but rather conditioned by visual stimuli: images were the visual entry point to interact with news 79% of the times. Vergara and colleagues argue that "by shaping how news surfaces and who gets to receive it, algorithms thus play a key role in the incidental exposure to news" (215–234).

However, algorithms are not the only gatekeepers of exposure to news. Social filtering also plays a role, as Valenzuela, Bachmann, and Bargsted (2019) find in their panel survey on how users in Chile share content on WhatsApp during the 2017 presidential campaign. Although respondents reported using WhatsApp to share more personal information, sharing of public affairs information increased as the campaign progressed. Moreover, sharing personal or public affairs content on WhatsApp did not vary across age, gender, educational attainment, or income. Those who used WhatsApp to share public affairs content were more likely to be knowledgeable about politics and to participate in civic activities. Despite warnings about echo chambers of digital platforms, increased use of WhatsApp for political content was not associated with increased issue position extremity. Valenzuela and co-authors propose that "from a normative perspective, it is an important finding that WhatsApp use is not linked to mass ideological polarization" (155–175). This finding suggests that the link between use of platforms and polarization, which has been mostly studied in the Global North, might be contingent on particular national cultural features, rather than an inevitable consequence of engagement with social media. Sarah Ganter and Fernando Oliveira Paulino look into Independent Digital Journalism in Brazil. By combining analysis of documents, industry data, and interviews, they find that Independent Digital Journalism is embedded within wider networks. These networks provide organizations and reporters with the opportunity to build resilience against professional, physical, and psychological attacks, and are also involved in an ongoing process of institutionalization to enhance journalists' safety. The "positive dependence" of Independent Digital Journalism in Brazil, "a situation in which dependence on various collaborators and partners exists" (p. 12), complements European and North American conceptualizations about independent journalism.

From Chile to Mexico and from television to WhatsApp, these six papers show how high-quality scholarship conducted in Latin America may illuminate contemporary phenomena in digital journalism, and communication more generally, in other regions of the world. It is our sincere hope that this special issue on Digital Journalism in Latin America sparks a multitude of other regionally specific special issues fostering comparative understanding and positional sensibility in a world in which the Global North is no longer treated as a *primus inter pares*.

Disclosure Statement

No potential conflict of interest was reported by the author(s).

ORCID

Eugenia Mitchelstein http://orcid.org/0000-0001-7355-8740
Pablo J. Boczkowski http://orcid.org/0000-0002-9446-8303

References

Cueva Chacón, L. M., and M. Saldaña. 2020. "Stronger and Safer Together: Motivations for and Challenges of (Trans) National Collaboration in Investigative Reporting in Latin America." *Digital Journalism* 9 (2): 196–214. doi:10.1080/21670811.2020.1775103.
Dorfman, A. 2016. "Now, America, You Know How Chileans Felt." *New York Times*, Accessed 28 November 2020. https://www.nytimes.com/2016/12/16/opinion/now-america-you-know-how-chileans-felt.html
García-Perdomo, V. 2020. "Re-Digitizing Television News: The Relationship between TV." *Online Media and Audiences. Digital Journalism* 9 (2): 136–154. doi:10.1080/21670811.2020.1777179.
Harlow, S. 2020. "Protecting News Companies and Their Readers: Exploring Social Media Policies in Latin American Newsrooms." *Digital Journalism* 9 (2): 176–195. doi:10.1080/21670811.2020.1738254.
Sarah Anne, G., and Fernando Oliveira P. 2020. "Between Attack and Resilience: The Ongoing Institutionalization of Independent Digital Journalism in Brazil." *Digital Journalism*. 9 (2): 235–254. doi:10.1080/21670811.2020.1755331.
Shapin, S., and S. Shaffer. 1985. *Leviathan and the Air-Pump: Hobbes, Boyle, and the Experimental Life*. Princeton: Princeton University Press.
Valenzuela, S., I. Bachmann, and M. Bargsted. 2019. "The Personal is the Political? What Do Whatsapp Users Share and How It Matters for News Knowledge, Polarization and Participation in Chile." *Digital Journalism* 9 (2): 155–175. doi:10.1080/21670811.2019.1693904.
Vergara, A., I. Siles, A. C. Castro, and A. Chaves. 2020. "The Mechanisms of "Incidental News Consumption": an Eye Tracking Study of News Interaction on Facebook." *Digital Journalism* 9 (2): 215–234. doi:10.1080/21670811.2020.1813047.

Re-Digitizing Television News: The Relationship between TV, Online Media and Audiences

Víctor García-Perdomo

ABSTRACT
This study takes a socio-technical approach, and uses ethnography, participant observation, and in-depth interviews to analyze the online operations of two major Colombian TV news organizations—Caracol TV and Citytv—and the interaction between traditional media and online news teams during a moment in which television is experiencing renewed technological pressures coming from innovative forms of online video production and distribution and unprecedented access to digital platforms such as social media that offer live social broadcasting features. Findings show that complicated organizational arrangements between traditional and online media conditioned the adoption of digital technology, the transition of television media to online settings, and the production of online content at Caracol TV and Citytv. Likewise, the relationship between online teams working for TV stations and online users mimics the traditional relationship between television professionals and TV viewers in national and local contexts.

Innovations in digital technology, audience fragmentation, and the abundance of online media and video content are now significantly impacting traditional television. Television newsrooms started their digital transition with timid efforts in the late 1990s, establishing small online news divisions to support their traditional TV programming and strengthen their presence on the Web. Partially because of bandwidth limitations, newsmaking costs, and copyrights that protected professional video production, TV channels avoided making their broadcast content openly available online, as newspapers did with their print stories to increase online readership, hoping to capture future advertising revenue (Chyi 2013). TV outlets were reluctant to share their programming for free, but they were eager to use their websites for branding and TV promotions (Gillan 2010).

At the beginning of the digital process, TV news, especially prosperous cable operations like Comcast and Time Warner in the U.S. (Pew Research Center 2013), did not experience the same level of disruption faced by other media industries, in part, thanks to networked structural limitations such as the lack of bandwidth to watch videos online or follow live transmissions. Since 2009, however, the increasing popularity of social video platforms (YouTube and Vimeo), devices (Chromecast, Apple TV), video streaming applications (Netflix, Hulu, and Amazon), and more recently, social video live broadcasting tools (Facebook Live, Instagram Live and Periscope) has exacerbated those tensions, forcing the TV industry to rapidly respond to the digital environment to find solutions to incorporate technologies, implement innovation, and counter audience fragmentation.

Native online video providers and platforms are gaining momentum and drawing users' attention away from television screens as video sharing through social media has become an increasingly prevalent form of news consumption, ironically thanks, in part, to the interaction between traditional TV and online platforms (Nielsen Insights 2015, 2018). Therefore, digital technology is having a significant but delayed impact on TV news media, fomenting similar socio-economic and professional tensions that newspapers already experienced (Lotz 2007; Sanchez 2016).

The growing importance of the online news teams at TV stations and the way they are adopting technological innovations raise questions about how the online operations of traditional TV news organizations are responding to current digital challenges such as online video abundance, technological disruptions, multi-platform content consumption, and the dismantling of traditional media business models. It is also relevant to understand how online teams are implementing digital affordances to create emerging forms of broadcasting, journalistic practices, and routines in the online media ecosystem.

To respond to these challenges, this study takes a socio-technical approach (Boczkowski 2004, 2011; Domingo 2008; Lewis and Westlund 2016) and uses ethnography to analyze the online operations of two major Colombian TV news organizations—Caracol TV and Citytv—and the interaction between traditional media and online news teams during a moment in which television is experiencing renewed technological pressures coming from innovative forms of online video production and distribution and unprecedented access to digital platforms that offer live social broadcasting features.

Theoretical Framework

The relationship between traditional media and their online initiatives appears to influence the adoption of technology, journalistic practices, content production, and interactions with the audience. This research is particularly interested in applying Boczkowski's (2004) empirical findings about U.S. newspapers' implementation of technological innovations at the beginning of the 21st century to TV news settings. In his seminal work *Digitizing the News* (2004), Boczkowski describes the efforts of print news media to establish their initial online presence, and given the disruption that television currently is experiencing, this article aims to test some of his findings in TV newsrooms.

Boczkowski (2004) found three generalizable patterns that shape newspapers' innovation processes in online endeavors. First, Boczkowski identified that the greater the effort of traditional media to organizationally integrate their print and online news work, the more newspapers' practices and norms are reproduced in the online environment. Conversely, newspapers that maintain print and online as independent media projects tend to incorporate more innovative online practices and multimedia content.

Second, Boczkowski emphasizes that newspapers' perceptions of their audiences' technological capabilities affect the adoption of technology and innovation within the organization. In fact, the more newspapers believe they are producing content for tech-savvy users, the more they integrate multimedia and other web capabilities into their platforms. On the contrary, if traditional newsrooms perceive that their users are technologically unsavvy, they tend to use more textual and still images in their content.

Third, newspapers' conceptualization of their online users—either as consumers or producers—affects the way they implement technology and present content. According to Boczkowski (2004), the more newspaper newsrooms believe their online readers are passive consumers of information, the more gatekeeping and traditional routines journalists put in place. Meanwhile, when traditional newsrooms view their online readers as potential content producers, they include features that allow interactivity and great flow of information in their editorial process. In this sense, according to Boczkowski (2004, 2011), traditional media norms and practices influence content and technology, affecting users' online experience.

TV Media's Transition to Online Spaces

The transformation of television newsmaking in the digital age has been accelerated due to the increasing relevance of video platforms, social media, and streaming tools. TV was seen as a "safe" traditional medium for a while when the Internet blossomed because the television industry did not foresee current online video capabilities or the powerful influence of platforms in the distribution and shaping of video consumption. As a consequence, media researchers have focused extensively on the relationship between newspapers and their online operations and have paid less attention to television news operations and their digital transition. Television has not received as much scholarly analysis in its transition to the digital world in comparison to newspapers largely because the print medium has been considered the backbone of democracy, and its long-anticipated (though it has not yet occurred) disappearance has been cause for alarm. Moreover, television has been blamed for eroding political life and civic engagement (Putnam 2000), imposing a cynical view of events (Bourdieu 1998), and even stoking fear among communities (Gerbner and Gross 1976).

However, recent studies have dropped that approach and instead focus on the influence of digital technology, platforms, and social media on television newsmaking. For instance, media studies have shown how some TV news organizations with profuse video archives adopted technological innovations at a fast pace to digitize video, but without fully understanding the purpose of this process (Weiss and Domingo 2010). Other broadcasters established work practices that valued multimedia journalists who could labor as "one-man bands" to produce video for both broadcasters and websites (Bock 2012, 2016). Interactivity and verification seem to be fundamental elements of TV's transition to online spaces. For instance, research has revealed how TV journalists at the BBC use fact-checking norms to implement new forms of interaction with social media users who can provide reliable breaking news information through those platforms (Belair-Gagnon 2015). Video distribution is also an essential practice for TV journalism (Braun 2015). For example, MSNBC has opened multiple online video distribution routes to meet audiences at their mobile screens, incorporating several digital technologies and intermediaries that are not typically visible inside newsrooms or for the end user (Braun 2015). More recently, in the contexts of the United States, United Kingdom, and Germany, the video legacy of broadcasters has been found to constrain the development of digital native video and shape online content according to what audiences want, and what platforms like Facebook prioritize (Kalogeropoulos and Nielsen 2018). In spite of this, researchers have noticed that TV news organizations are adopting entrepreneurial approaches to digital media and investing in new opportunities to ensure their online transition (Kalogeropoulos and Nielsen 2018).

A more critical approach to the transition of traditional media to online settings has focused on analyzing the significance of journalism as a provider of social order and cohesion. In a special Journalism Studies and Journalism Practices issue, editors Gutsche and Hess (2018) gathered research that looked closely at this transition and found important factors that are shaping media such as "the imagined and geographic boundaries of news audiences in digital spaces," and the "changing relationships to norms and conventions of journalism practice" (p. 474). The editors concluded that the way journalists "identify," "imagine," or "satisfy" the needs of their audiences in online settings can play an active role in building and repairing communities, but may also reinforce negative aspects of media, including abuse of power, influence, and social control (Gutsche & Hess, p. 475).

Media trust, legitimacy and the ability to connect with communities seem to be fundamental journalistic aims that shape the adoption of digital tools and networks in this new media ecology. For instance, Nelson (2018) has shown how non-profit and newspaper organizations are using live events and digital technologies to establish a stronger and "more conversational" relationship between news producers and their audiences. Despite this laudable intention, Nelson (2018) points out that the traditional mass audience approach to news production does not facilitate online conversation, as hordes of users usually engage in non-civic discussions that attack journalists and editors. Conversely, segmentation and small audiences allow media to build strong bonds with their readers and viewers. In this sense, intimate or offline spaces seem to be better settings for reporters, editors, and media to interact with audiences (Nelson 2018). In the same vein, Muscat (2018) found that commercial television news channels "cultivate a sense of local journalistic authority" (p. 231) by creating connections with specific communities in Sydney, Australia. "Being local" seems to be a fundamental asset of journalistic authority for broadcast television news operations because this practice not only determines newsworthiness by proximity, but also produces civic and social capital for TV news outlets. However, audiences react to this local strategy with conflicting attitudes because they perceive a disconnect between their reality and what they see on TV, and therefore suspect that this kind of coverage is an effort to surveil or exclude certain communities or groups (Muscat 2018). Similarly, Bodrunova et al. (2018) found that, despite technological advancements, mainstream media remained faithful to traditional geographic markets because they want to maintain legitimacy among their core audiences.

Additionally, the transition of traditional media to online settings has created some tension between business strategies and journalistic practices. For instance, journalists and scholars have been concerned about the fact that online enterprises increase the risk of blurring the historical wall between news and business, raising concerns about journalistic ethical norms (Coddington 2015; Singer 2003). However, as Coddington (2015) argues, more than a wall, this historical division has become a curtain in the digital era, and the erosion of this boundary is not necessarily a bad thing for journalism, as, without it, the traditional commercial interests behind media become more transparent and journalists become more aware of their professional vulnerability to the "fluctuations of market forces" (p. 79).

Digital Technology and Mainstream Media

Another consistent finding in regards to traditional dynamics of newsrooms in online settings has to do with the fact that journalists tend to *normalize* technology; that is, despite creators' initial intentions when building technological networks and platforms, journalists modify those tools to make them fit their journalistic norms, values, and practices (García-Perdomo, 2017a; Ekdale et al. 2015; Lasorsa, Seth, and Holton 2012; Singer 2005). Journalists' acceptance of innovation seems to depend on whether digital tools can be adapted to existing routines (Ekdale et al. 2015). Media scholars have found that journalists oppose technological innovations that they consider to be disruptive of journalistic autonomy or damaging to the news product (Weiss and Domingo 2010). For instance, social media platforms are designed to incentivize dialogue among users, but traditional media—including TV—are using them mainly to distribute content, access sources, and understand the reaction of their audiences (Artwick 2013; Broersma and Graham 2013; García-Perdomo 2017b; García-Perdomo et al. 2018; Hermida 2010; Vis and Court 2013). Furthermore, news organizations primarily are using their social media accounts to promote their own reporting (Malik and Pfeffer 2016), and struggle with how to encourage interaction and dialogue.

Research shows that one of the reasons traditional journalists continue to resist changes related to the presence of audiences in the media space is that they believe most content produced by the public through social media is harmful, puts news accuracy at risk, or does not meet journalistic quality standards (Ekdale et al. 2015). Despite this concern, social media has become part of journalists' daily activities (Ekdale et al. 2015), and traditional media have incorporated social platforms into their news operations (Coddington 2018; Dwyer 2010) and their news sourcing practices (Van Leuven et al. 2018). TV media are not necessarily reluctant to adopt digital technologies because they have been constantly evolving and experiencing the "challenges of embracing" new tools during disruptive times (Braun 2015, p. 12). Consequently, mainstream media journalists aim to take control of news during the editorial process, under the argument that the information produced by online users is not as journalistically worthy and has to be fact-checked and processed like raw material (Ekdale et al. 2015).

Some questions that arise after reviewing previous research findings include: How can Boczkowski's general findings about newspapers' technological innovation in online settings be applied to television news organizations? How do the diverse expectations of online audiences (e.g. local, national, tech-savvy, etc.) condition the use of technology within TV media? And, finally, does the relationship between television and online media influence the adoption of technology, journalistic practices, and content production?

Methodology

This research utilized two of the most prominent methodological tools used to collect data for qualitative studies: participant observation and in-depth interviews. Participatory observation for two months (one month per case) and semi-structured interviews with online newsroom managers, directors, editors, and reporters who handle the digital operations of two major TV news organizations in Colombia were applied. Participatory observation was conducted for one month inside Caracol TV from July 5th to August 5th, 2016, and one month of observation inside Citytv (El Tiempo Publisher House) from August 10th to September 10th, 2016. Participant observation is usually used in qualitative studies to capture social practices as they occur in the field (Schutt 2012). The qualitative approach particularly "emphasizes observation about natural behavior and artifacts" in order to capture social life in its everyday course, and from the way participants experience it (Schutt 2012, p. 282).

To complement observation, a total of 45 in-depth interviews (20 people at Caracol TV and 25 people at Citytv) were conducted for this research. In all cases, audio was recorded and stored in digital files. Personal identifying information was included in the audio at the beginning of each conversation and in notes only when the interviewees granted the right to be mentioned in the research with their full name and title. Otherwise, recordings and notes remained anonymous. Qualitative interviews are usually semi-structured conversations that seek to gather as much information as possible from participants in the field (Schutt 2012; Weiss 1994). The interviews were transcribed electronically. To conduct the analysis, the transcriptions of the interviews and the observation notes were transferred to NVivo, qualitative data analysis computer software that has been designed to examine text-base information. Initially, the theoretical framework illuminated the construction of broad themes, such as journalistic practices, adoption of technology, audiences, online-offline relationships, etc. The themes were highlighted and reviewed several times. Then, NVivo nodes were created to gather related material in one place and establish associations between themes and cases. Those associations were very helpful for analyzing the two cases and finding patterns that emerged from the data (Hammersley and Atkinson 2007), including differences and similarities between newsrooms.

Two cases were selected for this research: First, Caracol TV is the largest and most-watched national television channel in Colombia. Caracol TV belongs to the same media conglomerate that owns the operations of El Espectador newspaper, Blu Radio, and online products such as noticias.caracoltv.com, gol.caracoltv.com, and shock.co. The online video strategy of the conglomerate mainly depends on Caracol TV and

Caracol Next. Meanwhile, Citytv is a local, for-profit, private broadcaster that operates under government concession and provides information for Bogotá, the capital and most populous city in Colombia. Despite its local nature, it occupies the third place in ratings when compared to other national over-the-air TV news channels. It operates inside the headquarters of El Tiempo Publishing House, whose main product is the newspaper El Tiempo and its website www.eltiempo.com. At the beginning of its online endeavors, the publishing house considered Citytv to be the appropriate platform to distribute all video input from El Tiempo. However, El Tiempo has changed its video strategy and has relegated, to a certain extent, the Citytv website.

Findings

The most prominent finding of this investigation was that the relationship between television and online media influences the adoption of technology, journalistic practices, and content production at both Caracol TV and Citytv.

This research aimed to test Boczkowski's (2004) theoretical findings on newspapers, which postulates that the greater the effort of traditional media to integrate the news work between print and online enterprises, the more traditional media practices and norms are reproduced in the online environment. In the case of Caracol TV, observations of journalistic practices show that there was a large effort to integrate television and online media, and as a result, more television media practices and norms were reflected in the online media system. Practices and routines of Caracol TV's online professionals matched television newscasts and programing, and the traditional newscast editorial structure was reflected on Caracol TV's web pages and social media accounts. As a result, the adoption of digital technology and innovation were conditioned by the traditional needs of television news operations. Though the deployment of digital technology was very enthusiastic, it happened at a very slow pace because digital enterprises were anchored to traditional media practices. Even though Caracol TV was making a substantial effort to integrate traditional and online media, the relationship between the two media was unbalanced because online professionals were subordinate to television professionals and had to supply the traditional medium with content and technology.

Conversely, Boczkowski (2004) also postulates that news media that maintained print and online as independent projects tend to incorporate more innovative and multimedia elements in their news production. El Tiempo Publishing House does not make efforts to integrate Citytv and its online platforms, as its focus relies on the relationship and convergence between print and online operations. Moreover, the link between Citytv and online media was very lacking inside the media company. Only two frail points of interaction preserved the relationship between Citytv and online platforms. The first point of interaction was between Citytv and community managers who promoted programing in advance through social media using official accounts created on Twitter, Facebook, and Instagram. The second point of interaction was between Citytv and the video unit at El Tiempo newspaper, which clipped and uploaded five news packages from the traditional newscast to the Web every day. However, the video unit at El Tiempo worked as an independent team that mainly produced original native online content for eltiempo.com without integrating its work with Citytv. As a result of that independence from TV, there is evidence of online video and technological innovations that have emerged from the video unit of this media organization, such as news products designed exclusively for social media and long documentary formats that use digital features (e.g. animation). However, other factors in the case of Citytv seem to be more important for determining what shapes online content production and the adoption of digital technology, and, as explained below, the traditional relationship between Citytv and its audience.

Conflicting Relationships between TV and Online Media

The relationship between traditional and online media is challenging at both Caracol TV and Citytv. For instance, online journalists at Caracol TV mentioned that there is a certain level of disdain toward their work because the main focus of the news organization continues to be the traditional media business. They said that they continued to be considered a small part of the media company. Participants at Caracol TV pointed out that television is still their company's cash cow, and participants at Citytv made similar statements about print media at El Tiempo. In other words, traditional media are the main focus of these media organizations, while online operations keep struggling to find revenue and sustainability. That economic reality generates some imbalance in the distribution of resources. For instance, during my fieldwork at Caracol TV, the online news team was excited about the possibility of sending one of its digital journalists and a videographer to the Summer Olympic Games in Rio de Janeiro to produce special video news stories from Brazil, a country that was experiencing social unrest and political instability at the time. However, the decision to send an online duo to Brazil depended on whether two sponsors supported the trip by advertising in the special online section that the team had created for its coverage of the Olympics. The editorial decision was predicated on securing funding for the trip. In the end, the online team could not go to Rio de Janeiro because the marketing team did not close the deal with the sponsors. Meanwhile, the traditional Caracol TV news operation sent a large crew of reporters, cameramen, editors, and anchors to the event. This imbalance in the distribution of resources generated frustration within the online team.

As a consequence of this professional and budget imbalance, online journalists struggle on a daily basis to gain professional recognition and relevance inside media companies. Members of the online news team think that members of the traditional media team perceive them as less professional, so online news workers have to make great efforts to produce content for both online and television to be considered worthy by traditional journalistic standards. Hence, one of the main online enterprises consists of showing traditional journalists that they can produce valuable, innovative multimedia content that could air as TV news packages in their newscasts. The team members who were interviewed said it is part of the "online evangelization" to add significance to the digital work. When the online teams were asked why they invested their scarce resources in producing and airing TV packages when television had often more resources at its disposal, the online editors explained they do it to obtain journalistic respect and show the caliber of their work. In this way, online teams are able to prove they can produce high quality stories and master the TV and video crafts.

The struggle between television and online media has intensified with the decision of Caracol TV and El Tiempo Publisher House—owner of Citytv—to increase the production of its native digital content while continuing to clip a large volume of television news to reinforce their traditional brands and augment online distribution. Clipping TV news stories is already a big part of the digital culture in television settings, but the new direction of these media companies consists of producing more original online content to supply the needs of a young audience. Online leaders interviewed during my fieldwork said TV audiences are aging, and the new generations of viewers are not necessarily engaged with TV screens. In that sense, the strategy of TV news organizations consists of giving away portions of its traditional news content on the Web to reinforce their brands while capturing new online audiences with stories produced and designed exclusively for online platforms and social media.

A point of intersection that improves the relationship between TV and online teams occurs when the online teams implement tools that support or extend the TV news coverage. According to participants, any action in this direction contributes to gaining respect and acknowledgment from members of the TV team. Proof of that can be seen in the fact that most of the online teams' activities happen during the newscasts and TV broadcasting schedule because one of the fundamental goals of Caracol TV and Citytv is to reinforce their television brands on online platforms using all available technological resources. When the TV newscasts are on the air, online journalists, in conjunction with social media managers, tweet the TV news instantly as it is being presented on TV screens, reporting "live" on Twitter and Facebook what is going on during newscasts as if the act of broadcasting news on TV was, in and of itself, news. Online journalists from Caracol TV called this practice a "hot report," while professionals from Citytv referred to this activity as *twitterazo*. The "hot report," or *twitterazo*, about what is happening on the newscast has three main goals, according to participants. First, its intention is to reinforce TV news brands in the minds of young users who are on social media and follow news online, but do not necessarily watch TV. Second, it seeks to attract online users to television viewing at specific times of the day. Third, it sparks the reactions of users who are only on social media or viewers who are second screening with mobile devices while watching TV.

Similarly, social media managers at Citytv and Caracol TV utilized Facebook Live to stream headlines and promote every newscast, and they had established direct interactions with anchors and reporters in order to report the TV journalists' newsmaking process and announce breaking news. As a result of this practice, social media managers are very close to the traditional TV news operations. Because content seems to be converging on social media for distribution purposes and branding, community managers seem to be at the center of the TV news operation. In this sense, social media workers said they are able to bridge the online teams that produced content for digital platforms and the traditional television journalists who produced content for traditional media.

Relationship with the Audience: From Surveillance to Sources of Information

The relationships between digital teams working for television and online users vary in both case studies depending on the nature of local and national television outlets. While a national TV station like Caracol TV applies social listening and surveillance to understand the reaction of the audience to its content and the perception that users have about its programing and TV personalities, local Citytv considers online users to mainly be informants who can serve as sources of information for the newsmaking process.

Likewise, the main objective of the interaction between the organization and users for Caracol TV is to strengthen the brand, while the goal for Citytv is to keep local communities very close to TV journalists so users can report on local issues. In both cases, the influence of the audiences on social media is changing content, but in different stages of the newsmaking process. In the case of Caracol TV, online and TV content only change after the organization analyzes and processes the reaction of the audience towards stories. In the case of Citytv, online and TV content are nurtured during the reporting stage because users directly contribute to the newsmaking process with tips and complaints.

Caracol TV is more concerned about analyzing user input on social media and reacting to it in defense of their news professionals and brand. A good example of this tendency is that a team of social media analysts at Caracol TV works intensely to listen to users who mentioned Caracol's brands on the Web and gather information about online influencers in order to produce reports about what participants called "social media crisis" and send those comments to the top brass of the TV organization. Social media analysts are responsible for monitoring the Web, surveilling the audience, and writing assessments about users' discussions on social media about Caracol TV's brands and talent. The analysts used software with algorithms that mine and explore big data, targeting conversations that mentioned specific phrases, words, brands, and people from Caracol TV. This practice goes beyond monitoring @mentions, comments, or paying attention to notifications because it tracks individuals and groups who are talking about Caracol TV's programing and talent in their online updates and discussions even when they do not use Caracol TV's handles, replies, or hashtags. Social media analysts primarily monitor Facebook and Twitter, but also follow blogs, webpages, and other media. They generate alerts that try to anticipate crises involving brands or reporters.

Television and traditional news workers at Caracol TV have created a dependency of sorts on these social media analyses. Monthly reports from the monitoring unit are considered the eyes and ears of television on social media and the pulse with which to measure audience's sentiment toward the newscasts. Team members said TV is learning about its audience and how to approach it thanks to these reports. Paola Andrea Viva, Analyst of Digital Information at Caracol Next, revealed the reason why TV anchors and traditional journalists rely heavily on those analyses:

> They are public figures, and users talk about them or to them directly on social media. Many times, TV people approach us and tell us 'look, I've received an attack about this' or 'users are talking about this issue, please see how this conversation develops.' The relationship with TV is incredible, and we are always working on benefiting our talent.

They ask us for reports, they call us or email us asking about what's going on. (July 2016).

Monitoring and listening to the audience on social media is having a direct impact on both television and online content in that organization. Caracol TV gathers enough information to identify what content online audiences like and react to on social media. Interaction with users often does not intend to establish an open dialogue, but rather seeks to respond as a news brand to their requests, questions, and angst. Above all, monitoring allows social media experts to identify news that generates a negative reaction from the audience almost in real time. When that happens, social media analysts and managers usually warn television about coverage that digital audiences consider inappropriate or offensive. Caracol TV usually reacts quickly and pulls down controversial content from its platforms, including its broadcasting system, online pages, and social media.

Listening but not necessarily dialoguing with or incorporating the editorial input of audiences strengthens the traditional media concept of online users as consumers, affecting the way online journalists implement digital technology and present content at Caracol TV. In fact, most online journalistic activities do not intend to establish open conversations with users about public issues, but to grasp content preferences and measure sentiment and reactions of the general public in order to make content decisions that ultimately increase traffic and preserve brand reputation.

By thinking of users mainly as consumers, online professionals put in place more traditional TV journalistic routines in their projects and used digital technologies and networks as distribution channels. That dynamic transforms online news mainly in a one-way communication medium. Also, the traditional concept of audiences as consumers conditions the perception of users' technological capabilities, as Boczkowski (2004) showed with newspapers. Caracol TV believes it is producing content for technologically unsavvy online users who need support during the news consumption process, so online teams implement technologies that make it really easy for users to navigate the Web, interact on social media, distribute content, and find information.

Meanwhile, Citytv is more interested in establishing a limited collaboration with online users who utilize social media. With this practices, TV journalists can get tips from local communities on social media to improve their newsmaking process. Being close to the audience has been a traditional practice for Citytv, as that station strongly believes local communities are its main source of information. Now, the local channel is transferring those reporting practices and relationships with the audience to digital platforms like social media. As some online journalists recognized, however, citizen journalism "reaches the ceiling soon," and the input of the audience on social media and other platforms is valid until journalistic boundaries are drawn by traditional media. Therefore, the conceptualization of the audience varies notably from one media outlet to another depending on the media's traditional arrangements with their audience.

Citytv' norms and practices shaped the relationship between television reporters, online media, and audiences. Citytv began broadcasting in 1999 with the following journalistic principle: The main sources of information for Citytv reporters were citizens and local communities—not public officials or powerful elites. Thus, Citytv' model implied that reporters had to contact citizens, social groups, and community leaders firsthand to broadcast their problems, complaints, and points of view. The relationship between Citytv journalists and local communities in Bogotá led the newsroom to train communal leaders in order to obtain first-hand reports. That meant the information was structured to include the perspectives of common people and communities as primary sources of information, which were very close to their viewers. Only after reporters had presented people's version of events could they contact (mostly confront) officials in the public and private sectors in order to obtain answers from them and solve community problems. In short, journalistic norms and practices at Citytv gave priority to people and relegated the status quo.

That historical relationship has now facilitated dialogue between journalists and users through social media platforms. The proximity between the local station and local communities created a strong connection that is currently reflected on social media. Local TV reporters who rely on communities to accomplish their reporting are now using Twitter, Facebook, and WhatsApp to channel complaints from the public and gather local testimonies and complaints online. Given that one of the main journalistic goals of Citytv is to explain the news from the perspective of the Bogotá community, reporters are always looking for local information and tips that citizens on the ground can provide through social media. Darío Restrepo, Director of the Television System at Citytv, argued that the essence of reporting for local television has been transferred to the online media ecosystem:

> We already had in our DNA the vocation to consult and interact with citizens so when we began using social media—Twitter, Facebook, Instagram, all these platforms that allow us to connect with our people—what we were actually doing was the same thing that we did as part of our journalistic work on television. Only that we are doing it now on social media. For that reason, it is so easy for our reporters to develop that understanding and interaction with people on social media (August 2016).

That lasting link between television Citytv reporters and community viewers through citizen journalism has been transferred to social media. Social media users share information profusely via Twitter, Facebook, and WhatsApp with Citytv reporters and the official accounts of Citytv. This arrangement considered citizen informants to be primary sources of information in the field, but not necessarily content producers who can be part of the newsmaking process. In this sense, social media users contribute only to the newsgathering process as primary sources of information, reporting on issues in their communities (e.g. rampant robberies, lack of public transportation) so Citytv reporters could go to neighborhoods, corroborate the information, and produce a story. Usually, social media user participation does not go further than that because the content that they produced and shared on social media is considered low quality and legally risky.

Even that limited interaction has proved to be relevant for Citytv, as user participation on social media is higher at Citytv than at any other news outlet at El Tiempo Publishing House. For instance, participants interviewed recalled that, at the beginning of August 2016, social media managers found numerous complaints on social networks about criminal groups in Bogotá whose modus operandi was to steal objects from cars by breaking windows with bricks at red traffic lights. Perla Toro, former editor in chief of social media at El Tiempo, remembered that her team asked users to report via Facebook whether they had been victims of this kind of robbery and in what part of the city it happened in order to design a map of the crimes. The social media team posted these two questions on the Facebook pages of El Tiempo (2.8 million followers) and Citytv (750,000 followers). Most interactions and complaints came from Citytv, despite the fact that El Tiempo had more followers. Thanks to tips provided by Citytv users, El Tiempo Publishing House could design an interactive map reporting similar criminal incidents in Bogotá. Toro said that the good reaction from users happened because Citytv is closer to communities:

> City News has been on the streets in constant conversation with people. To reach this level of interaction with users, one has to move with coherence between different platforms. So, when City asks a question, people know that the question is important because that media outlet is going to take their complaints and inputs seriously. (August 2016).

In summary, there is a strong relationship between Citytv reporters and users on social media platforms, but that interaction has its limits when it comes to the newsmaking process, as citizens are solely considered local informants and primary sources of information.

Discussion

This ethnographic study of the transition of television to the digital ecosystem examines how news TV channels relate to their online media counterpart and how that relationship affects the adoption of technology. It also shows how long-established arrangements between traditional media and audiences condition the presence of television in online environments, and how users' interactions on social media exercise some power over the newsmaking process. This study makes an important contribution to the TV news media literature, as little research explores the intersection between television, online, social media, and audiences in the Latin American context, which tends to be underrepresented in global academic discussions. This study compared differences and similarities between two case studies—Caracol TV and Citytv—with divergent organizational goals, practices, and audience reach. Thus, this research situates our understanding of the Colombian television mediascape during a time of online video disruption and abundance.

As previous research has shown in other contexts and media organizations (Boczkowski 2011; Paterson and Domingo 2008; Domingo and Paterson 2011; Anderson 2013; Braun 2015), this study found that the relationship between traditional and online media remained difficult during this period of increasing disruption because the structures of these two different types of media followed distinct logics and paces. Despite examples of some successful global media that have put digital first or at the center of the news operation (e.g. The New York Times), online teams at Colombian TV stations continue to struggle to make their professional work relevant in the eyes of traditional TV news organizations and journalists.

In this sense, finding online sustainability and mastering video storytelling seem to be fundamental for the future of online teams in their struggle to obtain professional recognition at Colombian TV news organizations. Particularly, the lack of a clear business model that provides economic sustainability to online endeavors creates professional and economic imbalances that spread skepticism among TV journalists towards the relevance of digital teams. As long as the traditional medium continues to be the main moneymaker for these news companies and there is no clear path towards online economic revenue, TV channels will continue to rely on the power of conventional news production, despite all the troubles faced by the existing TV business model.

To counter this lack of financial clarity, online teams present themselves as the group that bridge the gap between television and young audiences in the digital media ecosystem. In this way, online teams position themselves as a necessary bridge between the old and new media systems. Also, in an effort to emphasize their relevance, online teams aim to master online video production and social media community management. Both practices—which are still in uncharted waters—seem to be key for modifying TV journalism as young audiences continue to consume and interact more and more with multimedia content through social platforms and mobile devices, prompting TV to remain relevant and transition to the new media ecosystem. The creation of small online teams of video producers who generate innovation through new formats aims to open paths that shed light on the future of the TV industry. Although the future of television in online settings is still unclear, channels cautiously invest in people and technology to produce innovative content (mainly video) for online platforms while they continue clipping traditional TV stories to reinforce their digital presence and get younger users' attention without abandoning their core business. Establishing linkages across TV and the online environment, however, requires a more aggressive editorial strategy from Colombian TV stations, given the rapid decrease in traditional viewers. Nevertheless, the uncertainty of the new environment forces TV channels to be particularly cautious with their online endeavors.

Another important conclusion of this research—which partially confirms, in TV settings, Boczkowski's (2004) theoretical findings about newspapers—is that the greater the effort of TV outlets to integrate their traditional business with online media, the more traditional media practices and norms were reproduced in the digital environment. That interaction between TV and online media conditions the use and implementation of digital technology, as online platforms are considered valuable mainly when they support TV. Practices such as reporting "live" everything that happened during the newscasts on social media revealed a tendency to favor TV's needs using digital technological resources that were available, a practice that is in line with traditional media's proclivity to normalize technology according to their norms (García-Perdomo 2017a; Ekdale et al. 2015; Lasorsa, Seth, and Holton 2012; Singer 2005). When television is at the center of the company's operation, most online activities revolve around newscasts and other television programing, including extensive clipping of TV news stories and editorial dependency. Also, this research found some evidence of video innovation and disruption when the integration of TV and online was weak, although, in this case, other factors were more relevant.

Findings from this research add to that theoretical framework by showing how the traditional arrangement between Colombian TV news organizations and their audiences strongly conditions the relationship between online media and users in the digital ecosystem, as well as the adoption of technology. These results show how TV channels' long-established conceptualization of their audiences still plays a significant role in the digital realm, as that traditional "image" of the audience is transferred to online settings, shaping the way TV produces information and interacts on the Web. This particular finding is much in line with Gutsche and Hess (2018)'s conclusion that the way traditional journalists imagine and establish the geographical boundaries of news audiences in digital spaces may play an active role in their interaction with communities and the production of content, helping media to either restore public cohesion or even monitor users. Despite all the technological advancements, as Bodrunova et al. (2018) argues, mainstream media continue to serve their traditional geographic markets to maintain legitimacy among their main TV audiences. Nevertheless, when TV media and journalists try to exercise that legitimacy in digital spaces, they realize that they need to establish a more conversational relationship with online audiences. Additionally, as Nelson (2018) found, television outlets are realizing that mass national audiences like that of Caracol TV do not facilitate online conversation, while a more local and segmented approach of news production like Citytv allows stations to build stronger bonds with their viewers. Being local for television, as Muscat (2018) argues, is a key aspect that enhances journalistic authority by providing civic and social capital to broadcasting in social media spaces.

Moreover, this study adds to the TV news literature by examining the differences between national and local television in regards to their online audience. While a national station like Caracol TV with a large audience is more interested in monitoring its users on social media to understand viewers' needs and defend its TV brand, local television tends to be closer to smaller communities, and it sees users as sources of information. This finding reveals that Caracol TV was constantly concerned about online audiences' perceptions regarding its brand and newsmaking process. National television in Colombia keeps its distance from users, reinforcing the TV journalism boundary between professional and amateur content. Meanwhile, this research revealed that the historical closeness of local television with local communities plays a significant role for these media outlets on digital platforms and social media. In fact, local TV media like Citytv seems to more easily incorporate user input in news making processes. That participation is still very limited in the Colombian context, and it mainly consists of story leads. In other words, Citytv, like Caracol TV, maintains a certain distance from its online audience likely in an effort to preserve authority and editorial independence.

This study contributes to television and online scholarship when it evidences the impact that users' interaction through social media is having on content produced by TV news media. In fact, monitoring the online audience (Caracol TV) or using the audience as sources of information (Citytv) is transforming the way television reports both off and online. This research shows how some controversial TV stories are actually taken out of regular news programing when users express a negative reaction towards it on social media. Meanwhile, TV channels are creating online video and multimedia content to supply the needs of young audiences who are not necessarily attached to TV screens. The relevance of the audience in the production of video and TV deserves future investigation because those active, often mobilized and almost always unrepresentative users may not always be beneficial to the editorial process or even to democracy given the technological designs of social media and discussions taking place on digital platforms.

Also, findings have some implications for the theory and practice of digital journalism. The dependency of online teams working for TV stations on social media platforms to produce and distribute information not only compromises innovation, audience reach and revenue in online settings but also produces what Ekström and Westlund (2019) have called the "dislocation of news journalism"; that is, "shifting power dependencies between news media and platform companies" (p. 259). This shift in power, in which TV news seems to depend heavily on social media to achieve its editorial goals and reach its audience, means less control and less journalistic epistemic knowledge for news producers as newsmaking becomes disconnected from the main principle and practices of traditional TV news production (Ekström and Westlund 2019, p. 264). The current research shows how—in the interaction between TV and online teams—news work around social media and other non-proprietary platforms has become one of the main practices for journalists in the new media ecosystem, transforming TV news and video production, norms and standards in unsuspected ways.

The socio-technical approach of this study helps to shed light not only on the particular cases of Caracol and CityTv, but also on the relationship between TV, online media and the audience. The combination of technology studies and the sociology of news helps researchers to unveil how multiple networked actors participate in the production and distribution of news, and how their practices become intertwined with platform and other artefacts. Socio-technical studies allow scholars to holistically see how the hybridity of old and new media, together with the "interpretation and validation of the audience" through digital networks (Ekström and Westlund 2019), is disrupting the distribution, production and consumption of traditional TV news. Similarly, adding a sociotechnical perspective to journalism studies helps reveal the influence that some platforms and digital networks exercise over TV journalism and its future. Zelizer (2019) convincingly argues that, "Technology does not become, replace or stand for journalism" (p. 344), but the power and mediation of platforms on news production and distribution shows, as Lewis and Westlund (2015) have argued, that journalism is becoming more and more interconnected with technology (e.g. social media) in ways that are difficult to analyse at least researchers take a closer look inside news organizations to capture the mutual shaping between professionals, tools and audiences. Finally, it is important to recognize that this study is limited in that it only analyzes two case studies in the Colombian context that cannot be generalized to other news organizations or countries in the region. Still, this study is valuable in that it extends the literature on television newsmaking and its challenging transformations in the digital age.

Acknowledgements

The author would like to thank Drs. Stephen Reese, Iris Chyi, Sharon Strover, Rosental Alves and Gina Chen, professors of the Journalism School at the University of Texas at Austin, for their advice and guidance through the process of refining this research. Also, many thanks to my proofreading editor, Andy East.

Disclosure statement

No potential conflict of interest was reported by the author(s).

Funding

This research was supported by the Jesse H. Jones Fellowship 2016-2017 from the Moody Communication Department at the University of Texas at Austin, and by Fulbright Colombia.

ORCID

Víctor García-Perdomo (iD) http://orcid.org/0000-0002-7187-1618

References

Anderson, C. W. 2013. *Rebuilding the News. Metropolitan Journalism in the Digital Age.* Philadelphia, PA: Temple University Press.
Artwick, C. G. 2013. "Reporters on Twitter." *Digital Journalism* 1 (2): 212–228.
Belair-Gagnon, V. 2015. *Social Media at BBC News. The Re-Making of Crisis Reporting.* New York, NY: Routledge.
Bock, M. A. 2012. *Video Journalism: Beyond the One-Man Band.* New York, NY: Peter Lang.
Bock, M. A. 2016. "Showing versus Telling: Comparing Online Video from Newspaper and Television Websites." *Journalism: Theory, Practice & Criticism* 17 (4): 493–510.
Boczkowski, P. 2004. *Digitazing the News. Innovation in Online Newspapers.* Cambridge, Mass: MIT Press.
Boczkowski, P. 2011. "Future Avenues for Research on Online News Production." In *Making Online News: Newsroom Ethnographies in the Second Decade of Internet Journalism*, edited by D. Domingo and C. Paterson, Vol. 2, 161–166. New York, NY: Peter Lang.
Bodrunova, S., A. Litivnenko, A. S. Smolyarova, I. S. Blekanov, and A. I. Maksimov. 2018. "Please Follow Us: Media Roles in Twitter Discussions in the USA, Germany, France and Russia." *Journalism Practice* 12 (2): 177–203.
Bourdieu, P. 1998. *On Television.* New York, NY: New Press.
Braun, J. 2015. *This Program is Brought to You by… Distributing Television News Online.* New Haven & London: Yale University Press.
Broersma, M., and T. Graham. 2013. "Twitter as a News Source." *Journalism Practice* 7 (4): 446–464.
Chyi, H. I. 2013. *Trial and Error: U.S. Newspapers' Digital Struggles toward Inferiority.* Pamplona, España: Servicio de Publicaciones Universidad de Navarra.
Coddington, M. 2015. "The Wall Becomes a Curtain: Revisiting Journalism's News–Business Boundary." In *Boundaries of Journalism*, edited by M. Carlson and S. Lewis, 67–82. New York, NY: Routledge.
Coddington, M. 2018. "Seeing Through the User's Eyes: The Role of Journalists' Audience Perceptions in Their Use of Technology." *Electronic News* 12 (4): 235–50. doi: 10.1177/1931243118767730.
Domingo, D. 2008. "Inventing Online Journalism: A Constructivist Approach to the Development of Online News." In *Making Online News: The Ethnography of New Media Production*, edited by D. Paterson and C. Domingo, 15–27. New York, NY: Peter Lang.

Domingo, D., and C. Paterson. 2011. *Making Online News: Newsroom Ethnographies in the Second Decade of Internet Journalism*, Vol. 2. New York, NY: Peter Lang.

Dwyer, T. 2010. *Media Convergence*. New York, NY: Open University Press.

Ekdale, B., J. Singer, M. Tully, and S. Harmsen. 2015. "Making Change: Diffusion of Technological, Relational, and Cultural Innovation in the Newsroom." *Journalism & Mass Communication Quarterly* 92 (4): 938–958.

Ekström, M., and O. Westlund. 2019. "The Dislocation of News Journalism: A Conceptual Framework for the Study of Epistemologies of Digital Journalism." *Media and Communication* 7 (1): 259–270.

García-Perdomo, V. 2017a. "Colombian Journalists on Twitter: Opinions, Gatekeeping, and Transparency in Political Coverage." *International Journal of Communication* 11: 1574–1596.

García-Perdomo, V. 2017b. "Diseminando Ando. La Obsesión de los Canales de TV por Distribuir Noticias en Twitter: El Caso de CNN en Español, Univision Noticias, Caracol Noticias y CityTV." [Obsessed with Disseminating News: Analysis of Four TV News Channels on Twitter: The case of CNNE, Univision News, Caracol News, and CityTv]. In *Titulares, Hashtags y Videojuegos*, edited by P. Boczkowski and E. Mitchelstein. Buenos Aires: Manantial.

García-Perdomo, V., R. Salaverría, D. K. Kilgo, and S. Harlow. (2018). "To Share or Not to Share." *Journalism Studies* 19 (8): 1180–1201. doi: 10.1080/1461670X.2016.1265896.

Gerbner, G., and L. Gross. 1976. "Living with Television: The Violence Profile." *Journal of Communication* 26 (2): 172–196.

Gillan, J. 2010. *Television and New Media: Must-Click*. New York, NY: Routledge.

Gutsche, R. E., and K. Hess. 2018. "Contesting Communities: The Problem of Journalism and Social Order." *Journalism Studies* 19 (4): 473–482.

Hammersley, M., and P. Atkinson. 2007. *Ethnography: Principles in Practices*. 3rd ed. London, UK, and New York, NY: Routledge.

Hermida, A. 2010. "Twittering the News." *Journalism Practice* 4 (3): 297–308.

Kalogeropoulos, A., and R. K. Nielsen. 2018. "Investing in Online Video News: A Cross-National Analysis of News Organizations 'Enterprising Approach to Digital Media." *Journalism Studies* 19 (15): 2207–2224.

Lasorsa, D., L. Seth, and A. E. Holton. 2012. "Normalizing Twitter." *Journalism Studies* 13 (1): 19–36.

Lewis, S. C., and O. Westlund. 2015. "Actors, Actants, Audiences, and Activities in Cross-Nedia News Work." *Digital Journalism* 3 (1): 19–37.

Lewis, S. C., and O. Westlund. 2016. "Mapping the Human–Machine Divide in Journalism.." In *The SAGE Handbook of Digital Journalism*, edited by T. Witschge, C. W. Anderson, D. Domingo and A. Hermida, 341–353. London, UK: Sage.

Lotz, A. 2007. *The Television Will Be Revolutionized*. New York, NY: New York University Press.

Malik, M. M., and J. Pfeffer. 2016. "A Macroscopic Analysis of News Content in Twitter." *Digital Journalism* 4 (8): 955–979.

Muscat, T. 2018. "Nurturing Authority: Reassessing the Social Role of Local Television News." *Journalism Practice* 12 (2): 220–235.

Nelson, J. L. 2018. "The Growing Appeal of the Niche News Audience." *Journalism Practice* 12 (2): 204–219.

Nielsen Insights. 2015. Screen wars: The battle for eye space in a TV-everywhere world. The Nielsen Global Survey. https://www.nielsen.com/us/en/insights/report/2015/screen-wars-the-battle-for-eye-space-in-a-tv-everywhere-world/

Nielsen Insights. 2018. Nielsen total audience report. The Nielsen Global Survey. https://www.nielsen.com/wp-content/uploads/sites/3/2019/04/q3-2018-total-audience-report.pdf

Paterson, C., and D. Domingo. 2008. *Making Online News: The Ethnography of New Media Production*. New York, NY: Peter Lang.

Pew Research Center. 2013. How Americans get TV news at home. https://www.journalism.org/2013/10/11/how-americans-get-tv-news-at-home/

Putnam, R. 2000. *Bowling Alone: The Collapse and Revival of American Community*. New York, NY: Simon and Schuster.

Sanchez, G. R. 2016. "Distributed Content Creates Challenges and Forces Newsrooms to Adapt." editors Tell ISOJ Audience. International Symposium of Online Journalism. https://online.journalism.utexas.edu/detail.php?story=501&year=2016.

Schutt, R. 2012. *Investigating the Social World: The Process and Practices of Research*. Thousand Oaks, CA: Sage Publications.

Singer, J. B. 2003. "Who Are These Guys? The Online Challenge to the Notion of Journalistic Professionalism." *Journalism: Theory, Practice & Criticism* 4 (2): 139–163.

Singer, J. B. 2005. "The Political J-Blogger: 'Normalizing' a New Media Form to Fit Old Norms and Practices." *Journalism: Theory, Practice & Criticism* 6 (2): 173–198.

Van Leuven, S., S. Kruikemeier, S. Lecheler and L. Harmans. 2018. "Online And Newsworthy." *Digital Journalism* 6 (7): 798–806.

Vis, F., and R. Court. 2013. "Twitter as a Reporting Tool for Journalists: Tweeting the 2011 UK Riots." *Digital Journalism* 1 (1): 27–47.

Weiss, R. S. 1994. *Learning from Strangers: The Art and Method of Qualitative Interview Studies*. New York, NY: The Free Press.

Weiss, A. S., and D. Domingo. 2010. "Innovation Processes in Online Newsrooms as Actor-Networks and Communities of Practice." *New Media & Society* 12 (7): 1156–1171.

Zelizer, B. 2019. "Why Journalism is about More than Digital Technology." *Digital Journalism* 7 (3): 343–350.

The Personal Is the Political? What Do WhatsApp Users Share and How It Matters for News Knowledge, Polarization and Participation in Chile

Sebastián Valenzuela [ID], Ingrid Bachmann [ID], and Matías Bargsted [ID]

ABSTRACT
Mobile instant messaging services (MIMs) are important gateways to news exposure and political conversations. Nevertheless, we still know little about the specific uses and consequences of using messaging apps on other aspects of democratic citizenship. This is especially true in Latin American countries, where usage of MIMs is more widespread than any other social media. Using a two-wave panel survey conducted in the context of the 2017 Chilean elections, this study examines the information sharing practices of WhatsApp users, comparing the antecedents and effects of the spread of personal (e.g., family, work) and public affairs content (e.g., news, political messages). Findings show that sharing on WhatsApp was rather equal across social groups, and that it could exert a significant influence on learning about politics and issues in the news as well as on protesting and other political behaviors. We discuss possible explanations, limitations, and significance of these results for digital journalism research and practice.

"An age of perpetual contact, at least in terms of potential, is dawning," noted Katz and Aakhus (2002, 2) in reference to the mobile communication revolution at the turn of the 21st century. Two decades later, the potential has become a reality. Two thirds of the population worldwide own a mobile phone, most of them with internet access (Statista 2019). Currently, mobiles rival computers and television as the major gateway for accessing media content, including news (Correa, Pavez, and Contreras 2018; Newman et al. 2018).

As could be expected, in the past few years digital journalism scholars have turned their attention to studying how people use mobiles for getting news and with what effect, especially in terms of knowledge and political participation (Baek and Kim 2016; Campbell and Kwak 2014; Kim, Chen and Wang 2016; Yamamoto, Kushin, and Dalisay

2018). Due to their popularity, mobile instant messaging services (MIMs) such as WhatsApp, Messenger, and WeChat have become a particular area of focus. While the main purpose of MIMs is to facilitate "intimate and controlled conversations within small groups while on the go" (Valeriani and Vaccari 2018, 1726), research has found that using these apps contributes to news exposure and political conversations in distinct ways than other social applications and platforms (Boczkowski, Matassi, and Mitchelstein 2018; Karapanos, Teixeira, and Gouveia 2016).

Missing in the literature, though, are systematic, longitudinal studies of the antecedents and political consequences of MIMs—that is, studies that could be more comparable to the well-established research on the influence of traditional news use on democratic citizenship (e.g., Hollander 2007; Rains et al. 2018). Furthermore, and despite the popularity of MIMs in Latin America, scant empirical research exists on how users in this region are using the app to communicate and become informed. What little research exists suggests that MIMs play a central role in the contemporary media landscape (Dodds, 2019; Matassi, Boczkowski, and Mitchelstein 2019), and have helped in the diffusion of both factual and false content (Tardáguila 2019; also Bradshaw and Howard 2019).

To this end, the current article explores the types of content people in Chile share on WhatsApp, with a special focus on how news and political messages intertwine with personal and social affairs, and tests whether these exchanges can influence users' knowledge, attitudes and behaviors during an election campaign. Like in other Latin American countries, in Chile WhatsApp is the dominant mobile platform for both relational and informational purposes. Because the study relies on an original two-wave panel survey of a representative sample of adults, it is especially adequate for exploring the temporal dynamics of MIMs use and individual-level political outcomes.

Our results suggest a rather complex set of relationships. While WhatsApp access is almost universal and is used mostly for personal rather than public affairs, it does not have a uniform effect on democratic citizenship. Specifically, we found statistically significant relationships between WhatsApp use, political knowledge and participation, the strength of which far supersede the contribution of traditional media and social network sites. This was not the case with issue position extremity and intention to vote, which we found to be rather independent of WhatsApp usage. The study, thus, confirms the importance of studying MIMs as a gateway for digital news.

The article is organized as follows. We first review the literature on public and private spheres as applicable to WhatsApp use. Then we summarize what we know about media use and political involvement, and discuss the similarities and differences of traditional, online, and mobile media. After listing the research questions, we describe the Chilean context and detail our research methods. Results are organized into two sections, one related to the antecedents of WhatsApp usage, the other on the consequences of using this mobile app for political outcomes. We close with a discussion on likely explanations for our findings and directions for future study.

The Personal/Private and the Political/Public Domains

Traditionally, people's lives have been deemed as occupying two domains of action— the personal, contained by the family, home and private aspects of life, and the political, the realm of power, policy, and authority. For some authors, the latter is the substance of the so-called public sphere, a forum of discursive interaction that eventually guides the affairs of the state. While Habermas' (1991 [1962]) influential conceptualization of a deliberative public sphere did not equate the public with the political, the concepts are closely tied and the seeming parallel has long permeated scholarly understandings of these terms (Dahlberg 2005; Hickerson and Gastil 2008). Further, the dualism between what is personal and what is political is quite pervasive and has been linked to other paired constructs, such as subjective/objective and individual/social (Gal 2002).

Admittedly, the distinction between the personal and political domains is somewhat artificial. Conceptually speaking neither the personal nor the political are as clear-cut as suggested by the term "divide." Indeed, the boundaries of either space are not clearly defined, as they tend to overlap and are interrelated (Chinkin 1999; Pateman 1989). Indeed, in the 1960s and 1970s, feminists in the US made popular the dictum that "the personal is political" to draw attention to the fact that even personal choices —such as those regarding women's everyday lives— are intrinsically political (Bachmann, Loke, and Harp 2018).

Even if not accurate, the dichotomy has proven to be a useful framework through which human life is organized (Gal 2002). Much of people's actions are understood, negotiated, analyzed and interpreted within a distinction of the personal and the political, including legal, cultural and practical matters (Chinkin 1999; Dahlberg 2005). Thus, theoretically and empirically, an individual's private and intimate affairs are still considered separate, albeit interdependent, of the public matters that concern politics and policy.

Media use is not an exception and there is ample evidence that people use media for different purposes and motivations, sometimes in response to personal, private or social needs to satisfy, and others to enable citizens to participate in public affairs (Wyatt, Katz, and Kim 2000).

Media and Political Involvement

Past research has shown a positive correlation between consuming news about public affairs and becoming socialized into politics (Rojas, Shah, and Friedland 2011; Valenzuela, Bachmann, and Aguilar 2019). News media provide individuals not only with factual information or knowledge to be involved in politics and community affairs, but it is also connected to other important resources determining people's participation in the political and civic spheres, such as interest, trust, efficacy, discussion, and mobilization. News use—or lack of thereof—influences participation and all kinds of political outcomes.

With the growth of the internet in terms of content and users, much attention has been paid to the role of digital media in people's engagement in public life. Scholars have focused in recent years on social media in particular, given their almost ubiquitous presence in people's lives. Research on this area has focused on social media use, its antecedents and effects. A bulk of this literature has paid attention to social media's impact on politics, with most studies finding positive effects of social media use on civic engagement (Boulianne 2015; 2019), trust (Ceron 2015), and political participation, both online and offline (Skoric et al. 2016). Research on social media's impact on knowledge offers mixed evidence, with findings showing both positive and negative impact, as well as little or no effects whatsoever (Dimitrova et al. 2014).

Along these lines, empirical and anecdotal evidence stresses that news consumption on social media is not necessarily intentional, with people stumbling upon news regularly when scrolling through posts on a social media feed for other purposes (Anspach 2017; Boczkowski, Mitchelstein and Matassi 2018; Fletcher and Nielsen 2018). Müller and colleagues (2016) suggested that incidental news exposure could induce both the illusion of knowledge among users and that news-seeking behaviors are not needed (Gil de Zúñiga and Diehl 2019).

Scholars have also stressed that social media facilitate the expression of multiple opinions, a good thing in a deliberative democracy approach, but which also contributes to political polarization by increasing the salience of partisan, biased or extreme information, and exacerbating selective exposure to it (Anspach 2017; Lee, Shin, and Hong 2018). The evidence on this regard is mixed as well and seems to be contingent on media platform and specific uses. Thus, examining social media as if they were a homogenous outlet is not necessarily an appropriate approach. Indeed, it is important to analyze the difference between and within various digital communication technologies, since each one entails diverse affordances, and a more nuanced understanding of political engagement in the current media environment should take that into consideration (Bode 2017; Valeriani and Vaccari 2018).

One area ripe for further research has to do with mobile instant messaging services, which are increasingly important in people's daily life (Newman 2018; Valeriani and Vaccari 2018; Yamamoto, Kushin, and Dalisay 2018). MIMs allow users for "instantaneous, synchronous exchange of small, seemingly inconsequential interactions [...] and information" (Goh et al. 2017, 2) and are increasingly popular for sharing, discussing and commenting on news (Newman 2018). Indeed, if digital media have facilitated sharing news—anyone can post links or publish content—mobile messaging apps allow people to access and discuss news and public affairs anywhere, anytime and on the go (Boczkowski, Mitchelstein and Matassi 2018). On them, users "create and maintain personal networks as they move through daily activities" (Baek and Kim 2016, 177). As MIMs are mobile native applications, they can easily blend informational (smartphone use with relational (i.e., social) mobile use [Lee et al. 2014]).

With 1.5 billion users worldwide as of 2019, WhatsApp is the single most popular MIM (Facebook Messenger, another popular messaging app, has 1.3 billion users). It serves as an "increasingly important means to receive, share, and discuss news with friends, colleagues, and family in a more private setting" (Swart, Peters, and Broersma 2017, 1351). Because news, discussion and participation are part of a "virtuous circle" (Norris, 2000) in democratic societies, examining the role WhatsApp plays in terms of political engagement is a relevant scholarly task.

Sharing Personal and Public Affairs on WhatsApp

Compared to other social media platforms such as Facebook or Twitter, WhatsApp serves as a more intimate setting, with users interacting privately with individual contacts or clearly defined groups (Newman 2018; Valeriani and Vaccari 2018; Yamamoto,

Kushin, and Dalisay 2018). For that reason, it enables perpetual contact in relatively more intimate, closed, and controlled environments. In fact, scholarship has described WhatsApp as enabling a more conversational, multimodal media than other texting apps (Dodds 2019; Matassi et al. 2019). Since it identifies other users based on the mobile number—something one shares more often among closed network ties—it is "tailor-made for maintaining strong tie and social support networks" (Chan 2018, 260). To the degree that WhatsApp use is largely related to communication with family, friends and colleagues, its affordances have specific consequences for both the personal and political realms.

WhatsApp use has been related to social support and well-being (Chan 2018). It favors political expression and conversation not only among politically active individuals, but also of people who are less confident in posting their political views on public online networks and would rather discuss in more controlled, less confrontational settings (Newman et al. 2018; Valeriani and Vaccari 2018; Vaccari and Valeriani 2018).

WhatsApp users also report a heightened sense of presence and togetherness when communicating through the application, with near-real-time sharing and synchronous exchanges (Karapanos, Teixeira, and Gouveia 2016; Matassi et al. 2019). Its multimodality also opens the door for news consumption and sharing of political information, including links to media content and personal commentaries about public affairs (Yamamoto, Kushin, and Dalisay 2018), as well as images, audios, videos, and emojis. While there is some evidence of a negative correlation between WhatsApp use and incidental exposure to news (Mitchelstein and Boczkowski 2018), some research suggests that selective content curation on WhatsApp is one feature highly valued by users, who consider that news sharing on the app is not haphazard or casual, but a strategic choice by their contacts that results in multiple information flows (Anspach 2017; Goh et al. 2017).

In this context, WhatsApp is quite different from other social platforms for news sharing and social messaging. While political talk on Facebook and Twitter has been linked positively to political involvement (Vaccari and Valeriani 2018), the conversational-yet-private nature of WhatsApp enables a different context for open dialogue among trusted ties (Yamamoto, Kushin, and Dalisay 2018).

Users of WhatsApp also report relying less on Facebook for news nowadays, due to content fatigue and exposure to undesirable content, and preferring to go to WhatsApp to take part in a private discussion about news or to discuss personal and public affairs with their contacts (Karapanos et al. 2016; Newman 2018; Newman et al. 2018). In the words of Swart, Peters, and Broersma (2018, 3), "people continue to make sense of and interpret news within specific social contexts," but need to access and maintain interpersonal relationships with family and friends (Chan 2018). Not surprisingly, then, Valeriani and Vaccari (2018) argued that WhatsApp plays a specific role in the digital environment of people's everyday life.

More so, past research points to WhatsApp gaining relevance as means to access information and discuss with others. Goh and colleagues (2017) found that users exchange information they feel would help their interpersonal relationship prosper, a willingness to cooperate that favors social cohesion. Empirical evidence also shows that individuals perceive that Facebook is "becoming less conducive to open discussion" and users are migrating their conversations to the privacy of WhatsApp and other messaging apps (Newman 2018, 13).

Similarly, Vaccari and Valeriani (2018) found that mobile communication encourages more and more diverse citizens to participate in discussion, thus exposing users to diverse points of view. This is important because conversations feed into political engagement. People learn from talking to others, even if they do not necessarily change their minds about different issues (Lee et al. 2018). Yamamoto and colleagues (2018) found evidence that use of MIMs such as WhatsApp indirectly leads to online and offline political participation.

While the popularity of WhatsApp for information exchange among users has been linked to the diffusion of news and information regarding all kinds of topics, there are concerns about its role in the spread of low-quality content, such as rumors and so-called fake news. Resende et al. (2019) found that fabricated images were commonly shared in WhatsApp groups during the 2018 presidential campaign in Brazil. Similarly, Bradshaw and Howard (2019) noted the increasingly prominent role of WhatsApp in organized social media manipulation campaigns in Argentina, Australia, Brazil, India, Italy, Mexico, and Nigeria.

The available evidence notwithstanding, research on the antecedents and consequences of MIMs is scant, especially in Latin America. This prevents us from positing directional hypotheses. Instead, the present study is guided by two overarching research questions:

RQ1: What are the sociodemographics, political predispositions, and news media orientations of users of WhatsApp?

RQ2: How does the differential uses of WhatsApp (i.e., sharing public and public affairs) influence users' political engagement during an election campaign, as measured by knowledge of public affairs news, attitudes towards contentious issues in the news, and participation in various political activities?

Overall, we want to explore what is the contribution of MIMs like WhatsApp to contemporary repertoires of digital media use and news consumption. Before going over the methods and empirical results, it is important to provide an overview of the context in which the study took place, which should help in the interpretation of the findings (Boczkowski and Mitchelstein 2019; Rojas and Valenzuela 2019).

The Chilean Context

Chile has a rather homogeneous, concentrated, and small news media system for a 17-million-people country, which largely operate in a commercially oriented environment (Gronemeyer and Porath 2015; Orchard 2018). At the same time, it has an active digital sector, with high penetration levels of social media and mobile devices (Harlow and Salaverría 2016). The online population represents more than three-fourths (77%) of the total population, and 82% of internet users use their smartphone to get news (Fernández 2018). Not surprisingly, messaging applications are extremely popular, both as a source of communication and for acquiring information, rivaling in prominence with social network sites like Facebook. According to the *2018 Reuters Digital News Report* (Newman et al. 2018), up to 36% of Chilean online users get their news through

WhatsApp, Facebook Messenger, and/or Snapchat; the equivalent figure is 16% on average for the nearly 40 countries covered. News consumption through traditional media, while still prevalent, has continued to decline. For instance, readership of print newspapers and viewership of TV news decreased 8% and 13%, respectively, between 2015 and 2018 (Valida 2015, 2018; Consejo Nacional de Televisión 2016, 2019).

Changes in the Chilean media ecosystem over the past few years have coincided with important transformations in the political sphere. Once regarded as the 'poster child' for democratic stability, clean government and economic growth in Latin America (Siavelis 2016, 62), Chile has witnessed since 2005 a steep decline in party identification, with an ensuing drop in voter turnout and confidence in political institutions, while experiencing an uptake of mass protests and social movements that culminated in the violent riots of 2019 (Bargsted and Maldonado 2018; Somma and Medel 2017). That is, the Chilean context is one of technology-empowered, critical citizens who have become increasingly distrustful of political and media elites.

We conducted our study in Chile in the context of the 2017 presidential and legislative elections. Compared to a nonelection period, it is likely that interest in public affairs, especially through MIMs, as well as political knowledge and participation, were heightened. While the role of so-called fake news, bots, and other disinformation campaigns were discussed in the press, surveys and content analyses show that these tactics were not widespread (Santana and Huerta 2019; Valenzuela et al. 2019). Thus, our study is well-suited for finding significant relationships between differential uses of WhatsApp and key political outcomes.

Because we conducted a panel survey, we could track changes in WhatsApp usage over time and measure how these related to political involvement. In this sense, our research is an improvement over cross-sectional designs regarding the issue of causality. Nevertheless, we cannot rule out completely the possibility of a spurious relationship between WhatsApp and political variables. Thus, our view of causality in the current study is closer to the concept of Granger causality than to true causality (Hamaker, Kuiper and Grasman 2015).

Method

Data

We fielded an original face-to-face panel survey, with the first wave (N = 678) conducted in March-June 2016 and the second wave (N = 505) in September-November 2017. The Office of Sociological Research at Pontificia Universidad Católica de Chile (DESUC) fielded the survey using a multi-stage, probability-based sample of adult residents living in the Greater Santiago—the most populous metropolitan area of Chile. Using the American Association for Public Opinion Research (AAPOR) criteria, the response rate was 74.5%, whereas the attrition rate between waves was 25.5%. To provide representative estimates, the data were weighted according to the National Statistics Institute's (INE) population estimates of gender, age, education and area of residence. Comparing our sample to census data revealed few differences (see Table A1 in Supplementary Material).

Table 1. Assessing differences between WhatsApp users and nonusers.

	WhatsApp user W2 M or %	WhatsApp nonuser W2 M or %	F value	p value
Gender (female)	52.15	40.94	2.44	0.119
Age (years)	42.21	63.25	69.76	<0.001
Education	4.83	3.07	43.83	<0.001
Income	3.22	3.46	1.40	0.237
Political interest W1	2.37	1.94	7.04	0.008
Political interest W2	2.29	2.32	0.02	0.880
Left-right ideology W1	4.70	4.47	0.73	0.394
Left-right ideology W2	4.64	4.76	0.17	0.683
TV news W1	4.91	6.00	20.03	<0.001
TV news W2	4.70	5.94	20.90	<0.001
Radio news W1	2.88	2.99	0.09	0.770
Radio news W2	2.37	2.86	1.51	0.219
Newspaper W1	2.64	1.96	2.95	0.087
Newspaper W2	1.96	1.95	0.00	0.978
Social media news W1	3.09	0.61	66.18	<0.001
Social media news W2	2.73	0.76	44.21	<0.001
News attention W1	3.01	2.95	0.27	0.606
News attention W2	2.94	2.84	1.19	0.275

Notes. N = 505. W1 = wave 1, W2 = Wave 2. For all variables, except gender, F values were obtained from ANOVAs. For gender, the test statistic is the corrected weighted χ^2 statistic.

Variables

Following our theoretical expectations, we measured two dimensions of WhatsApp usage: *public affairs* (i.e., sharing news about current events and political messages) and *personal affairs* (i.e., talking about personal issues, family life, work and/or studies). To gauge these measures, respondents were first asked whether they used WhatsApp on their mobile devices. Those responding affirmatively (74% in wave 1; 83% in wave 2) were then asked: "With what frequency do you share information on WhatsApp about the following topics: (a) your personal and/or family life, (b) your work and/or studies, (c) news and general current affairs, (d) political issues?" Responses were coded using a 5-point scale, ranging from 1 (*never*) to 5 (*always*). Items (a) and (b) were averaged to produce a scale of WhatsApp use for personal affairs (wave 1: $M = 3.34$, $SD = 1.13$; wave 2: $M = 3.51$, $SD = 1.05$). Using the same process, items (c) and (d) were combined into a scale of WhatsApp use for public affairs (wave 1: $M = 1.94$, $SD = 0.96$; wave 2: $M = 2.35$, $SD = 0.90$). Certainly, these behaviors overlap. Nevertheless, they are different, at least in terms of consequences as we shall demonstrate, and their correlation is rather weak (wave 1: $r = .38$; wave 2: $r = .39$).

As could be expected, respondents reported using the app more frequently for personal, rather than public, affairs (see Figure 1). Nevertheless, there was a significant increase in the frequency of sharing news and political content on the platform over the course of the electoral campaign, $t(323) = 5.92$, $p < .001$. This was not the case with personal usage, which remained equally high between waves 1 and 2, $t(323) = 1.92$, $p = .056$.

We also measured a variety of political outcomes as well, including knowledge, attitudes, and behaviors. To gauge knowledge, respondents were asked seven factual multiple-choice questions, including identification of political figures and recall of current issues in the news. Each item had four response choices: one correct, two incorrect, and a "don't know" response. To distinguish between informed, uninformed and misinformed responses (Kuklinski et al. 2000; Mondak 2001), each item was coded as

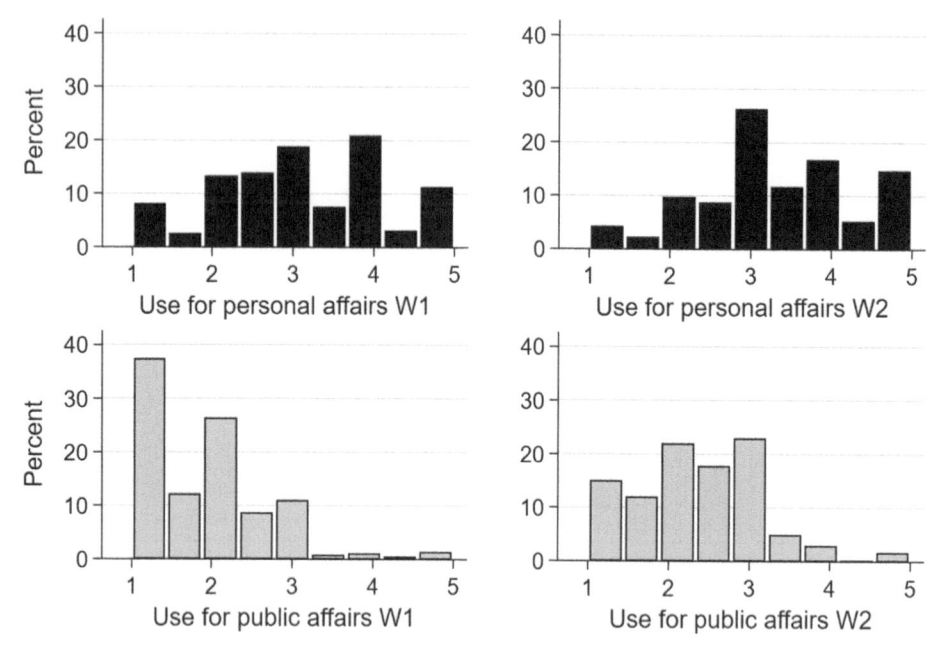

Figure 1. Frequency of WhatsApp usage across topics and waves.

follows: 1 = *correct*, 0 = *don't know*, and −1 = *incorrect*. Subsequently, we combined each item into an additive index (wave 1: $M = 2.54$, $SD = 2.14$; wave 2: $M = 3.06$, $SD = 1.93$).

To assess the relationship between WhatsApp use and political polarization, we measured respondents' issue position extremity (Mason 2015). Using a 5-point Likert scale, respondents indicated their level of agreement or disagreement towards seven politically contentious policies, including support for same-sex marriage, enacting a new law to control illegal immigration, and a proposal for a new Constitution. Each response was folded in half and rescaled into a 0 to 1 range, such that neutral responses were coded as 0 and more extreme responses (i.e., *strongly agree* and *strongly disagree*) were coded as 1. Subsequently, the individual items were averaged into a single scale (wave 1: $M = .57$, $SD = .18$; wave 2: $M = .52$, $SD = .14$). We chose this measure because it is independent of individuals' degree of ideological consistency across issues (i.e., how consistently liberal or conservative the respondent is across issues; see Broockman, 2016), which has been decreasing in Chile in the past few years (Saiegh 2015).

Political participation was measured with two variables. Because the second wave of the survey concluded right before Election Day, we could only ask for intention to vote—not actual voting. Thus, respondents were asked to estimate on a 5-point scale how likely they were to vote in the upcoming election, with 1 = *not likely at all* and 5 = *extremely likely* (wave 1: $M = 3.40$, $SD = 1.51$; wave 2: $M = 3.59$, $SD = 1.29$). Because nonelectoral forms of political participation in Chile are becoming increasingly prevalent, we also measured five other political behaviors, including protest activities, petitioning, and expressive participation (e.g., communicating with political leaders). We asked whether the respondent had engaged or not in each activity in the past 12 months, and then added the responses into a 0 to 5 index of political participation (wave 1: $M = 0.62$, $SD = 1.01$; wave 2: $M = 0.66$, $SD = 0.94$).

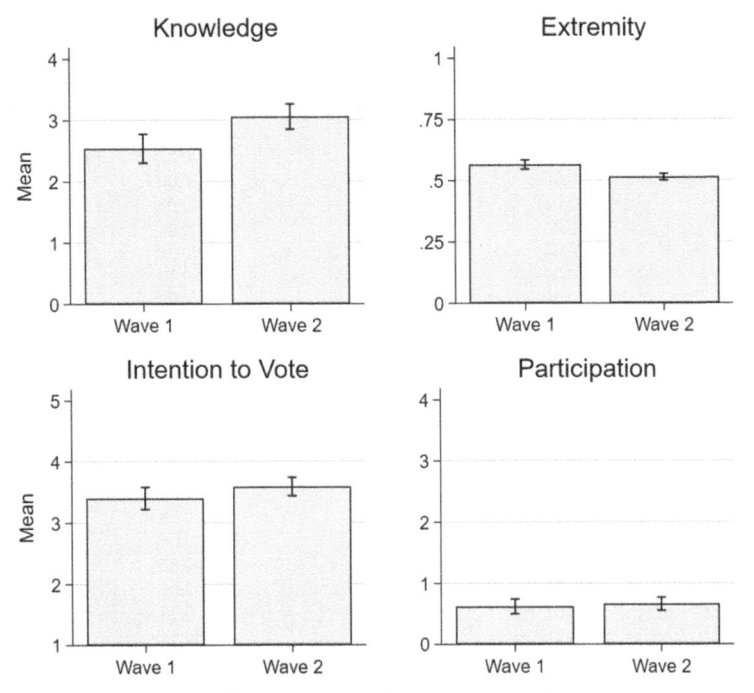

Figure 2. Average scores (and 95% CIs) of political outcome variables across waves.

As shown on Figure 2, between waves the sample became significantly more informed about public affairs, $t(504) = 4.06$, $p < .001$, and less extreme in their issue positions, $t(504) = -4.72$, $p < .001$. The trends for political participation, however, were less clear, as neither intention to vote, $t(428) = 1.78$, $p = .076$, nor expressive or protest behaviors, $t(504) = .69$, $p = .493$, changed in statistically significant terms.

In addition, we measured three sets of control variables (for the use of these, see Campbell and Kwak, 2011; Halpern et al. 2017; Vaccari and Valeriani 2018): sociodemographics, political orientations, and media use. Specifically, we measured respondents' gender (dummy-coded), age (in years), education, income, ideology (left-right), political interest, exposure to news on TV, radio, newspapers, Facebook and Twitter, and attention to news about politics, the economy, crime, sports, and entertainment. For details about these variables, (see Table A2 in Supplementary Material).

Statistical Analysis

We conducted a series of bivariate and multivariate analyses. First, we used analysis of variance (ANOVA) to compare the characteristics of WhatsApp users and nonusers. Subsequently, we analyzed the antecedents of sharing content on WhatsApp using two sets of longitudinal models: difference scores and lagged panel regressions. The difference score model answers the question of whose score in the dependent variable is most likely to increase or decrease over time, whereas the lagged regression addresses the question of which independent variables are a likely cause of the dependent variable (Newsom 2015). Lastly, we estimated lagged panel regression models for the study of the possible influence of WhatsApp uses on political

Table 2. Results of regression models of sharing content on WhatsApp.

	Sharing public affairs on WhatsApp		Sharing personal affairs on WhatsApp	
	Change score	Lagged regression	Change score	Lagged regression
Gender (female)	0.18	0.17	−0.12	−0.05
	(0.15)	(0.12)	(0.21)	(0.15)
Age	0.00	−0.00	0.00	−0.01
	(0.01)	(0.00)	(0.01)	(0.01)
Education	−0.00	0.02	0.05	0.02
	(0.04)	(0.03)	(0.06)	(0.04)
Income	0.01	0.00	−0.10	−0.03
	(0.05)	(0.04)	(0.08)	(0.06)
Political interest W1	−0.10	0.10	−0.09	0.06
	(0.07)	(0.06)	(0.10)	(0.08)
Left-right ideology W1	0.03	0.02	−0.01	0.02
	(0.04)	(0.03)	(0.04)	(0.03)
TV news W1	−0.01	0.01	−0.02	−0.00
	(0.03)	(0.03)	(0.04)	(0.03)
Radio news W1	0.04	0.03	0.02	0.01
	(0.03)	(0.02)	(0.04)	(0.03)
Newspaper use W1	−0.06	−0.04	−0.08*	−0.01
	(0.03)	(0.02)	(0.04)	(0.03)
Social media news W1	−0.03	−0.03	−0.02	0.01
	(0.03)	(0.02)	(0.04)	(0.03)
News attention W1	0.01	0.11	0.03	0.00
	(0.11)	(0.09)	(0.14)	(0.12)
Autoregressive term		0.30***		0.26***
		(0.07)		(0.07)
R^2	0.07	0.21	0.04	0.14

Notes. N = 346. Cell entries are unstandardized regression coefficients, with standard errors in parentheses.
*** $p < 0.001$, ** $p < 0.01$, * $p < 0.05$.

outcomes. Because prior research has found that the effect of digital media on outcomes such as political knowledge can be rather immediate, using the WhatsApp variables from wave 1 only could underestimate the potential influence of the messaging app (Eveland et al. 2005; Shah et al. 2005). Hence, we estimated both asynchronous and synchronous relationships between the WhatsApp variables and each outcome. We included a correlation table of all variables (see Table A3 in Supplementary Material). The data that support the findings of this study are openly available in .csv format at: http://bit.ly/whatsapp_data.

Results

Antecedents of WhatsApp Use

Considering the widespread adoption of WhatsApp in Chile, there was reason to expect that access to the messaging app would be relatively equal among sociodemographic groups. This was, indeed, the case. When comparing respondents who used the app to those who did not along the control variables, only seven out of 18 comparisons turned out to be statistically significant (see Table 1). There were no detectable differences along gender distribution, income, ideology, exposure to radio news and newspapers, and levels of attention to news. The initial difference in political interest also dissipated as Election Day approached. Nevertheless, WhatsApp use was more likely among younger, educated respondents who consumed TV news less frequently and—as could be expected—depended more on social media platforms as a source for news.

While these findings suggest that *access* to WhatsApp is rather homogenous along social groups, *uses* of the messaging application may still vary considerably along individual characteristics. To examine this possibility (**RQ1**), we studied the antecedents of the two dimensions of WhatsApp use, that is, personal and public affairs sharing.

As explained earlier, we estimated both difference score and lagged regression models. The most remarkable finding of these models, displayed in Table 2, is the lack of statistically significant relationships. That is, growth in sharing content through WhatsApp between waves 1 and 2 was not particularly different for app users with higher or lower education, income, interest in politics, news media use, and so forth. If anything, there was a strong inertia in usage patterns; using WhatsApp for public or personal affairs in wave 1 was a potent predictor of continuing to do by the time of wave 2. The only exception is the negative, statistically significant coefficient for newspaper use in the change score model of personal usage of WhatsApp. This result means that respondents who read the newspaper more frequently in wave 1 became, over time, less likely to share content about family, studies or work with their WhatsApp contacts. Still, this is a rather weak relationship ($p < .05$), and there is the strong possibility that it resulted from chance alone.

If anything, the results suggest that the two uses of the messaging app are well engrained across the different segments of the Chilean population, such that no particular group with access to WhatsApp is significantly more or less likely to use the app to share personal and public affairs.

Consequences of WhatsApp Use

We now turn to analyzing the possible consequences of using WhatsApp on various individual-level political outcomes during the 2017 Chilean election (**RQ2**). Because we are interested in the issue of causal precedence, we estimated lagged regression models, in which each political outcome is predicted from the WhatsApp variables, while controlling for the likely influence of sociodemographics, political orientations, news media use, and initial levels of each dependent variable.

The results of the regression models are displayed in Table 3. Several findings are noteworthy. First, frequent use of WhatsApp for sharing news and political messages was associated to a significant increase in the correct recall of information. Second, higher levels of usage of WhatsApp for personal affairs, in contrast, were associated with lowers levels of knowledge. Third, for those who shared personal affairs over the app more frequently, the probability of participating in political activities such as protesting and petitioning was significantly greater. Last, there was no evidence that usage of WhatsApp was related to issue opinion extremity and vote intention in any consistent fashion.

To facilitate the interpretation of these results, Figure 3 plots the average marginal effects of the WhatsApp variables that had a statistically significant relationship with the outcome variables. With these plots, we are comparing two samples that are identical in all measured characteristics except in the frequency with which they use

Table 3. Results of regression models of knowledge, attitudes and behaviors.

	Knowledge Asynchronous OLS	Knowledge Synchronous OLS	Issue position extremity Asynchronous OLS	Issue position extremity Synchronous OLS	Intention to vote Asynchronous Ordinal	Intention to vote Synchronous Ordinal	Political participation Asynchronous Neg. bin.	Political participation Synchronous Neg. bin.
Public affairs on WhatsApp W1	0.30 (0.17)		−0.01 (0.01)		0.29 (0.16)		−0.05 (0.10)	
Public affairs on WhatsApp W2		0.43** (0.16)		−0.01 (0.01)		0.24 (0.22)		−0.08 (0.11)
Personal affairs on WhatsApp W1	−0.23* (0.11)		0.01 (0.01)		−0.15 (0.14)		0.17 (0.10)	
Personal affairs on WhatsApp W2		0.09 (0.13)		0.00 (0.01)		−0.19 (0.16)		0.41*** (0.09)
Gender (female)	−0.11 (0.30)	−0.23 (0.30)	0.01 (0.02)	0.01 (0.02)	−0.10 (0.32)	−0.12 (0.33)	0.06 (0.17)	0.15 (0.17)
Age	0.02* (0.01)	0.03** (0.01)	0.00 (0.00)	0.00 (0.00)	0.01 (0.01)	0.01 (0.01)	−0.01 (0.01)	−0.01 (0.01)
Education	0.11 (0.06)	0.12* (0.06)	0.00 (0.00)	−0.00 (0.00)	0.03 (0.08)	0.03 (0.09)	0.07 (0.04)	0.05 (0.05)
Income	−0.14 (0.10)	−0.16 (0.10)	0.00 (0.01)	0.00 (0.01)	−0.06 (0.13)	−0.07 (0.13)	0.05 (0.07)	0.05 (0.07)
Political interest	0.19 (0.14)	0.15 (0.14)	−0.01 (0.01)	−0.01 (0.01)	−0.04 (0.17)	−0.02 (0.17)	0.12 (0.09)	0.12 (0.09)
Left-right ideology	0.05 (0.06)	0.03 (0.05)	0.00 (0.00)	0.00 (0.00)	−0.03 (0.07)	−0.05 (0.08)	0.04 (0.05)	0.03 (0.04)
TV news	0.08 (0.05)	0.08 (0.05)	0.00 (0.00)	0.00 (0.00)	−0.08 (0.07)	−0.08 (0.08)	0.11* (0.05)	0.11** (0.04)
Radio news	0.05 (0.06)	0.04 (0.06)	−0.00 (0.00)	−0.00 (0.00)	−0.02 (0.07)	−0.02 (0.08)	0.00 (0.03)	0.02 (0.03)
Newspaper (print and online)	−0.07 (0.04)	−0.07 (0.04)	0.00 (0.00)	0.00 (0.00)	−0.03 (0.08)	−0.01 (0.08)	−0.02 (0.04)	−0.02 (0.04)
Social media news use	−0.00 (0.05)	−0.01 (0.05)	0.00 (0.00)	0.00 (0.00)	0.07 (0.07)	0.08 (0.07)	−0.00 (0.03)	−0.00 (0.03)
News attention	0.20 (0.19)	0.19 (0.19)	0.04* (0.02)	0.04* (0.02)	0.62* (0.27)	0.65* (0.28)	−0.10 (0.14)	−0.10 (0.13)
Autoregressive term	0.14 (0.07)	0.11 (0.07)	0.17** (0.06)	0.18** (0.06)	0.24* (0.12)	0.23 (0.12)	0.25** (0.08)	0.27*** (0.08)
R^2	0.20	0.22	0.12	0.11	0.06	0.05	0.09	0.13

Notes. N = 346 (except for vote intention, where N = 296). OLS = ordinary least squares regression. Ordinal = ordinal logit regression. Neg. bin. = negative binomial regression. Cell entries are unstandardized regression coefficients, with standard errors in parentheses.
***$p < 0.001$, **$p < 0.01$, *$p < 0.05$.

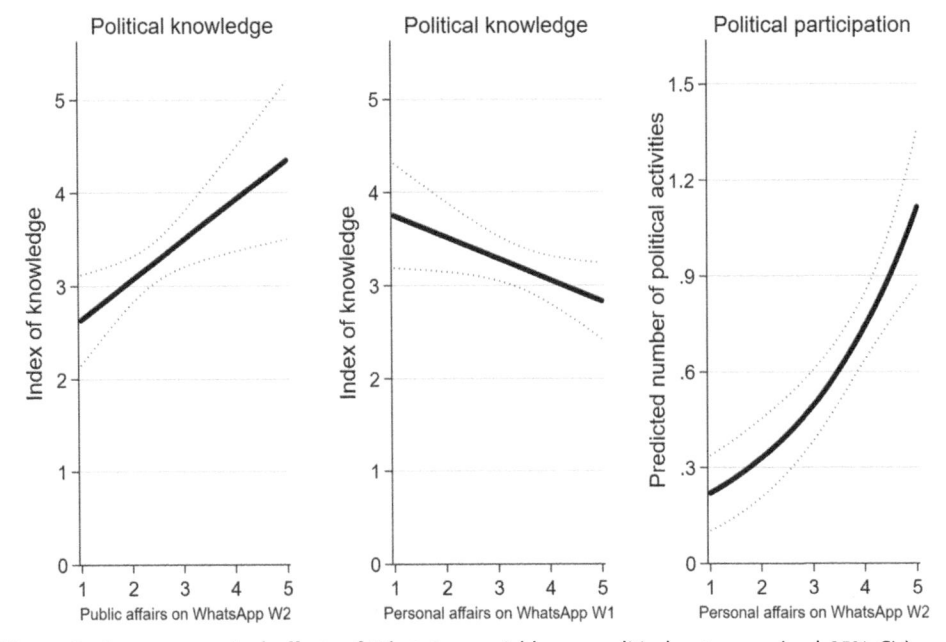

Figure 3. Average marginal effects of WhatsApp variables on political outcomes (and 95% CIs).

WhatsApp for sharing public and private affairs. For instance, frequently sharing public affairs on the messaging app was associated to correctly answering one additional question of the seven we asked to gauge political knowledge. Frequent sharing of personal affairs on the app, while associated to a one-point decrease in the index of knowledge, produced a fourfold increase in the mean number of political activities, from close to .3 to 1.2.

Discussion

Mobile instant messaging services (MIMs) such as WhatsApp are among many digital services available to online users. They have neither replaced television, websites or social network sites on most people's media diet, nor they constitute the most important source for news about public affairs. Its usage requires material (i.e., having a smartphone with internet access), cognitive (i.e., digital skills) and social resources (i.e., social capital), which are not equally distributed across the population. This is especially true in highly unequal countries, such as Chile.

Yet, there is growing evidence that the widespread use of MIMs not only makes them one of the most universal communication technologies, but also one that is exerting a unique influence on the conduit of news and political information. In this sense, the current study's findings are enlightening. By employing a panel survey fielded over the course of the 2017 elections in Chile, we found that few of the typical markers of the digital divide are applicable to WhatsApp. Age and education may well determine whether people have access to the application, but they do not structure in any noticeable way the type of content people share once they have access. Furthermore, we did not find that other indicators of interest in public affairs, such as attention to issues in the news or general political interest, were predictive of sharing personal or political news on WhatsApp, either. Instead, we found that WhatsApp users of all makeups are adopting this new technology for a variety of purposes, including communication about family, friends, work, news, and politics. While these findings differ from similar studies conducted in Europe (e.g., Valeriani and Vaccari 2018), they are similar to those from other Latin American countries (e.g., Matassi et al. 2019).

A likely explanation for our results has to do with the incidental nature of news in the context of WhatsApp use in Chile. In platforms built for relational or social purposes, news consumption and sharing does not result from an instrumental motivation to become informed—a motivation that is strongly determined by political predispositions and traditional media routines (Gil de Zúñiga, Valenzuela and Weeks 2016). Rather, it is more a means to enable users to fulfill relational and social goals, which are more universal across groups. This seems particularly applicable to countries in which MIMs are popular. As Boczkowski, Mitchelstein, and Matassi (2018, 3534) found in their study of WhatsApp in Argentina, "news loses the privileged place it used to have when the main mode of consumption was through dedicated media. It is re-contextualized within a vast ocean of all kinds of other information that defies traditional definitions of newsworthiness." The multimodality of WhatsApp —where exchanges can include texts, audios, videos, images, and/or links— certainly favors that. Since users can easily forward messages to multiple groups —thus creating a viral effect (see Tardáguila 2019)— it is possible that users get redundant or reinforcing messages that also favors information accessibility, more so when it comes from seemingly trusted sources, such as close ties.

That the modal type of content shared in WhatsApp is personal, not public, affairs, is also consistent with the incidental character of how users experience news and politics. What is remarkable in this case, however, is that the type of content shared is significantly shaped by the political context. That is, it may well be that the individual differences we measured cannot explain the frequency with which WhatsApp users talk about family or the election. Nevertheless, we observed a significant increase in the amount of news and political messages exchanged by users between survey waves. The explanation, of course, is the impact of the campaign and the larger news environment: as electoral events and political coverage increased, so did political conversations on WhatsApp.

Importantly, we found evidence that two distinct types of WhatsApp use coexist, personal and political, with each having specific effects on political outcomes. On the one hand, these findings confirm prior research showing that in private digital environments where communication takes place mostly with close ties (or close enough), discussion about news and political affairs can prosper. On the other, they show that the effects of digital media on political outcomes, even in more distributed platforms such as WhatsApp, are still contingent upon specific uses, just as early research on social media and internet use found (Shah et al. 2005).

More specifically, we found that using WhatsApp for public affairs had a significant and positive relationship with political knowledge. This is noteworthy considering that most of the scholarly and public attention to the effects of WhatsApp in election campaigns in emerging democracies has been on the spread of misperceptions and so-called fake news. It is also remarkable due to the incidental character that news plays in WhatsApp conversations discussed before. Nevertheless, prior research on both incidental news exposure (Kobayashi, Hoshino, and Suzuki 2017) and offline, political talk (Eveland and Hively 2009) has found that these communication forms can produce considerable learning effects. It is important to note, however, that the relationship between WhatsApp and knowledge is somewhat weak. A possible explanation—noted by a reviewer of this article—is that WhatsApp users may conceive as "news" content that does not follow the standards of professional journalism, such as content freely produced and posted online by regular citizens or, in the worst case, false or misleading political stories.

We also found that personal uses of WhatsApp were strongly predictive of engagement in protest and expressive forms of political participation. In this aspect, the results are quite consistent with the available evidence on social media and protest behavior, as summarized by the meta analyses of Boulianne (2015, 2019). More surprising seems the finding that public affairs sharing was not significantly related to intention to vote and political participation. Nevertheless, an early study conducted in Chile found a similar null result for the effects of Facebook news use on protest behavior, while finding a positive result for relational uses of the platform (Valenzuela 2013). A possible interpretation is that personal uses of WhatsApp are more apt for producing social reinforcement (e.g., peer pressure), which is more determinant of the decision to engage in costly political activities (e.g., street demonstrations) than information acquisition (Valenzuela, Correa, and Gil de Zúñiga, 2018). Public affairs usage, in turn, would be more apt for information gains, as demonstrated by its positive effects on knowledge.

We did not find that WhatsApp usage had a clear-cut relationship with issue position extremity, which has been used as a marker of political polarization (Mason 2015). This can be interpreted in a number of ways. It is consistent with the notion that the risks of digital platforms creating so-called echo chambers is "overstated" (Dubois and Blank 2018). It could also confirm Lee and colleagues' (2018) point that thanks to WhatsApp conversations, people do not change their minds so much as they are more understanding of others' opinions and their own. However it may be, from a normative perspective, it is an important finding that WhatsApp use is not linked to mass ideological polarization.

While we did not find a direct relationship between using WhatsApp and the propensity to vote, it is possible that the relationship operates in indirect fashion. An obvious channel of influence would be political knowledge—that is, WhatsApp produces political learning, which in turn increases the likelihood of voting. Future research, of course, needs to confirm this possibility.

As in any study, ours has limitations that future research can address. While the panel design enables the temporal ordering of the variables, it is not based on random assignment. Despite the extensive list of control variables, with these data we cannot rule out the possibility that other, omitted variables explain the observed changes in political knowledge, attitudes and behaviors between waves. Thus, the issue of causality remains elusive. Field experiments could thus complement the type of study reported here. For instance, participants without an account on WhatsApp could be recruited, a subset of which could be randomly assigned to create and use WhatsApp for some time (see, e.g., Theocharis and Lowe 2016). With panel surveys, sensitization may also become an issue. Given the relatively long time that elapsed between the first and second waves, this may be less of an issue.

Limitations notwithstanding, the current study has scholarly and practical implications for digital journalism, especially in Latin America. Studies on the role played by digital news need to incorporate MIMs such as WhatsApp in the repertoire of major news gateways. To date, most of the literature still revolves around Facebook, Twitter and YouTube. Journalists and news media organizations could invest more in making their content amenable for news sharing on social platforms such as WhatsApp. Thus, experimentation with user engagement on WhatsApp may provide a valuable future return. For instance, in 2014–2015 the BBC used WhatsApp to reach readers with its coverage of the Ebola outbreak in West Africa. The special Ebola service had over 19,000 subscribers, and users sent back questions and local news, which in turn helped the BBC staff to better cover this health crisis (Barot 2015). Since several other news media organizations have been experimenting with a conversational format for news delivery within the context of private messaging services (Ford and Hutchinson 2019), this is a line of inquiry worth pursuing.

Disclosure Statement

No potential conflict of interest was reported by the authors.

Funding Statement

This work was supported by a grant from the Vice Provost for Research, Pontificia Universidad Católica de Chile. The first author also received funding from: the National Commission for Scientific and Technological Research (CONICYT) under grant Fondap/CIGIDEN/15110017; and the Millennium Science Initiative under grant ICM/2018/Millennium Institute for Foundational Research on Data (IMFD).

ORCID

Sebastián Valenzuela http://orcid.org/0000-0001-5991-7364
Ingrid Bachmann http://orcid.org/0000-0002-2805-5148
Matías Bargsted https://orcid.org/0000-0001-5617-6230

References

Anspach, Nicolas M. 2017. "The New Personal Influence: How Our Facebook Friends Influence the News We Read." *Political Communication* 34 (4): 590–606.
Bachmann, Ingrid, Jaime Loke, and Dustin Harp. 2018. "Feminist Commentary by Women a Whisper among Op-Ed Voices." *Newspaper Research Journal* 39 (1): 93–104.
Baek, Kanghui, and Yeolib Kim. 2016. "Exploring the Relationship between Mobile Application Use and Political Information Seeking and Political Discussion." *Journal of Information Technology & Politics* 13: 175–186.
Bargsted, Matías, and Luis Maldonado. 2018. "Party Identification in an Encapsulated Party System: The Case of Postauthoritarian Chile." *Journal of Politics in Latin America* 10 (1): 29–68.

Barot, Trushar. 2015. "How BBC Ebola WhatsApp Service is Battling Virus and Finding Great Stories." BBC Blogs. https://www.bbc.co.uk/blogs/collegeofjournalism/entries/0f944ab7-9f96-4091-a927-db826630d997

Boczkowski, Pablo J., Mora Matassi, and Eugenia Mitchelstein. 2018. "How Young Users Deal with Multiple Platforms: The Role of Meaning-Making in Social Media Repertoires." *Journal of Computer-Mediated Communication* 23 (5): 245–259.

Boczkowski, Pablo J., and Eugenia Mitchelstein. 2019. "The Politics of Contextualization in the Contextualization of Political Communication Research." *Political Communication*, 1.

Boczkowski, Pablo J., Eugenia Mitchelstein, and Mora Matassi. 2018. "'News Comes across When I'm in a Moment of Leisure': Understanding the Practices of Incidental News Consumption on Social Media." *New Media & Society* 20: 3523–3539.

Bode, Leticia. 2017. "Closing the Gap: Gender Parity in Political Engagement on Social Media." *Information, Communication & Society* 20: 587–603.

Boulianne, Shelley. 2015. "Social Media Use and Participation: A Meta-Analysis of Current Research." *Information, Communication & Society* 18: 524–538.

Boulianne, Shelley. 2019. "Revolution in the Making? Social Media Effects across the Globe." *Information, Communication & Society* 22: 39–54.

Bradshaw, Samantha, and Philip Howard. 2019. *Global Disinformation Order: 2019 Global Inventory of Organised Social Media Manipulation*. Oxford: University of Oxford, Oxford Internet Institute.

Broockman, David E. 2016. "Approaches to Studying Policy Representation." *Legislative Studies Quarterly* 41 (1): 181–215.

Campbell, Scott W., and Nojin Kwak. 2011. "Political Involvement in 'Mobilized' Society: The Interactive Relationships among Mobile Communication, Network Characteristics, and Political Participation." *Journal of Communication* 61 (6): 1005–1024.

Campbell, Scott W., and Nojin Kwak. 2014. "Mobile Media and Civic Life: Implications of Private and Public Uses of the Technology." In *The Routledge Companion to Mobile Media*, edited by Gerard Goggin and Larissa Hjorth, 409–418. New York: Routledge.

Ceron, Andra. 2015. "Internet, News, and Political Trust: The Difference between Social Media and Online Media Outlets." *Journal of Computer-Mediated Communication* 20 (5): 487–503.

Chan, Michael. 2018. "Mobile-Mediated Multimodal Communications, Relationship Quality and Subjective Well-Being: An Analysis of Smartphone Use from a Life Course Perspective." *Computers in Human Behavior* 87: 254–262.

Chinkin, Christine. 1999. "A Critique of the Public/Private Dimension." *European Journal of International Law* 10 (2): 387–395.

Consejo Nacional de Televisión. 2016. "Anuario Estadístico de Oferta y Consumo de Televisión Abierta 2015." Accessed 13 October 2019. https://www.cntv.cl/cntv/site/artic/20160729/asocfile/20160729173754/anuario_estad__stico_de_oferta_y_consumo_2015.pdf

Consejo Nacional de Televisión. 2019. "Anuario Estadístico Oferta y Consumo de Televisión 2018." Accessed 13 October 2019. https://www.cntv.cl/cntv/site/artic/20190329/asocfile/20190329114753/anuario_estadistico_de_oferta_y_consumo_2018.pdf

Correa, Teresa, Isabel Pavez, and Javier Contreras. 2018. "Digital Inclusion through Mobile Phones?: A Comparison between Mobile-Only and Computer Users in Internet Access, Skills and Use." *Information, Communication & Society*.

Dahlberg, Lincoln. 2005. "The Habermasian Public Sphere: Taking Difference Seriously." *Theory and Society* 34 (2): 111–136.

Dimitrova, Daniela V., Adam Shehata, Jesper Strömbäck, and Lars W. Nord. 2014. "The Effects of Digital Media on Political Knowledge and Participation in Election Campaigns: Evidence from Panel Data." *Communication Research* 41 (1): 95–118.

Dodds, Tomás. 2019. "Reporting with WhatsApp: Mobile Chat Applications' Impact on Journalistic Practices." *Digital Journalism* 7 (6): 725–745.

Dubois, Elizabeth, and Grant Blank. 2018. "The Echo Chamber is Overstated: The Moderating Effect of Political Interest and Diverse Media." *Information, Communication & Society* 21: 729–745.

Eveland, William P., Jr., and Myiah Hutchens Hively. 2009. "Political Discussion Frequency, Network Size, and "Heterogeneity" of Discussion as Predictors of Political Knowledge and Participation." *Journal of Communication* 59: 205–224.

Eveland, William P., Jr., Andrew F. Hayes, Dhavan V. Shah, and Nojin Kwak. 2005. "Understanding the Relationship between Communication and Political Knowledge: A Model Comparison Approach Using Panel Data." *Political Communication* 22 (4): 423–446.

Fernández, Francisco. 2018. "Chile." *Digital News Report*. Reuters Institute for the Study of Journalism, Oxford University. http://www.digitalnewsreport.org/survey/2018/chile-2018/

Fletcher, Richard, and Rasmus Kleis Nielsen. 2018. "Are People Incidentally Exposed to News on Social Media? a Comparative Analysis." *New Media & Society* 20: 2450–2468.

Ford, Heather, and Jonathon Hutchinson. 2019. "Newsbots That Mediate Journalist and Audience Relationships." *Digital Journalism*, 1–19.

Gal, Susan. 2002. "A Semiotics of the Public/Private Distinction." *Differences* 13 (1): 77–95.

Gil de Zúñiga, Homero, and Trevor Diehl. 2019. "News Finds Me Perception and Democracy: Effects on Political Knowledge, Political Interest, and Voting." *New Media & Society* 21: 1253–1271.

Gil de Zúñiga, Homero, Sebastián Valenzuela, and Brian E. Weeks. 2016. "Motivations for Political Discussion: Antecedents and Consequences on Civic Engagement." *Human Communication Research* 42 (4): 533–552.

Goh, Debbie, Richard Ling, Liuyu Huang, and Doris Liew. 2017. "News Sharing as Reciprocal Exchanges in Social Cohesion Maintenance." *Information, Communication & Society* 8: 1128–1144.

Gronemeyer, María Elena, and William Porath. 2015. "A Study on Homogeneity between Editorials and News Sources Opinions in the Chilean Reference Press." *Cuadernos.info* 36: 139–153.

Habermas, Jürgen. 1991. *The Structural Transformation of the Public Sphere: An Inquiry into a Category of Bourgeois Society*. Cambridge, MA: MIT Press. (Original work published 1962.)

Halpern, Daniel, Sebastián Valenzuela, and James E. Katz. 2017. "We Face, I Tweet: How Different Social Media Influence Political Participation through Collective and Internal Efficacy." *Journal of Computer-Mediated Communication* 22 (6): 320–336.

Hamaker, Ellen L., Rebecca M. Kuiper, and Raoul P. P. P. Grasman. 2015. "A Critique of the Cross-Lagged Panel Model." *Psychological Methods* 20 (1): 102–116.

Harlow, Summer, and Ramón Salaverría. 2016. "Regenerating Journalism: Exploring the 'Alternativeness' and 'Digital-Ness' of Online-Native Media in Latin America." *Digital Journalism* 4 (8): 1001–1019.

Hickerson, Andrea, and John Gastil. 2008. "Assessing the Difference Critique of Deliberation: Gender, Emotion, and the Jury Experience." *Communication Theory* 18 (2): 281–303.

Hollander, Barry A. 2007. "Media Use and Political Involvement". In *Mass Media Effects Research: Advances through Meta-Analysis*, edited by Raymond W. Preiss and Barbara Mae Gayle, 377–390. Mahwah, NJ: Erlbaum.

Karapanos, Evangelos, Pedro Teixeira, and Ruben Gouveia. 2016. "Need Fulfillment and Experiences on Social Media: A Case on Facebook and WhatsApp." *Computers in Human Behavior* 55: 888–897.

Katz, James E., and Mark Aakhus, eds. 2002. *Perpetual Contact: Mobile Communication, Private Talk, Public Performance*. Cambridge, UK: Cambridge University Press.

Kim, Yonghwan, Hsuan-Ting Chen, and Yuan Wang. 2016. "Living in the Smartphone Age: Examining the Conditional Indirect Effects of Mobile Phone Use on Political Participation." *Journal of Broadcasting & Electronic Media* 60: 694–713.

Kobayashi, Tetsuro, Takahiro Hoshino, and Takahisa Suzuki. 2017. "Inadvertent Learning on a Portal Site: A Longitudinal Field Experiment." *Communication Research*.

Kuklinski, James H., Paul J. Quirk, Jennifer Jerit, David Schwieder, and Robert F. Rich. 2000. "Misinformation and the Currency of Democratic Citizenship." *The Journal of Politics* 62 (3): 790–816.

Lee, Changjun, Jieun Shin, and Ahreum Hong. 2018. "Does Social Media Use Really Make People Politically Polarized? Direct and Indirect Effects of Social Media Use on Political Polarization in South Korea." *Telematics and Informatics* 35 (1): 245–254.

Lee, Hoon, Nojin Kwak, Scott W. Campbell, and Rich Ling. 2014. "Mobile Communication and Political Participation in South Korea: Examining the Intersections between Informational and Relational Uses." *Computers in Human Behavior* 38: 85–92.

Mason, Lilliana. 2015. "'I Disrespectfully Agree': The Differential Effects of Partisan Sorting on Social and Issue Polarization." *American Journal of Political Science* 59 (1): 128–145.

Matassi, Mora, Pablo J. Boczkowski, and Eugenia Mitchelstein. 2019. "Domesticating WhatsApp: Family, Friends, Work, and Study in Everyday Communication." *New Media & Society*.

Mitchelstein, Eugenia, and Pablo J. Boczkowski. 2018. "Juventud, Estatus y Conexiones. Explicación del Consumo Incidental de Noticias en Redes Sociales." *Revista Mexicana de Opinión Pública* 13 (24): 131–145.

Mondak, Jeffrey J. 2001. "Developing Valid Knowledge Scales." *American Journal of Political Science* 45 (1): 224–238.

Newman, Nic. 2018. "News in Social Media and Messaging Apps." Reuters Institute for the Study of Journalism. https://reutersinstitute.politics.ox.ac.uk/sites/default/files/2018-09/KM%20RISJ%20News%20in%20social%20media%20and%20messaging%20apps%20report%20_0.pdf

Newman, Nic, Richard Fletcher, Antonis Kalogeropoulos, David A. L. Levy, and Rasmus Kleis Nielsen. 2018. "Reuters Institute Digital News Report." Reuters Institute for the Study of Journalism. http://media.digitalnewsreport.org/wp-content/uploads/2018/06/digital-news-report-2018.pdf.

Newsom, Jason T. 2015. *Longitudinal Structural Equation Modeling: A Comprehensive Introduction*. New York: Routledge.

Norris, Pippa. 2000. *A Virtuous Circle: Political Communications in Post-Industrial Democracies*. Cambridge: Cambridge University Press.

Orchard, Ximena. 2018. "Precarious Balance: How Journalists Negotiate Notions of Autonomy in the Trade-Off with Political Actors." *Journalism Practice* 12 (4): 422–439.

Pateman, Carole. 1989. *The Disorder of Women: Democracy, Feminism and Political Theory*. Cambridge: Polity Press.

Rains, Stephen A., Timothy R. Levine, and Rene Weber. 2018. "Sixty Years of Quantitative Communication Research Summarized: Lessons from 149 Meta-Analyses." *Annals of the International Communication Association* 42 (2): 105–124.

Resende, Gustavo, Philipe Melo, Hugo Sousa, Johnnatan Messias, Marisa Vasconcelos, Jussara M. Almeida, and Fabrício Benevenuto. 2019. "(Mis)information dissemination in WhatsApp: Gathering, analyzing and countermeasures." Proceedings of the 2019 World Wide Web Conference (WWW '19), May 13-17, 2019, San Francisco, CA, USA.

Rojas, Hernando, Dhavan V. Shah, and Lewis A. Friedland. 2011. "A Communicative Approach to Social Capital." *Journal of Communication* 61 (4): 689–712.

Rojas, Hernando, and Sebastián Valenzuela. 2019. "A Call to Contextualize Public Opinion-Based Research in Political Communication." *Political Communication*, 1.

Saiegh, Sebastián M. 2015. "Using Joint Scaling Methods to Study Ideology and Representation: Evidence from Latin America." *Political Analysis* 23 (3): 363–384.

Santana, Luis, and Gonzalo Huerta. 2019. "Are They Bots? Social Media Automation during Chile's 2017 Presidential Campaign." *Cuadernos.info* 44: 61–77.

Shah, Dhavan V., Jaeho Cho, William P. Eveland, Jr., and Nojin Kwak. 2005. "Information and Expression in a Digital Age: Modeling Internet Effects on Civic Participation." *Communication Research* 32: 531–565.

Siavelis, Peter M. 2016. "Crisis of Representation in Chile? The Institutional Connection." *Journal of Politics in Latin America* 8 (3): 61–93.

Skoric, Marko M., Qinfeng Zhu, Debbie Goh, and Natalie Pang. 2016. "Social Media and Citizen Engagement: A Meta-Analytic Review." *New Media & Society* 18: 1817–1839.

Somma, Nicolás, and Rodrigo Medel. 2017. "Social Movements and Institutional Politics in Contemporary Chile". In *Social Movements in Chile. Organization, Trajectories, and Political Consequences*, edited by Sofia Donoso and Marisa von Bülow, 29–61. New York: Palgrave Macmillan.

Statista. 2019. "Number of Mobile Phone Users Worldwide from 2015 to 2020 (in Billions)". Accessed 13 October 2019. https://www.statista.com/statistics/274774/forecast-of-mobile-phone-users-worldwide/

Swart, Joëlle, Chris Peters, and Marcel Broersma. 2017. "Navigating Cross-Media News Use." *Journalism Studies* 18 (11): 1343–1362.

Swart, Joëlle, Chris Peters, and Marcel Broersma. 2018. "Sharing and Discussing News in Private Social Media Groups." *Digital Journalism* 7 (2): 187–205.

Tardáguila, Cristina. 2019. "Falsehoods Outperform Facts in Brazilian WhatsApp Groups, Study Shows." Poynter.org. https://www.poynter.org/fact-checking/2019/falsehoods-outperform-facts-in-brazilian-whatsapp-groups-study-shows/.

Theocharis, Yannis, and Will Lowe. 2016. "Does Facebook Increase Political Participation? Evidence from a Field Experiment." *Information, Communication & Society* 19: 1465–1486.

Vaccari, Cristian, and Augusto Valeriani. 2018. "Digital Political Talk and Political Participation: Comparing Established and Third Wave Democracies." *SAGE Open* 8 (2).

Valenzuela, Sebastián. 2013. "Unpacking the Use of Social Media for Protest Behavior: The Roles of Information, Opinion Expression, and Activism." *American Behavioral Scientist* 57 (7): 920–942.

Valenzuela, Sebastián, Ingrid Bachmann, and Marcela Aguilar. 2019. "Socialized for News Media Use: How Family Communication, Information-Processing Needs, and Gratifications Determine Adolescents' Exposure to News." *Communication Research* 46 (8): 1095–1118.

Valenzuela, Sebastián, Teresa Correa, and Homero Gil de Zúñiga. 2018. "Ties, Likes, and Tweets: Using Strong and Weak Ties to Explain Differences in Protest Participation across Facebook and Twitter Use." *Political Communication* 35 (1): 117–134.

Valenzuela, Sebastián, Daniel Halpern, James E. Katz, and Juan Pablo Miranda. 2019. "The Paradox of Participation versus Misinformation: Social Media, Political Engagement, and the Spread of Misinformation." *Digital Journalism* 7 (6): 802–823.

Valeriani, Augusto, and Cristian Vaccari. 2018. "Political Talk on Mobile Instant Messaging Services: A Comparative Analysis of Germany, Italy, and the UK." *Information, Communication & Society* 21: 1715–1731.

Valida. 2015. "Boletines de Circulación y Lectura 2° Semestre 2015." Accessed 13 October 2019. http://www.valida-chile.cl/wp-content/uploads/2015/09/Boleti%CC%81n-de-Circulacio%CC%81n-y-Lectura-2%C2%B0-Semestre-2015.pdf

Valida. 2018. "Boletín de Circulación y Lectura Diarios 2° Semestre 2018." Accessed 13 October 2019. http://www.valida-chile.cl/wp-content/uploads/2019/03/Boletin-Circulacio%CC%81n-y-Lectura-Diarios-2%C2%B0semestre-2018.pdf

Wyatt, Robert, Elihu Katz, and Joohan Kim. 2000. "Bridging the Spheres: Political and Personal Conversation in Public and Private Spaces." *Journal of Communication* 50 (1): 71–92.

Yamamoto, Masahiro, Matthew J. Kushin, and Francis Dalisay. 2018. "How Informed Are Messaging App Users about Politics? A Linkage of Messaging App Use and Political Knowledge and Participation." *Telematics and Informatics* 35 (8): 2376–2386.

Protecting News Companies and Their Readers: Exploring Social Media Policies in Latin American Newsrooms

Summer Harlow

ABSTRACT
This study uses a survey of journalists from throughout Latin America ($n = 1,094$) to understand the relationship between policies (or lack thereof) and journalists' work environments and editorial decisions. Results show most journalists work in newsrooms with no policy in place. Country, newsroom size, geographic scope, and revenue source all are significantly related to presence of a policy. Despite differences in organizational factors and country contexts, this study suggests newsrooms in Latin America mostly approach the use and regulation of social media in the same ways. Journalists' descriptions of policies suggest they extend traditional practices and ethics to the social media realm, representing a missed opportunity as journalists lack the guidance they need to deal with the latest technological advancements. Journalists described outward-facing policies focused on protecting the news companies' brands, readers, and sources, rather than protecting journalists.

Social media have become an essential part of reporting and branding processes, affecting journalists' roles and workflows and how they interact with audiences (Ferrer-Conill and Tandoc 2018; Hanusch and Bruns 2017). The introduction of social media into newsrooms, however, also has been fraught with confusion and uncertainty (Lewis and Molyneux 2018) as journalists and news outlets struggle to understand best practices that would allow them to take advantage of the affordances of emerging digital technologies (Bachmann and Harlow 2012). While newsrooms encourage social media use, they're not necessarily regulating that use in the most effective ways (Ihlebaek and Larsson 2018; Opgenhaffen and Scheerlinck 2014), which could be contributing to underutilization and normalization of digital tools (Garcia de Torres et al. 2011; Molyneux and Mourão 2017). Although some news companies and journalist organizations have issued industry guidelines for social media use, scholarly research is only starting to examine the policies media outlets have enacted to regulate journalists' conduct on social media (Bloom, Cleary, and North 2016), and studies have yet to specifically explore the role of social media policies in Latin American news media.

With this in mind, this study relies on a survey of journalists from throughout Latin America ($n = 1,094$) to 1) explicate the relationship between policies (or lack thereof) and journalists' work environments and social media practices, and 2) understand, via a Competitive Values Framework (Quinn et al. 1991), how journalists describe and understand the social media policies in place where they work. These two goals are linked in that journalists' conceptions of the policies guiding their practices could influence the usage decisions they make. Offering a foundational understanding of policies in Latin America helps shed light on how journalists use social media, as without policies, or with inefficient or misunderstood policies, journalists might be hesitant to experiment or use social media in innovative ways, furthering normalization and potentially hindering the institutionalization of social media (Mergel and Bretschneider 2013) in journalism throughout the region. Further, considering the dearth of research on social media policies in Latin American newsrooms, exploring how journalists describe the contents of policies provides insight into what newsrooms in different countries view as "professional" online behavior, illuminating the opportunities and challenges they see in using social media in innovative, non-normalized ways.

Literature review

An extensive body of scholarship has explored journalists' use of social media in news gathering, content sharing, branding, and audience relations (e.g. Bloom, Cleary, and North 2016; Canter 2013; Gulyas 2013; Hermida, Lewis, and Zamith 2014; Lasorsa, Lewis, and Holton 2012; Saldaña et al. 2017). While some studies simultaneously consider the opportunities and challenges that social media present for journalism (e.g. Belair-Gagnon 2015), often research tends to focus either on the "bright side" or on the "dark side" (Baccarella et al. 2018). Lewis and Molyneux (2018) found that the narrative of "control" dominates research about journalists' use of social media, with scholars approaching it as a "boon" for journalism in terms of audience access and interactivity, or a hindrance in terms of tensions arising over perceived loss of journalistic control. Understanding how journalists perceive and use social media in the newsroom offers insight into why it is important to examine how the presence or absence of social media policies might influence the extent to which journalists incorporate social media into their work. Social media policies, like social media use, tend to be evaluated in terms of the opportunities or risks they present (Lee 2016; Newman, Dutton, and Blank 2012). In this light, the following sections consider previous research that analyzes the bright side of using social media in journalism, in terms of facilitating reporting, dissemination, and audience interaction processes, as well as the challenges and risks that come with adopting such participatory tools. Subsequent sections consider social media journalistic uses in Latin America specifically, as well as how social media policies have been enacted in various newsrooms around the world. The benefits and challenges of social media for journalism offer a framework for better understanding the role of social media policies and how they might change journalists' social media uses.

Using social media in journalism

Research identifies sourcing, story ideas, awareness, gatekeeping, branding, and audience interaction as some of the main ways journalists have taken advantage of the opportunities social media afford (Broersma and Graham 2012; Lawrence 2015; Tandoc and Vos 2016). When news is breaking, journalists often turn to social media to stay up-to-date with what is happening until they can get to the scene (Canter 2013), or to fill a void when journalists don't have on-the-ground access or when media are censored (Hermida, Lewis, and Zamith 2014; Lotan et al. 2011). Social media also are potentially facilitating transparency and accountability in journalists' work (Lasorsa, Lewis, and Holton 2012), contributing to the evolution of journalists' roles and prompting new understandings of how journalists can or should interact with audiences (Ferrer-Conill and Tandoc 2018; Weber and Monge 2014).

Over all, research suggests journalists have embraced social media in their work, yet tend to underutilize it or adapt it into traditional norms and routines via normalization (Lasorsa, Lewis, and Holton 2012; Tandoc and Vos 2016). Garcia de Torres et al. (2011) showed Iberoamerican media outlets used social media to drive traffic to their websites, rather than to interact with readers. Likewise, some U.S. studies have shown little interaction between journalists and audiences on Twitter (Greer and Ferguson 2011; Molyneux and Mourão 2017). In their study of Latin American newspapers' websites, Bachmann and Harlow (2012) found the newspapers did not take full advantage of the multimedia, interactive, or participatory digital features afforded by being online. Similarly, Harlow and Salaverría (2016) showed that participatory features were uncommon at online-only news sites in Latin America. The underutilization of social media and digital tools can be viewed as a product of "normalization," wherein journalists have "normalized" digital practices by applying traditional ways of doing journalism to the online realm (Artwick 2013; Gulyas 2013; Lasorsa, Lewis, and Holton 2012). In contrast, Bruns (2018) noted another potentially problematic normalization process, whereby social media platforms have normalized news companies, rather than the other way around. Such normalization processes demand research into social media policies, raising questions about how journalists' social media practices might change depending on the presence of a social media policy to guide their use.

Risks of social media

Griffin (2012) noted that social media ranks among the top five risks for businesses, particularly in terms of branding and reputation, creating a need for policies that guide social media use (Lenartz 2012; Short 2012). One concern with employees using social media to serve as brand ambassadors is the control the company loses over published content (Berthon et al. 2012; Fuduric and Mandelli 2014). For journalists, the participatory opportunities of social media go hand-in-hand with potential risks, as participation in online spaces pushes the boundaries of professional norms and values (Reed 2013; Singer 2005). The lines between the "personal" and the "professional" are blurred on social media, raising concerns about journalists' ability to maintain traditional values like objectivity and professional distance (Canter 2013).

The potential to spread hoaxes and trivial or inaccurate information, and the difficulties associated with verifying sources and user-generated content, also are risks accompanying the incorporation of social media into news processes (Lee 2016). Such risks can threaten the professionalism of journalism (Reed 2013), potentially influencing journalists' social media use. Additionally, news organizations and journalists increasingly are raising concerns over their social media presence and dependence on third-party social media platforms (Chua and Westlund 2019), and the way news outlets have been normalized into these platforms (Bruns 2018). Ekström and Westlund (2019) highlighted the power imbalance between news organizations and social media platforms, and identified a "dislocation of news journalism" as news outlets' dependency on non-proprietary platforms potentially damages their journalistic authority and truth and knowledge claims. It is worth considering then, how social media policies might help diminish or at least control some of the risks involved with journalists' social media use, thereby potentially enabling uses that could help balance the outlet-platform power relationship.

The Latin American context

Studies increasingly explore how journalists in Latin America use social media in their work, but few look specifically at how social media policies influence use. Herscovitz (2012) found Brazilian journalists used social media for keeping up with the news, accessing databases, getting press releases, and branding. More recently, Schmitz Weiss (2015) showed that Argentine, Brazilian, and Mexican journalists used social media for news gathering, research, and fact-checking. In their Latin America-wide study of journalists, Saldaña et al. (2017) found evidence of social media used to monitor the news, find story ideas, and promote journalists' work. Interviews with online news managers and a content analysis of journalists' Facebook and Twitter use in various Iberoamerican countries described the usefulness of social media to gather, receive, and circulate the news, but also expressed a need for policies specifying what to post, who to "friend," and how much time to spend on social media (Said-Hung et al. 2014).

Social media policies

Social media have prompted questions over what constitutes "proper" use, leading some news outlets to create social media guidelines in order to optimize the opportunities and minimize the risks (Newman, Dutton, and Blank 2012). For example, The New York Times' policy, while acknowledging the "vital role" social media play in journalism, also notes the "potential risks" social media present to the newspaper (NYT 2017). The policy prohibits political or partisan expression, suggests that nothing online is private so journalists should follow the same rules for their public/professional accounts as for their private accounts, and mandates that exclusives should be published on the newspaper's platforms before social media. The BBC's policy, although less detailed than the Times', specifies that journalists' social media use must not do anything to "risk undermining the BBC's impartiality" (BBC, n.d.). It also calls for journalists to use "editorial judgment" when considering what to post. While many of the larger U.S. and European news outlets publish their social media policies online, in Latin America, if such policies exist, they are not always readily available online. According to Mergel and Bretschneider (2013), development of a policy is a natural part of the social media adoption process. Their three phases of adoption start with experimentation, followed by constructive chaos. The final stage, institutionalization, is characterized by the creation of formal policies to guide use.

Research is starting to examine social media policies in an attempt to understand, despite variations in journalistic cultures and "professionalism" around the world (Waisbord 2013; Weaver and Willnat 2012), whether there is a universally "correct" way for journalists to use social media that takes advantages of its affordances while still protecting news organizations and the professional tenets that help define journalism (Opgenhaffen and Scheerlinck 2014; Sacco and Bossio 2016). A few studies have considered the content of such policies (Opgenhaffen and d'Haenens 2015) and how they are perceived (Opgenhaffen and Scheerlinck 2014; Sacco and Bossio 2016). For example, Ihlebaek and Larsson (2018) study of Norwegian journalists found many did not know whether their news organizations had social media guidelines, and any policies tended to be informal. They concluded that the goal of encouraging, rather than restricting, social media use has resulted in journalists' self-regulation. This is in line with research from Opgenhaffen and Scheerlinck (2014) suggesting Flemish journalists saw social media guidelines as unnecessary since "common sense" guided their practices. Similarly, Sacco and Bossio (2016) interviews with Australian media workers showed that while most believed social media guidelines were important, they saw them as "'common sense' extensions of the norms of journalistic practice" (p. 185). This follows Bloom, Cleary, and North (2016) findings that social media policies were absent from many international news agencies, and when they did exist, they "stretch[ed] existing editorial guidelines to cover social media" (p. 349). This represents another form of normalization, happening in the realm of journalistic social media policies.

Using an opportunities and risk framework, Lee (2016) conducted a content analysis of social media policies at major U.S. and British news outlets and found that most focused on the risks associated with social media, especially in terms of accuracy, objectivity, and the outlet's reputation. Such "prevention-focused" rather than "promotion-focused" guidelines potentially stifle "the collaborative relationship between news providers and consumers" (Lee 2016, p. 123). Lysak, Cremedas, and Wolf (2012) noted the need for clearer guidelines for local TV journalists that instead of telling them what *not* to do, would provide best practices that would help them better use social media as a newsgathering tool. Opgenhaffen and d'Haenens (2015) concluded there is "no homogeneity" in how outlets think journalists should use social media, and argued against any kind of universal policy for news organizations around the world. Ihlebaek and Larsson (2018) noted the need for more research not just into the content of social media guidelines, but also "how guidelines might differ across various countries, between smaller and larger media organizations, as well as across journalistic work cultures" (p. 917). Using the Competing Values Framework (CVF) as an analytical lens, this present study answers that call.

```
                        Relational awareness
        Relational                    │        Transformational
       communication                  │         communication
                                      │
    Conventional  ────────────────────┼──────────────── Dynamic
     structure                        │                 content
                                      │
       Informational                  │       Instructional/persuasive
       communication                  │          communication
                                      │
                         Instrumental logic
```

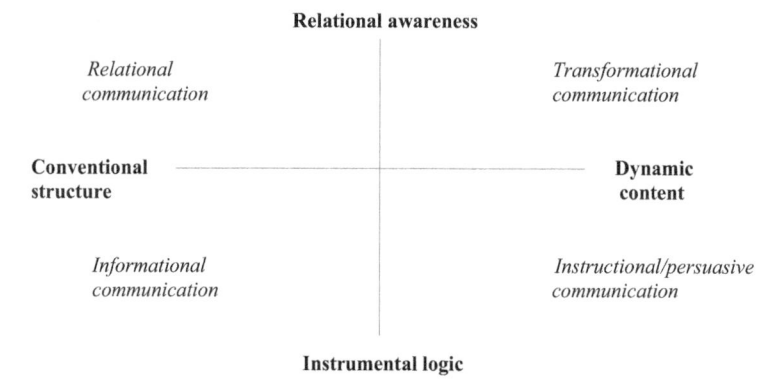

Figure 1. Competing values framework of managerial communication, from Quinn et al. (1991).

Competing values framework

The Competing Values Framework (CVF) is aimed at assessing organizational culture and categorizing organizational and managerial performance and effectiveness (Quinn and Rohrbaugh 1983). The competing values model has two axes defining four quadrants: the horizontal axis ranges from an internal to an external focus, and the vertical axis ranges from flexibility to control. Together, these quadrants demonstrate an organization's competing, or conflicting, values that are not necessarily mutually exclusive.

Quinn et al. (1991) built on the original CVF to create a modified model to evaluate businesses' oral and written communications from a managerial standpoint, such as instruction manuals, technical briefings, or sales presentations. This present study relies on this modified model as most appropriate for understanding social media policies of newsrooms. Quinn et al.'s multi-dimensional model presents the CVF along two dimensions (see Figure 1): conventional structure to dynamic content ranges along a horizontal axis, and instrumental logic to relational awareness along a vertical axis. The four quadrants suggest opposing perceptions of managerial communications: *informational communication* represents the lower left quadrant and encompasses the presentation of logical, organized facts; *transformational communication* in the upper right quadrant represents the competing value, and is characterized by descriptors such as powerful, insightful, expansive, mind-stretching and visionary, with the goal of inspiring change. The lower right quadrant, *instructional/persuasive communication*, is aimed at prompting specific actions and includes descriptors like decisive, action oriented, interesting, stimulating, and engaging. The contrasting value in the upper left quadrant, *relational communication*, is focused on creating trust and a rapport. Ultimately this model suggests that effective communication requires elements from each of the four quadrants.

Fuduric and Mandelli (2014) used Quinn et al. (1991) modified CVF to examine the social media guidelines at 20 multinational corporations spanning various industries. Their content analysis showed most policies were informative and relational, and fewer were transformational or instructional, pointing to an overall weakness in the policies' communication effectiveness. Bennett and Manoharan (2017) also brought up CVF in their examination of social media policies of U.S. municipalities, showing that cities' policies tended toward control and internal communications.

While the communicational CVF offers a systematic way of evaluating business documents, including policies, Quinn et al. (1991) also suggested that its main qualification lies in its function as a theoretical tool to show the diversity of effective policy communication. For example, CVF was used as a theoretical framework for Brady, McLeod, and Young (2015) development of guidelines for social media use in social work classrooms. Noting that social media classroom policies are overly cautious, the authors suggested that CVF can help bridge the tensions between educators who view social media as beneficial and those who see it as a privacy threat, allowing for development of valuable yet still subjective, context-dependent policies to guide ethical social media use. With this in mind, this present study uses the CVF as a lens to help explain journalists' descriptions of social media policies at newsrooms throughout Latin America.

With the preceding in mind, this study poses the following research questions:

RQ1: Which characteristics of Latin American news outlets are related to the presence of social media policies?

RQ2: How does journalists' social media use change depending on whether their outlet has a social media policy?

RQ3: How do journalists describe and perceive the social media policies at the news organizations where they work?

Methods

This study relied on a 2017 Qualtrics survey of journalists ($n = 1,094$) from 20 Latin American countries, and is part of a larger research project focused on the evolution of journalism in Latin America. Respondents were recruited from the University of Texas-Austin's Knight Center for Journalism in the Americas' mailing list of approximately 15,500 subscribers comprised of journalists, journalism students, and educators throughout the Americas, resulting in a 10% response rate (American Association for Public Opinion Research 2016). Journalist respondents came from 20 Latin American countries, including Puerto Rico. Most (32.9%) were from Brazil, followed by Mexico (18.5%), Venezuela (7.8%), and Argentina (7.7%).

Newsroom characteristics

The following survey measures were used as independent variables for RQ1:

Country
Respondents identified which country they worked in.

Type
The questionnaire asked whether respondents worked at a broadcast TV, cable TV, newspaper, magazine, commercial radio, community radio, news wire, a digital native/

online-only outlet, or other. These categories were collapsed into the following during analysis: broadcast/cable TV, newspaper/magazine, commercial/community radio, news wire, and digital/online-only outlet.

Size

Respondents noted how many people worked at their news outlets: 1–5, 6–10, 11–20, 21–50, 51–100, or more than 100 persons. For analysis, these categories were collapsed into 1–20, 21–50, 50–100, and 100+.

Geographic scope

Respondents were asked whether they worked at local, regional, national, or international outlets.

Ownership

Respondents specified whether the outlets they worked at were owned by one of the following: a private individual or family without direct political ties, a politician, a private foundation, a non-profit organization, a commercial media company traded publicly on the stock market, a workers' cooperative, a conglomerate of media and non-media companies traded publicly on the stock market, the state controlled by the government, funded but not controlled by the state, joint public-private venture, or other. For analysis, these options were collapsed into individuals/families, foundations/non-profit, corporation/conglomerate, cooperative, and government.

Funding

Respondents were asked to identify their outlets' main source of revenue: direct sales, subscriptions, advertising, events, subsidies/foundation grants, reader donations, or other. During analysis, government funding emerged as a prominent "other" category. As such, these categories were collapsed into traditional funding (direct sales, subscriptions, advertising), non-traditional funding (events, foundations, reader donations), and government.

Social media

Policies

Respondents were asked if their outlets had a social media policy. This dichotomous variable served as the dependent variable for RQ1 and the independent variable for RQ2.

Use

On a scale of 1–5, where 1 = never and 5 = all the time, respondents noted how often they used social media for the following: to find story ideas, to find sources, to communicate with readers about your stories, to conduct interviews, to receive information from sources, to receive feedback from readers on your stories, to receive/read press releases, to stay in touch with friends/family, to write about/discuss daily life events, to stay up-to-date on the news, to know what people are talking about, to verify information, to provide more information about your job, to transmit events live, to promote your own work, or for entertainment/distraction. These use variables were used to answer RQ2 in two ways. First, the individual uses were analyzed separately as dependent variables in multiple independent samples t-tests. Next, based off a principal components factor analysis with Varimax rotation that revealed four dimensions with Eigenvalues above 1, composite use variables were created and their reliabilities reported (Spector 1992). The four factors accounted for 58.67% of variance. The first factor, which had an Eigenvalue of 5.197 and accounted for 32.48% of variance, was used to create the *reporting function* composite variable (to find story ideas, to find sources, to conduct interviews, to receive information from sources, and to receive press releases; $\alpha=.787$). The second dimension, with an Eigenvalue of 1.57 explained 9.79% of variance, became the composite variable of the *audience function* (to communicate with readers about your stories, to receive feedback from readers on your stories, to transmit events live, to promote your own work, and to provide behind-the-scenes information; $\alpha=.795$). The third, which had an Eigenvalue of 1.5 and explained 9.36% of variance, became the *monitor function* (to stay up-to-date on the news, to know what people are talking about, to verify information; $\alpha=.66$). The final dimension, which had an Eigenvalue of 1.13 and accounted for 7.04% of variance, related to a *non-journalistic function* (to stay in touch with friends/family, to write about/discuss daily life events, entertainment/distraction; $\alpha=.58$), and so was not relevant for this analysis.

Open-ended responses

The final research question relied on a two-pronged approach to analyze responses to an open-ended question that asked journalists to describe their outlets' social media policies, if they existed ($n=317$). First, the *Provalis WordStat* software was employed to conduct topic modeling on the open-ended responses. Topic modeling uses algorithmic techniques to discover patterns in the text, relying on "probabilistic models for uncovering the underlying semantic structure of a document collection" (Blei and Lafferty 2009, p. 1). Media analyses increasingly use topic modeling (Jacobi, van Atteveldt, and Welbers 2016; Shahin 2019). According to Shahin (2019), topic modeling produces: "(1) a series of 'topics,' each comprising keywords that have a statistically high probability of co-occurrence and together produce a meaningful theme, and (2) the proportion of use of each topic in the documents." (p. 6).

Lemmatization and stop words were used. Topic modeling first yielded the maximum number of possible topics. Subsequent rounds reduced the number of topics, producing different models, until one resulted that was theoretically and statistically appropriate, with Eigenvalues above one and with each topic clearly defined with relevant keywords (see Table 1).

Once the topics had been identified, a thematic analysis (Lindlof and Taylor 2002) of journalists' open-ended responses ($n=317$) to the same question that asked respondents to describe their outlets' social media policies was conducted using CVF as an analytical lens to look for common themes and patterns that emerged from within the different topics. Respondents' open-ended responses categorized into the

Table 1. Topics of journalists' open-ended survey responses.

	Category	Keywords	Eigenvalue (%)
Topic 1	Traditional practices/roles/ ethics of journalists	confirmar; noticiar; difundir; publicar; deber; fuente; información; medir	4.1
Topic 2	Protect company image	político; empresa; opiniões; público; dar; evitar, opinión; deber; personar; tener; personal	4.05
Topic 3	Respect for readers/sources	dirigir; respetar; verificación; personar; fuente; hacer; ético	1.43

topics identified via Topic Modeling were closely read and re-read to identify recurring themes, commonalities, and articulations within each topic until no new themes emerged (Strauss and Corbin 1998). This step allowed for interpretation of how these themes and topics fit within the CVF, thus providing a more nuanced analysis of how journalists understood the social media policies in their newsrooms. Such a qualitative approach is useful for exploring undeveloped research areas (Brennen 2013), as well as for helping reveal and interpret the communicative constructs of journalists' "lived experience" (Lindlof and Taylor 2002, p. 237).

Results

Overall, results show that only about a third of journalists (33.9%, $n = 371$) reported working in a newsroom with a social media policy. About half (50.6%, $n = 554$) said there was no policy, and about 15% ($n = 169$) did not know or did not answer. Most respondents worked at a digital/online-only outlet (49.2%, $n = 456$) or newspaper/magazine (31.3%, $n = 290$), followed by broadcast/cable TV (9%, $n = 83$), commercial/community radio (6.9%, $n = 64$), or a news wire (3.6%, $n = 33$). Most of the outlets where respondents worked were small, with 1–20 employees (63.7%, $n = 619$), or large with 100+ employees (16.4%, $n = 159$), followed 21–50 employees (11.6%, $n = 113$) and 50–100 employees (8.2%, $n = 80$). Generally the outlets where respondents worked were national in scope (43.4%, $n = 442$), followed by regional (23.7%, $n = 242$), local (19%, $n = 194$), and international outlets (13.8%, $n = 141$). In terms of ownership, most journalists said their outlets were owned by individuals/families (61.6%, $n = 614$), followed by foundations/non-profit (19.8%, $n = 197$), the government (10.9%, $n = 109$), a corporation/conglomerate (5.3%, $n = 53$), and cooperatives (2.4%, $n = 24$). These outlets were journalists worked relied mostly on traditional funding (direct sales, subscriptions, advertising, 72.8%, $n = 593$), followed by non-traditional funding (events, foundations, reader donations, 16.8%, $n = 137$), and government (10.4%, $n = 85$).

Organizational influences

In answering RQ1, which considered how various organizational-level factors of Latin American news outlets related to the presence of social media policies, results of chi-square tests showed significant differences when it came to size, geographic scope, country, and revenue source (see Table 2). Journalists working in larger newsrooms (55.7%), significantly more than smaller ones, reported having social media

Table 2. Crosstabulation of organizational factors and presence of social media policies in Latin American newsrooms.

	No policy	Policy	χ^2
Geographic scope	%	%	13.649**
Local	70.5	29.5	
Regional	57.4	42.6	
National	58.6	41.4	
International	50	50	
Total	59.5	40.5	
Size			15.601***
1–20	62.3	37.7	
21–50	62.6	37.4	
51–100	57.4	42.6	
100+	44.3	55.7	
Total	59	41	
Revenue source			6.423*
Traditional	57.8	42.2	
Non-traditional	66.7	33.3	
Government	48.6	51.4	
Total	58.4	41.6	
Ownership			3.678
Individual or family	59.7	40.3	
Foundation	63.1	36.9	
Corp. or conglomerate	47.6	52.4	
Coop	59.1	40.9	
Government	56.8	43.2	
Total	59.5	40.5	
Type of media			7.119
TV	59.7	40.3	
Print	62.3	37.7	
Radio	69.1	30.9	
Online only	57.1	42.9	
Wire	43.3	56.7	
Total	59.3	40.7	
Country			37.199**
Argentina	63.8	36.2	
Bolivia	80.0	20.0	
Brazil	56.9	43.1	
Chile	74.2	25.8	
Colombia	51.4	48.6	
Costa Rica	44.4	55.6	
Cuba	33.3	66.7	
Dom. Republic	89.5	10.5	
Ecuador	67.6	32.4	
El Salvador	46.2	53.8	
Guatemala	52.0	48.0	
Honduras	65.7	35.3	
Mexico	51.1	48.9	
Nicaragua	64.3	35.7	
Panama	75.0	25.0	
Paraguay	100	0.0	
Peru	78.4	21.6	
Puerto Rico	50.0	50.0	
Uruguay	64.3	35.7	
Venezuela	66.2	33.8	
Total	59.9	40.1	

*$p < .05$,
**$p < .01$,
***$p < .001$.

policies ($x^2 = 15.601$, df $= 3$, $p < .001$). Significantly more respondents from national (41.4%) and international (50%) outlets had social media policies ($x^2 = 13.649$, df $= 3$, $p < .01$) compared with those working at local or regional outlets.

Country where the journalists worked made a significant difference in presence of a social media policy ($x^2 = 37.199$, df = 19, $p < .01$). More journalists from Cuba (66.7%), Costa Rica (55.6%), and El Salvador (53.8%) worked at outlets with social media policies compared with journalists from other Latin American countries.

Outlets' main revenue source also made a significant difference ($x^2 = 6.423$, df = 2, $p < .05$). More respondents working at outlets with government funding (51.4%) or traditional revenue sources (42.2%) had social media policies compared with those working at outlets with non-traditional (33.3%) funding.

Ownership and type of media outlet (i.e. television, newspaper, etc.) were not significant.

Social media uses

To answer RQ2, which considered whether the way journalists use social media changes depending on whether their outlet has a social media policy, independent samples T-tests were conducted. However, results showed that none of the composite variables (reporting function, interacting with audiences function, or monitoring the news function) was significantly related to the presence of a social media policy. However, when considering social media uses individually, having a social media policy was significantly related to how often respondents said they used social media to broadcast live events [$t(671.500) = -2.346$, $p < .05$]. Respondents from a newsroom with a social media policy had a higher frequency of broadcasting live via social media ($M = 3.17$, SD = 1.498) than those working in newsrooms without a policy ($M = 2.90$, SD = 1.549). Other individual social media uses were not significant.

Perceptions of social media policies

The final research question relied on topic modeling and thematic analysis to better understand journalists' perceptions of Latin American outlets' social media policies, especially in relation to the Competing Values Framework for managerial communications (Quinn et al. 1991). With topic modeling, journalists' responses to an open-ended question to describe their outlets' social media policies were categorized into three main topics. **Topic 1**, identified as *traditional journalistic practices/roles/ethics*, refers to journalists who discussed social media policies in terms of guidelines for how they can use social platforms to fulfill traditional journalistic responsibilities. This topic is characterized by words such as publish, spread, information, tell the news, and confirm. **Topic 2**, identified as *protecting the company's image*, included discussion of guidelines in terms of putting the media outlet's reputation first, and was characterized by words such as company, responsibility, public, avoid, personal, and opinions. Finally, **Topic three** was identified as *respecting readers and sources*. This topic included key words such as respect, verification, source, and ethics. Using these topics as a guiding framework, a thematic analysis of journalists' open-ended responses then was conducted.

TOPIC 1: Within the *traditional journalistic practices/roles* topic, three main themes emerged as to how journalists characterized policies: *news diffusion, fact-checking,* and *ethics*. The policies that journalists described as aimed at *news diffusion* were those that specified what to post, when to post, and which platforms to use. A few even mentioned the need to use proper grammar. One journalist noted, "Reporters are allowed to post only the news they make or some stories (which are previously identified). It is not allowed to publish photos of bodies (dead) or very strong images. We have different ways of working on Facebook and Instagram. In Instagram, for example, stories are allowed when the news is still happening." Journalists' responses also indicated, though, that policies ended up focusing more on what *not* to do, potentially leaving them in the dark as to what to do.

Fact-checking policies were those journalists described as specifying that social media content should be subject to the same strenuous verification processes as content that is printed or broadcast. "Verify content, just as the veracity of the source," one journalist said. Another noted, "Always search on different platforms; don't believe the first thing you read/see." Social media also could be used to help verify information, journalists noted in their responses.

Journalists also highlighted policies that mentioned the importance of traditional *ethics* being maintained on social media. "Separate the professional and personal, and nothing partisan," one respondent said. Another noted, "Avoid expressing personal or controversial opinions." Some said that policies stipulated social media were strictly for professional use only. One respondent even referred to a policy that prohibited "expressing political opinions or explicitly endorsing a soccer team."

TOPIC 2: Within the *respect the company's image* topic, the main theme to emerge was that of social media as a risk. Journalists said policies specified that journalists should "avoid ... covering any topics outside our editorial line." Similarly, another said to only publish that which agrees with the company's editorial line. One journalist said, "Respect the business' principals" and another noted, "Don't criticize the outlet" or do something that could "jeopardize" the company. "Take care of the company's reputation" another journalist responded.

Lastly, the final topic of *respecting readers and sources* revealed two main themes among journalists' perceptions of social media policies: a division over how to respond to readers on social media, and privacy. Some respondents said the policies said to "always" respond to readers' comments, no matter what. "Interact, even with criticism," one journalist said. Others took the opposite position: interact, but "don't respond to complaints or insults." Another noted, "Don't argue with sources or readers in public." A few even went so far as to call for "little interaction with users."

The privacy theme showed how journalists described social media policies as specifying the need to maintain respect for readers and sources' privacy. "Defend and maintain privacy of sources. Avoid insults and slander," one respondent noted. Many journalists also linked privacy with a respect for human rights.

Discussion and conclusions

This study used a survey of Latin American journalists to explore the link between the presence of social media policies in newsrooms and journalists' work environments and editorial decisions. Research is only starting to explore the impact of social media policies on journalism, and to date little research has examined this topic in Latin

America, allowing this study to fill a gap in the literature. Further, as Ihlebaek and Larsson (2018) noted, more interrogation of the content of social media guidelines and policies is needed across countries and different organizational sizes. By looking at such policies at different types and sizes of outlets throughout Latin America, this present study advances our understanding of how guidelines might be hindering or helping journalistic social media practices.

Findings show that only about 40% of journalists reported working at media outlets with social media policies, which extends to Latin America findings from other countries that suggest while newsrooms increasingly are adopting policies, formal guidelines are still not an institutionalized practice (Bloom, Cleary, and North 2016; Ihlebaek and Larsson 2018). As Mergel and Bretschneider (2013) noted, social media policies are the third and final phase of social media adoption, indicating that most Latin American news outlets have yet to reach that institutionalization stage and remain in early phases of adoption. Such a finding makes sense considering that previous research suggests media outlets in Latin America do not necessarily take full advantage of the interactive and participatory affordances of the Internet (Bachmann and Harlow 2012; Harlow and Salaverría 2016). Further, as this study showed, when newsrooms do adopt social media policies, journalists describe them as more oriented at what *not* to do or protecting the company's image, focusing on the potential risks rather than rewards of using social media. This finding is in line with Lee's (2016) finding about the prevalence of "prevention-focused" social media policies at U.S. and British news outlets. Policies more about control than flexibility (Quinn et al. 1991) normalize traditional journalistic practices to fit a social media context, thereby clinging to old understandings of journalism, rather than pushing the boundaries of what could be considered "professional." Despite differences in organizational factors and country contexts, this study thus suggests newsrooms in Latin America for the most part approach the use and regulation of social media in the same ways.

This study advances social media scholarship by showing that an outlet's country, size, geographic scope, and type of revenue all are related to presence of social media policies, indicating that organizational level factors are important influencers in how journalists will be able to use social media in their jobs. Interestingly, in terms of country, the region's countries with the worst (Cuba) and best (Costa Rica) press freedom records are those where journalists were most likely to say they worked at outlets with social media policies. Future research should explore the role of countries further. One possible explanation is that Cuba's policies see social media more as a risk—low press freedom could indicate low tolerance for social media and its potential democratizing capacity. In contrast, Costa Rica's policies could approach social media as more of an opportunity, since high press freedom could indicate higher tolerance for experimentation and innovative uses of social media. Thus, Lee's (2016) finding that U.S. and British news outlets' social media policies focused on risk and preventative measures could be at play in the country differences found in this current study.

Journalists working in larger newsrooms, as well as national and international outlets and those with traditional funding mechanisms (advertising), also were more likely to say their companies had social media policies. Larger newsrooms have more employees, making the risks of not having a formal policy greater, simply because more people are posting on social platforms. Further, larger, potentially more established media outlets might see social media policies as a way to curb any potential risks and protect their company's reputations, while smaller outlets not beholden to advertisers might feel as if they have more freedom to experiment and thus see less of a need to explicitly regulate their journalists' social media use. It is noteworthy that neither type of outlet (i.e. online, print, etc.) nor ownership (i.e. family, foundation, government, etc.) made a significant difference in presence of a social media policy. This is further evidence of the lack of institutionalization of social media use in Latin American newsrooms, as newspapers and digital-native sites are no different when it comes to whether they have a policy or not.

Presence of social media policies only somewhat mattered when it came to how journalists used social media at work. Except for livestreaming, which was significantly associated with presence of a policy, having a social media policy did not make a difference in how journalists used social media. In other words, regardless of whether there was a policy in place, journalists used social media mostly in the same ways. The fact that live streaming was the only use associated with having a policy could be because journalists are not taking full advantage of social media because they are unsure what is allowed and what is not. This finding points to a potential weakness of social media policies and their inability to adequately guide journalists' practices, and prepare them for the next technological development.

This study also examined journalists' open-ended responses describing social media policies, and results showed responses were categorized into three topics, according to 1) traditional journalistic practices/roles/ethics, 2) protecting the company's image, and 3) respecting readers and sources. The first topic lends itself toward a normalization view (Gulyas 2013; Molyneux and Mourão 2017), as journalists described policies as about preserving traditional ways of doing and thinking about journalism. From a CVF (Quinn et al. 1991) perspective, such policies have an internal focus and are more control-oriented than flexible. Based on journalists' characterizations, these policies would seem to fit best within the *informational communication* quadrant of the modified CVF, as they follow conventional structure and instrumental logic. In other words, these policies are about communicating logical information about what journalists should and should not do on social media, based on what they should and should not do in print or on television. Similarly, the second topic, *protecting the company's image*, also is control- and internally focused, and fits within the relational communication quadrant of the modified CVF. These policies aimed at controlling posts to align with the company's editorial line and protect its reputation seemingly represent conventional structure and relational awareness. Just like with policies in the first topic, content is not dynamic or transformational, but rather aimed at protecting the status quo instead of implementing change. Both of these topics potentially point to weaknesses in transformational and instructional communication effectiveness, in line with Fuduric and Mandelli (2014) content analysis of social media policies at multinational corporations. While it can be argued that news companies with their public service missions should have a different agenda than a profit-focused corporation, any potential similarities in CVF approaches to social media policies could suggest that news companies' policies are missing the mark: perhaps they are too focused on preserving traditional definitions of journalism and professionalism (Reed 2013; Waisbord 2013) and protecting the bottom line, thereby missing out on innovative and transformative ways of using social media.

At the same time, the third topic, *respect for readers and sources*, and the way journalists described social media policies as divided over how to respond to readers, suggests an internal *and* external focus, as well as control *and* flexibility. As a result, based on open-ended survey responses, policies within this topic could separately fit within multiple quadrants of the modified CVF. Those policies suggesting a more open, expansive way of looking at the producer-consumer relationship—such as directing journalists to respond to all reader comments, even the negative ones—could fit into the *transformational communication* quadrant, as the policy ultimately could be seen as aimed at overhauling audience interaction. In contrast, those more restrictive policies that called for little interaction, or to never respond to negative comments, fit better within the *informational communication* or *relational communication* quadrants that emphasize conventional structure. As Quinn et al. (1991) originally suggested with their modified CVF, the most effective managerial communication combines elements from all four quadrants; journalists' survey responses, however, indicate policies take mostly informational or relational approaches to communicating social media guidelines, mostly missing out on transformational and instructional/persuasive communication. No wonder, then, that previous studies show journalists often are unaware whether their newsroom even has a social media policy, or think a policy is unnecessary (Ihlebaek and Larsson 2018; Opgenhaffen and Scheerlinck 2014). It also is noteworthy that a few respondents of this current study noted they were unclear what their outlets' social media policies entailed, or that guidelines were actually informal, and not written policies, potentially leading to further confusion about how to behave professionally on social media.

One limitation of this research is that it relied on a mailing list of self-subscribed journalists, so it is not generalizable to all journalists in Latin America. The qualitative analysis, while providing nuance to journalists' understandings of their policies, also prevents generalization, so findings should be understood within this particular Latin American context. Another limitation is that this study relied on journalists' assessments of social media policies, rather than quantitatively measuring components of the actual policies, so it is likely some journalists were unaware of whether their outlets had policies or what they actually said. Additionally, this study used CVF as an analytical lens to help interpret journalists' qualitative descriptions of social media policies, rather than the policies themselves. Future studies should conduct a content analysis of social media policies to better understand how CVF might be at play, especially when it comes to journalists who are unaware of their newsrooms' policies. Lastly, these findings should be interpreted critically: any social media study should not assume that incorporating social media into the newsroom is inherently beneficial *or* problematic. Further, considering news publishers' over-reliance on third-party social platforms (Schwartz, 2018), this study's findings should not be interpreted as promoting social media guidelines to encourage journalistic social media use at any cost, but rather to consider how social media policies might promote "platform counterbalancing" (Chua and Westlund 2019, p. 162) that lessens both the pressure to have a social media presence and the dependence on such non-proprietary platforms.

Overall this study contributes to research by suggesting that the lack of social media policies in newsrooms across Latin America represents missed opportunities and vulnerabilities. This study adds to scholarship by showing that Latin American journalists see social media policies as more risk- and prevention-focused, similar to such policies in the U.S. and U.K. (Lee 2016). Further, findings answered Ihlebaek and Larsson (2018) call for more research into social media policies across countries, media type, and journalistic culture, by showing use and regulation of social media mostly followed similar patterns across Latin America. Following Quinn et al. (1991) CVF, this study suggests social media policies can be put in place that not only aim to transform practices, but that also are persuasive, showing journalists why they are necessary, and informational – clear and precise, communicating not only what *not* to post, but offering guidelines that leave no questions as to what *to* post. Further, simply extending traditional practices and ethics to the social media realm, as this study and Bloom, Cleary, and North (2016) found, rather than transforming them, represents a missed opportunity as journalists will not have the guidance they need to deal with whatever the latest technological advancements are in the field. Importantly, this study identified a focus on protecting the news companies' brands, and protecting readers and sources. Such outward-facing social media policies, while they might protect a company's image and even potentially build trust with audiences, do nothing to protect journalists. The absence of mentions of protections for journalists being harassed on social media is a striking vulnerability that must be addressed if social media use is truly to become institutionalized in Latin America.

This is not to suggest that a universal social media policy should be applied in newsrooms throughout the region. Just as tenets of journalism and understandings of professionalism vary by country (Waisbord 2013; Weaver and Willnat 2012), it follows that social media policies would differ, as well. Still, in light of the similar media systems across the region, and the findings of this research, some commonalities related to the incorporation of transformational, persuasive, informational, and relational communication techniques could underlie social media policies across countries to make them more effective, even as owners and editors implement policies specific to their country and organizational contexts.

Acknowledgements

The author would like to thank the Knight Center for Journalism in the Americas at the University of Texas at Austin, and its director, Rosental Calmon Alves, for supporting this study.

Disclosure statement

No potential conflict of interest was reported by the author(s).

ORCID

Summer Harlow http://orcid.org/0000-0001-6079-1439

References

American Association for Public Opinion Research. 2016. *Standard Definitions: Final Dispositions of Case Codes and Outcome Rates for Surveys*. 9th ed. AAPOR. https://www.aapor.org/AAPOR_Main/media/publications/Standard-Definitions20169theditionfinal.pdf.

Artwick, C. 2013. "Reporters on Twitter." *Digital Journalism* 1 (2): 212–228.

Baccarella, C. V., T. F. Wagner, J. H. Kietzmann, and I. P. McCarthy. 2018. "Social Media? It's Serious! Understanding the Dark Side of Social Media." *European Management Journal* 36 (4): 431–438.

Bachmann, I., and S. Harlow. 2012. "Opening the Gates: Interactive and Multimedia Elements of Newspaper Websites in Latin America." *Journalism Practice* 6 (2): 217–232.

BBC. (n.d.). "Use of Social Media." *BBC*. https://www.bbc.com/editorialguidelines/news/use-of-social-media.

Belair-Gagnon, V. 2015. *Social Media at BBC News: The Re-Making of Crisis Reporting*. New York: Routledge.

Bennett, L. V., and A. P. Manoharan. 2017. "The Use of Social Media Policies by US Municipalities." *International Journal of Public Administration* 40 (4): 317–328.

Berthon, P. R., L. F. Pitt, K. Plangger, and D. Shapiro. 2012. "Marketing Meets Web 2.0, Social Media, and Creative Consumers: Implications for International Marketing Strategy." *Business Horizons* 55 (3): 261–271.

Blei, D. M., and J. D. Lafferty. 2009. "Topic Models." In *Text Mining*, 101–124. New York: Chapman and Hall/CRC.

Bloom, T., J. Cleary, and M. North. 2016. "Traversing the 'Twittersphere': Social Media Policies in International News Operations." *Journalism Practice* 10 (3): 343–357.

Brady, S. R., D. A. McLeod, and J. A. Young. 2015. "Developing Ethical Guidelines for Creating Social Media Technology Policy in Social Work Classrooms." *Advances in Social Work* 16 (1): 43–54.

Brennen, B. S. 2013. *Qualitative Research Methods for Media Studies*. New York: Routledge.

Broersma, M., and T. Graham. 2012. "Social Media as Beat: Tweets as a News Source during the 2010 British and Dutch Elections." *Journalism Practice* 6 (3): 403–419.

Bruns, A. 2018. *Gatewatching and News Curation: Journalism, Social Media, and the Public Sphere*. New York, NY: Peter Lang.

Canter, L. 2013. "The Interactive Spectrum: The Use of Social Media in UK Regional Newspapers." *Convergence: The International Journal of Research into New Media Technologies* 19 (4): 472–495.

Chua, S., and O. Westlund. 2019. "Audience-Centric Engagement, Collaboration Culture and Platform Counterbalancing: A Longitudinal Study of Ongoing Sensemaking of Emerging Technologies." *Media and Communication* 7 (1): 153–165.

Ekström, M., and O. Westlund. 2019. The dislocation of news journalism: A conceptual framework for the study of epistemologies of digital journalism.

Ferrer-Conill, R., and E. C. Tandoc. Jr. 2018. "The Audience-Oriented Editor: Making Sense of the Audience in the Newsroom." *Digital Journalism* 6 (4): 436–453.

Fuduric, M., and A. Mandelli. 2014. "Communicating Social Media Policies: Evaluation of Current Practices." *Journal of Communication Management* 18 (2): 158–175.

Garcia de Torres, E., L. Yezers'ka, A. Rost, M. Calderin, M. Rojano, C. Edo, E. Sahid, et al. 2011. See you on Facebook or Twitter? The use of social media by 27 news outlets from 9 regions in Argentina, Colombia, Mexico, Peru, Portugal, Spain and Venezuela. Paper presented at International Symposium on Online Journalism, Austin, TX.

Greer, C., and D. Ferguson. 2011. "Using Twitter for Promotion and Branding: A Content Analysis of Local Television Twitter Sites." *Journal of Broadcasting & Electronic Media* 55 (2): 198–214.

Griffin, J. 2012. "Social Media Ranked as a Top Source of Risk." *The Australian*, September 10. http://www.theaustralian.com.au/media/opinion/social-media-ranked-as-a-top-source-of-risk/story-e6frg99o-1226468478717.

Gulyas, A. 2013. "The Influence of Professional Variables on Journalists' Uses and Views of Social Media: A Comparative Study of Finland, Germany, Sweden and the United Kingdom." *Digital Journalism* 1 (2): 270–285.

Harlow, S., and R. Salaverría. 2016. "Regenerating Journalism: Exploring the "Alternativeness" and "Digital-Ness" of Online-Native Media in Latin America." *Digital Journalism* 4 (8): 1001–1019.

Hanusch, F., and A. Bruns. 2017. "Journalistic Branding on Twitter: A Representative Study of Australian Journalists' Profile Descriptions." *Digital Journalism* 5 (1): 26–43.

Hermida, A., S. C. Lewis, and R. Zamith. 2014. "Sourcing the Arab Spring: A Case Study of Andy Carvin's Sources on Twitter during the Tunisian and Egyptian Revolutions." *Journal of Computer-Mediated Communication* 19 (3): 479–499.

Herscovitz, H. 2012. "Brazilian Journalists in the 21st Century." In D. Weaver & L. Wilnat (Eds.). *The Global Journalist in the 21st Century*, 365–381. New York, NY: Routledge.

Ihlebaek, K. A., and O. Larsson. 2018. "Learning by Doing." *Journalism Studies* 19 (6): 905–920.

Jacobi, C., W. van Atteveldt, and K. Welbers. 2016. "Quantitative Analysis of Large Amounts of Journalistic Texts Using Topic Modelling." *Digital Journalism* 4 (1): 89–106.

Lasorsa, D., S. Lewis, and A. Holton. 2012. "Normalizing Twitter: Journalism Practice in an Emerging Communication Space." *Journalism Studies* 13 (1): 19–36.

Lawrence, R. G. 2015. "Campaign News in the Time of Twitter." In V. Farrar-Meyers & J.S. Vaughn (Eds.) *Controlling the Message: New Media in American Political Campaigns*, 93–112. New York and London: New York University Press.

Lee, J. 2016. "Opportunity or Risk? How News Organizations Frame Social Media in Their Guidelines for Journalists." *The Communication Review* 19 (2): 106–127.

Lenartz, A. J. 2012. "Establishing Guidelines for the Use of Social Media in Higher Education." In *Misbehavior Online in Higher Education*, ed. L. A. Wankel and C. Wankel, 333–353. Bingley, England: Emerald Publishing.

Lewis, S. C., and L. Molyneux. 2018. "A Decade of Research on Social Media and Journalism: Assumptions, Blind Spots, and a Way Forward." *Media and Communication* 6 (4): 11–23.

Lindlof, T. R., and B. C. Taylor. 2002. *Qualitative Communication Research Methods*. USA: Sage.

Lotan, G., E. Graeff, M. Ananny, D. Gaffney, I. Pearce, and D. Boyd. 2011. "The Revolutions Were Tweeted: Information Flows during the 2011 Tunisian and Egyptian Revolutions." *International Journal of Communication* 5: 1375–1405.

Lysak, S., M. Cremedas, and J. Wolf. 2012. "Facebook and Twitter in the Newsroom: How and Why Local Television News is Getting Social with Viewers?" *Electronic News* 6 (4): 187–207.

Mergel, I., and S. I. Bretschneider. 2013. "A Three-Stage Adoption Process for Social Media Use in Government." *Public Administration Review* 73 (3): 390–400.

Molyneux, L., and R. R. Mourão. 2017. "Political Journalists' Normalization of Twitter: Interaction and New Affordances." *Journalism Studies*. 20 (2): 248–266.

Newman, N., W. H. Dutton, and G. Blank. 2012. "Social Media in the Changing Ecology of News: The Fourth and Fifth Estates in Britain." *International Journal of Internet Science* 7 (1): 6–22.

NYT. 2017. "The Times Issues Social Media Guidelines for the Newsroom." The *New York Times*. https://www.nytimes.com/2017/10/13/reader-center/social-media-guidelines.html.

Opgenhaffen, M., and L. d'Haenens. 2015. "Managing Social Media Use: Whither Social Media Guidelines in News Organizations?" *International Journal on Media Management* 17 (4): 201–216.

Opgenhaffen, M., and H. Scheerlinck. 2014. "Social Media Guidelines for Journalists." *Journalism Practice* 8 (6): 726–741.

Quinn, R. E., and J. Rohrbaugh. 1983. "A Spatial Model of Effectiveness Criteria: Towards a Competing Values Approach to Organizational Analysis." *Management Science* 29 (3): 363–377.

Quinn, R. E., H. W. Hildebrandt, P. S. Rogers, and M. P. Thompson. 1991. "A Competing Values Framework for Analyzing Presentational Communication in Management Contexts." *Journal of Business Communication* 28 (3): 213–232.

Reed, S. 2013. "American Sports Writers' Social Media Use and Its Influence on Professionalism." *Journalism Practice* 7 (5): 555–571.

Sacco, V., and D. Bossio. 2016. "Don't Tweet This!" *Digital Journalism* 5 (2): 1–17.

Said-Hung, E., A. Serrano-Tellería, E. García-De-Torres, M. Calderín, A. Rost, C. Arcila-Calderón, … J. Sánchez-Badillo. 2014. "Ibero-American Online News Managers' Goals and Handicaps in Managing Social Media." *Television & New Media* 15 (6): 577–589.

Saldaña, M., V. D. M. Higgins Joyce, A. Schmitz Weiss, and R. C. Alves. 2017. "Sharing the Stage: Analysis of Social Media Adoption by Latin American Journalists." *Journalism Practice* 11 (4): 396–416.

Schwartz, J. 2018. "A Pullback from Platforms and a Focus on Products." *Nieman Journalism Lab.* Retrieved from http://www.niemanlab.org/2018/12/a-pullback-from-platforms-and-a-focus-on-product.

Schmitz Weiss, A. 2015. "The Digital and Social Media Journalist: A Comparative Analysis of Journalists in Argentina, Brazil, Colombia, Mexico, and Peru." *International Communication Gazette* 77 (1): 74–101.

Shahin, S. 2019. "Facing up to Facebook: How Digital Activism, Independent Regulation, and Mass Media Foiled a Neoliberal Threat to Net Neutrality." *Information, Communication & Society* 22 (1): 1–17.

Short, M. 2012. "Play Nice in Social Media Sandpit." *The Age.* http://www.theage.com.au/opinion/society-andculture/play-nice-in-social-media-sandpit-20120907-25jwt.html.

Singer, J. B. 2005. "The Political J-Blogger: 'Normalizing' a New Media Form to Fit Old Norms and Practices." *Journalism: Theory, Practice & Criticism* 6 (2): 173–198.

Spector, P. E. 1992. *Summated Rating Scale Construction.* Newbury Park, Calif: Sage.

Strauss, A. C., and J. M. Corbin. 1998. *Basics of Qualitative Research: Techniques and Procedures for Developing Grounded Theory.* Thousand Oaks, CA: Sage.

Tandoc, E. C., Jr, and T. P. Vos. 2016. "The Journalist is Marketing the News: Social Media in the Gatekeeping Process." *Journalism Practice* 10 (8): 950–966.

Waisbord, S. 2013. *Reinventing Professionalism: Journalism and News in Global Perspective.* Cambridge: Polity.

Weaver, D., and L. Willnat. 2012. *The Global Journalist in the 21st Century.* London: Routledge.

Weber, M. S., and P. R. Monge. 2014. "Industries in Turmoil: Driving Transformation during Periods of Disruption." *Communication Research* 41: 1–30.

Stronger and Safer Together: Motivations for and Challenges of (Trans)National Collaboration in Investigative Reporting in Latin America

Lourdes M. Cueva Chacón and Magdalena Saldaña

ABSTRACT
Despite the growing scholarship on investigative journalism in Latin America, very few studies have addressed collaboration across newsrooms in the region. By analyzing the responses of 251 journalists who work for investigative units in Latin American news outlets, this study explores a) the reasons why Latin American journalists are increasingly seeking to participate in national and transnational collaborative enterprises, b) the challenges they identify, and c) the role digital technologies are playing in this trend of transnational collaboration. Using mixed methods, we found that collaborations occur to enhance the impact of investigative projects, to reach larger audiences, and to achieve a big-picture coverage. We also found that safety is an important motivation to work in conjunction with other newsrooms—by collaborating, journalists are able to strengthen security measures and challenge censorship. Yet, coordinating teams—especially at the transnational level—remains the biggest challenge to overcome. Digital technologies are significantly related to reporters' likelihood of collaborating, but these technologies require other reporting skills to be useful for investigative journalism. Implications for research and practice are discussed.

But from day one in 1997, there was one, simple operating principle within the consortium: collaboration, collaboration, collaboration! We are still only at the dawn of a new age. And amid a world of debilitating political dysfunction with the mostdire potential consequences, the crucial concept of public accountability cannot and should not be narrowly confined by local or national borders, or the rigid strictures, orthodoxies, conceits and insecurities of traditional journalism.

Charles Lewis, ICIJ, Founder, 2016

Introduction

Digital investigative journalism projects from Latin America are increasingly winning important awards worldwide (Mioli 2018; Nalvarte 2016). The region is undoubtedly producing high-quality data journalism (de Assis 2019; Mazote 2017). But there is another trend that can be observed among the award-winning projects in the region: collaboration across newsrooms either nationally or transnationally. For instance, in the 2018 Excellence in Journalism Awards by the Inter American Press Association, nine collaborative projects won awards among a total of 13 award categories (Sociedad Interamericana de Prensa 2018). The winner in the Data Journalism category—VíaSobrecosto, part of Investigate Lava Jato—was a collaborative effort that involved more than 20 journalists from 15 countries, most of them from Latin America (Convoca 2018). The project, conceived á lá Panama Papers, had internalized the philosophy of "radical sharing" sponsored by the International Consortium of Investigative Journalists (Romera and Gallego 2018), of which many of these news organizations are members.

More recently, at the 2019 International Symposium of Online Journalism (ISOJ), Pablo Fernández, from Chequeado—an Argentinian fact-checking news organization—said, "Collaboration is key. I know it's a trendy word, but it's totally real in our case" (Fernández 2019). Fernández's comment is an example of a growing attitude among some Latin American journalists that favors collaborative practices, and his experience might suggest that journalists are identifying benefits in collaborative projects. Graves and Konieczna (2015) in their analysis of collaboration in the U.S., attributed the move to support more open collaborations to a relief in "the tension between the field's commercial orientation and its democratic mission" (p. 1971) caused by the economic crisis in journalism.

Other signs of increasing interest and participation in collaborations can be observed through the creation of guides and manuals. For instance, the Red Internacional de Periodistas, a project from the International Center For Journalists (ICFJ), has included a new section in Spanish in their website devoted to collaborative journalism that includes guidelines and case studies (Red Internacional de Periodistas 2018).

However, the questions as of what are the main characteristics of these Latin American journalists, and the reasons they are increasingly seeking to participate in this type of enterprises have yet to be answered. Studies focused on investigative journalism in the U.S., Britain, and Australia have found that the industry has incorporated digital tools and collaboration to keep producing high-quality projects despite the lack of resources (Carson and Farhall 2018) and "to increase the impact of their own reporting" (Graves and Konieczna 2015, 1973). In Latin America, Schmitz Weiss et al. (2018) found that news entrepreneurs tied innovation and sustainability to the development of collaborative processes. Collaborative projects such as the Panama and Paradise Papers were possible because of technology affordances and because journalists were capable of exploiting those affordances (Lewis 2018). Even so, there is a gap in the research that analyzes the role that digital tools and journalists' digital nativeness play in these collaborative efforts. This project was designed to do just that. Journalists from 20 countries in Latin America answered an online survey with questions relevant to explore the goals of this study: a) the motivations for collaboration, b) the challenges of working on collaborative projects, and c) the role digital tools might play in these collaborations.

Theoretical Framework

The impetus and enthusiasm expressed by journalists about collaborative practices, coupled with the impact of large, but very rare, collaborative projects such as the Panama and Paradise Papers could, however, lead scholars to follow idealistic notions of the democratic potentials of technology. It is tempting to blindly consider the existence of a special breed of digital journalists imbued with norms and values of a digital culture (Deuze 2006) that not only expects, but demands participation. There is the need to contrast these idealistic approaches with more critical views to journalism norms and routines and the role of technology. Borger et al. (2013), for instance, in their genealogical analysis of participatory journalism as a field of study, have pointed to how "scholars observe(d) that participatory journalism's democratic ideal" has clashed" with professional journalism's core values of objectivity and autonomy" (p. 127), leading to disappointment with journalism's inflexibility to carry those ideals.

Nevertheless, technology has brought structural changes that must be considered. As opposed to the "highly competitive and mutually independent" attitude of journalists during the golden era of investigative journalism (Carson and Farhall 2018, 1900), in the networked society, digital journalists are interacting with—if not becoming themselves—technologists to "take advantage of the distinct way that programmers think about technology in terms of the hacker ethic... and to re-interpret this into the language of news" (Lewis and Usher 2013, 604). It is not that investigative journalism lacked a strong public-interest ethics, but that technological changes brought by the digital world are contributing to the creation of hybrid professional cultures (Waisbord 2013) where journalists are embracing the open-source mentality and its pro-social interest (Coleman 2012) in more overt ways than in the past (Graves and Konieczna 2015). They do not only use what is shared, but they themselves share what they have produced. In the same ISOJ presentation mentioned above, Fernández (2019) from *Chequeado* gave away a link to a free video transcription tool developed by his team. Actions like this one suggest reporters and media practitioners are more likely to openly share not only information, but also tools and other means to access and produce news content.

Trying to balance the factors expressed above, this project draws from three strands of research for its design: the particular history of investigative journalism in Latin America, the degree of digitalness of Latin American journalism, and research on digital collaborative journalism.

Investigative and Watchdog Journalism in Latin America

As Waisbord (2000) elaborately describes it, Latin American watchdog journalism grew strong in the 1980s and 1990s because of its integration as part of mainstream media and the support of corporations. That integration was an important shift in the way watchdog journalism had been conducted in the decades before when, alternating democratic governments with dictatorial ones, watchdog journalism was either marginal or clandestine (Waisbord 2000), respectively. Toward the change of the millennium, operating under steadier democracies and the economic changes brought by neoliberalism, conditions emerged for the development of "an independent journalism *á lá Americaine*" in the region (Alves 2005, 200). This meant independent, pro-democratic, aggressive, and, sometimes, objective journalism—an important change considering the long history of a press mostly submissive to the interests of the political class in Latin America (Alves 2005).

In these two decades of the 21st Century, investigative journalism is living a renewed era in Latin America. Following a worldwide trend (Houston 2010), investigative journalism in the region is expanding into different forms that include a vibrant field of news startups (SembraMedia 2017) and non-profit journalism (Requejo-Alemán and Lugo-Ocando 2014). Meneses (2016) argues that a new investigative journalism erupted in 2009 after Wikileaks' revelations and consolidated after the Panama Papers. Though Latin American news organizations' participation in Wikileaks was passive, this certainly changed during the Panama Papers investigation, when 96 journalists from 15 countries in the region were part of the International Consortium of Investigative Journalists team that reviewed 11.5 million records from a Panamanian law firm (Bueno, Mioli, and Higuera 2016).

The new millennium has also brought new challenges for investigative journalism in the region. Saldaña and Mourão (2018), in their study of the main challenges faced by Latin American investigative journalists, found that crime and corruption were the most common constraints identified by reporters. Crime and corruption were mentioned by reporters of 17 out of 18 countries in the sample. The researchers also found these constraints permeated multiple levels of influence when analyzing investigative journalism under the Hierarchy of Influences model (Shoemaker and Reese 2013). Reporters "emphasized that rampant crime in the region creates a culture of fear" that leaves reporters feeling unsafe "while covering controversial topics" (p. 314). Because corruption permeates mostly official institutions, reporters not only do not have access to official information, they also face retaliation, intimidation, and "disqualification from the political sector" (Shoemaker and Reese 2013, 315). González de Bustamante and Relly (2014) confirm these risks in their study of journalists covering violence in the U.S.-Mexico border. As a consequence, many journalists in Latin America self-censor to preserve their jobs and their personal integrity.

Another important challenge journalists in the region face is the lack of a strong investigative culture. In Saldaña and Mourão's study (2018), journalists pointed out that "audiences do not value investigative stories, there is little or no interest in fomenting a culture of free speech, news organizations do not invest in investigative projects, and reporters are too apathetic to take the initiative" (p. 315). This challenge is in tune with a region where at least five countries (Cuba, Ecuador, Honduras, Mexico, Venezuela) had their press cataloged as "not free," and 11 as "partly free" (Argentina, Bolivia, Brazil, Colombia, Dominican Republic, El Salvador, Guatemala, Haiti, Nicaragua, Panama, Paraguay, Peru) by the Freedom House (2019). In addition to that, only 43% of the population in Latin America trust the news and a low 25% believe the press is free from political influence (Salaverría 2017).

At the individual level, reporters in Latin America have complained about an inadequate training in investigative reporting techniques (Saldaña and Mourão 2018) and the overreliance on "tips and documents passed by officials" with little actual independent investigations (Waisbord 2000, 103). The effect is an exclusive focus on political and institutional wrongdoing at the cost of neglecting investigations of corporate abuses or important social issues (Waisbord 2000). Freedom House (2007) adds that the practice and abuse of *"denuncismo"* (denouncing political or corporate figures, not necessarily supported on facts) has contributed to the trivialization of investigative journalism.

These obstacles, of course, are also present in other parts of the world. According to the last report about the state of technology in global newsrooms (International Center for Journalists 2019), only 12% of the reporters worldwide see themselves as investigative journalists, and most of them complain about inadequate training to perform investigative tasks. South Asian journalists (33%) are the most likely group to do investigative journalism, while East/Southeast Asian journalists (17%) are the least likely to do so (International Center for Journalists 2019). In addition to that, in other similar democracies, journalists also self-censor to be safe, preserve their jobs, and save their news organizations with the consequence of diminished public accountability of government and international organizations (Iordanidou et al. 2020) and lack of freedom in the electoral process (Walulya and Nassanga 2020). Nevertheless, it is important to highlight that despite all these obstacles, investigative journalists in Latin America have persisted in their work, producing impactful reports as the award-wining projects mentioned above reflect.

Digital Journalism in Latin America

The development of digital media in the region starts in 1994 in Brazil. By 1996, Internet and digital news media had extended to all of Latin America (Salaverría, Rivera-Rogel, and Gonzales-Córdova 2019). Although Salaverría, Rivera-Rogel, and Gonzales-Córdova (2019) report that digital-native news organizations appeared early in the Internet age, Meléndez Yúdico (2016) indicates the period between 2009 and 2014 is when the explosion of digital natives occurred. Harlow and Salaverría's (2016) extensive analysis of "digitalness" and "alternativeness" of 67 Latin American online-native news sites shows that, even though none of the sites identified themselves as alternative media, about half of the sites "mentioned the importance of covering untold stories and reaching new and different audiences" and emphasized "their dedication to independent journalism free from the interests of business and political elites" (p. 1013). Furthermore, most of these digital-native organizations talked about "their commitments to strengthening democracy, bettering society, promoting diversity, or empowering smaller groups and communities" (p. 1013). Comparing themselves to mainstream media, these digital natives emphasized their digitalness and innovativeness. Yet, Harlow and Salaverría (2016) did not find their use of digital features more sophisticated than mainstream media's.

Globally, digital-native newsrooms have increased in size, while traditional news outlets have gotten smaller. Yet, the overall size of digital-native outlets is smaller than other workplaces, like traditional TV or print newsrooms (International Center for Journalists 2019). In terms of skills, more journalists are being hired with digital content creation skills as compared to previous years—33% in 2017 and 43% in 2019. Yet, Latin American journalists might be running behind—reporters from Latin America

(27%) and Eurasia (22%) are the most likely to have no technology skills when they are hired (International Center for Journalists 2019).

The digital world has brought with it risks for journalists too. Henrichsen, Betz, and Lisosky (2015) enumerate the many digital challenges and dangers that journalists are subjected to in addition to the traditional offline risks. These risks include traditional harassment facilitated by social media, digital surveillance to journalists and their sources, and more complicated attacks on hardware and software that might also impede the normal operation of websites.

Collaborative Journalism

Collaboration in journalism can be traced back to 1846, when six newspapers joined to form the Associated Press (Stonbely 2017), but Konow-Lund, Gearing, and Berglez (2019) indicate the founding of the Investigative Reporters and Editors (IRE) in 1976 as the breaking point when collaborative methods and processes were more extensively established. The current new era of collaboration started in the mid-2000s "when publishers, journalism scholars, and foundations began to look at the opportunities made possible by digital networking" (Stonbely 2017, 12). This new era is characterized by "qualitative difference in the consciousness and intentionality with which collaborations are now being undertaken" (p. 12). This characterization coincides with Howe et al. (2017) study which revealed, based on 72 interviews with data journalists, web developers, interactive graphics editors, and project managers from digital newsrooms around the world, that the current tendency among leading digital news organizations is to develop practices that promote a "collaborative, team-based news production; an ethos of open-source sharing, both within and between newsrooms; and the transition of 'digital-first' newsrooms into 'mobile-first' newsrooms" (p. 2). Graves and Konieczna (2015) have theorized that journalists who adopt sharing practices do it as a form of field repair, to carry a journalistic field reform moving away from a commercial and competitive ethos to a more democratic mission.

Research about collaboration across news organizations is still scarce. Westlund and Ekström (2020) analysis of 21st century newsroom routines showed that news organizations are adopting practices to "facilitate routines in which social actors in diverse departments coordinate everyday news work as well as innovation projects" (p. 80). However, as Konieczna (2020) highlights, the literature on convergence is richer in collaboration analysis but provides a look mostly into intra-organizational collaboration among journalists, technologists, and business people, and no so much into collaboration among journalists.

Within the most current research on collaboration across newsrooms, Stonbely (2017) defines collaborative journalism as "a cooperative arrangement (formal or informal) between two or more news and information organizations, which aims to supplement each organization's resources and maximize the impact of the content produced" (p. 14). This type of collaboration has to be across newsrooms or even better, across news organizations. The impact and quality of these collaborative journalism projects has been registered by their presence in prestigious awards. The U.S. has the earliest instance of an award-winning, cross-newsroom collaboration with

ProPublica, a non-profit news organization born in 2008, joining *The New York Times* and winning a Pulitzer Prize in 2010 (Carson and Farhall 2018). There is also an increasing presence of Latin American collaborative projects receiving recognition, as mentioned at the opening of this article.

In terms of the challenges to collaborative enterprises, Konow-Lund, Gearing, and Berglez (2019) highlight the importance of the development of trust because of the special demands of "confidentiality and sensitivity when it comes to information that can put everyone at risk" (p. 5). An area of research, they add, that hasn't been properly addressed by scholars. In their report on collaborative local journalism, Jenkins and Graves (2019) found that journalists participating in collaborative efforts in the UK, Italy, and Finland reported as their most common challenges the "need to develop a shared mission and goals, unite newsrooms with different ownership structures and funding models, teach local journalists how to incorporate data into their reporting, adapt their communication and management structures to reflect the needs of participants, and find ways to chart and measure the implications of their work" (p. 6).

In terms of benefits mentioned by participants in collaborative projects, Jenkins and Graves (2019) report that journalists" value opportunities to unite participants with diverse backgrounds, skills, and expertise as equal partners and offer both virtual and in-person opportunities for knowledge-sharing and mentorship" (p. 41). Finally, Stonbely (2017), based on a multi-method analysis of several collaborative projects mostly in the U.S., observed that successful collaborations required a common agreement in the editorial line early on in the project, a dedicated project manager, trust and good intentions among partners, and the attitude to learn new practices.

Research Questions and Hypotheses

Latin American digital newsrooms are increasingly producing high-quality investigative journalism. As evidenced by projects such as the Panama and Paradise Papers, this high-quality journalism has been driven also by collaborative efforts across newsrooms. However, there is a gap in the research to inform what are the main characteristics of the journalists who have participated in collaborative projects and how they compare to journalists who have not participated. As described in the literature review, previous research on collaboration mentions digital technologies and access to information as important factors to conduct investigative pieces. However, other factors are important to be considered as well. Studies aiming to understand journalistic practices usually include demographics (such as gender or age) to create more accurate profiles of journalists, especially in comparative contexts (e.g. Hovden and Kristensen 2018; Weaver and Willnat 2012) As such, this study asks:

> **RQ1.** Are there differences between journalists who have and have not participated in a) national and b) transnational collaborative projects in terms of age, gender, using savvy, digital investigative techniques, and using expert material?

Based on the findings and concepts developed by previous research (Deuze 2006; Howe et al. 2017; Schmitz Weiss et al. 2018), this study suggests a hypothesis to explain collaborations depending on the level of digitalness of the news organizations that journalists work for:

H1. Journalists working for digital-native outlets will be more likely to work on a) national and b) transnational collaborative projects than those who work for legacy media.

We also aim to identify if digital techniques and expert material use, along with demographic characteristics like gender, age, country of origin, and type of news organization they work for, are related to collaborations. Thus, we ask:

RQ2. Do gender, age, country of origin, news organization, savvy investigative techniques, and expert material use correlate with participation in collaborative projects at the a) national and b) transnational levels?

Finally, to understand why Latin American digital investigative journalists seek to participate in collaborative enterprises, we ask:

RQ3. What are the main motivations for working on a) national and b) transnational collaborative projects in Latin America?

RQ4. What are the most challenging aspects of working on a) national and b) transnational collaborative projects in Latin America?

Methods

This study combines quantitative and qualitative research techniques to understand factors affecting national and transnational collaboration in Latin America when it comes to investigative journalism projects. Data for this study come from an online survey conducted by the Knight Center for Journalism in the Americas at The University of Texas at Austin. The questionnaire was translated from English by native speakers of Portuguese and Spanish, and the survey was administered using Qualtrics between December 1st and 30th, 2017.

Respondents were recruited from a database of more than 15,000 journalists, journalism students, and journalism educators who had been enrolled in online training courses offered by the Knight Center between 2015 and 2017. These courses cover topics as diverse as fact-checking, data visualization, and freedom of expression, and usually enroll around 3,000 participants each. We applied a quota system by country to make sure each country was fairly represented in the sample. In total, 1,541 participants responded, yielding a participation rate of 10% (American Association for Public Opinion Research 2016). Out of this total, 1,049 respondents were journalists working for different news outlets. In this particular study, we analyzed responses from journalists working for an investigative unit within their organization ($n = 251$).

Variables

Savvy Digital Investigative Techniques
We asked respondents about several investigative techniques requiring computer/math skills. On a scale from 1 (never) to 5 (very often), they indicated how often they used the following techniques: accessing and downloading data, scholarly database searching, computer assisted reporting, web scraping, data analysis (textual analysis, computer-aided analysis), and statistical analyses (running averages, medians, modes,

pivot tables). We used these items to create an index of savvy techniques (six items; α = .77, range = 1–5, $M = 3.7$, SD = 0.8).

Access to Expert Material

To build this variable, we asked respondents how often they used academic studies, databases, official reports published by experts, and documents obtained through public access law mechanisms, on a scale from 1 (never) to 5 (very often). We used these items to create an index of access to expert material (four items; α = .71, range = 1–5, $M = 4.1$, SD = 0.8).

Type of Organization

Respondents indicated whether they worked for digital-native outlets (50.2%), or for legacy media outlets, such as print (newspapers and magazines, 36.3%), TV stations (broadcast and cable, 9.6%), and radio stations (commercial and community, 4%).

Collaboration in Investigative Journalism Projects

Based on Stonbely's (2017) definition of collaborative journalism, we asked respondents whether they had worked in collaboration with other news organizations in their own country (Yes = 60%) and with news organizations in another country (Yes = 45%) to conduct investigative journalism pieces.

Motivations and Challenges

To identify respondents' main motivations and challenges related to participating in collaborative projects, respondents answered two open-ended questions also based on Stonbely's (2017) definition of collaborative journalism: "what is the main motivation to work in collaboration with a news organization from a) your country and b) another country?" and "what is the most challenging aspect of collaborating with a news organization from a) your country and b) another country?".

Demographics

Respondents' ages ranged from 23 to 71 years old ($M = 41$, SD = 10.3), and they were mostly male (55%). In terms of country of origin, we built five geo-cultural regions replicating the classification used in Saldaña et al. (2017). The majority of respondents came from the Andean region (32%, including respondents from Bolivia, Colombia, Ecuador, Peru, and Venezuela), followed by Mexico (23%), Central America and the Caribbean (19%, with respondents from Guatemala, Honduras, Nicaragua, Costa Rica, Panama, El Salvador, Puerto Rico, Cuba, and Dominican Republic), Brazil (14%), and the Southern cone (12%, with Argentina, Chile, Paraguay, and Uruguay).

Statistical Analyses

To answer RQ1a and RQ1b, we conducted t-tests and Chi-square tests to observe whether reporters who had collaborated in investigative pieces (nationally and internationally) differed from reporters who had not, in terms of gender, age, using savvy investigative techniques, and accessing expert material. To test H1, we ran Chi-square tests to observe the association of collaboration and type of organization journalists work for. Finally, to answer RQ2a and RQ2b, we ran two logistic regressions with participation in national and transnational collaborations as dependent variables, respectively. Age, gender, home region, news organization, savvy investigative techniques, and accessing expert material were used as independent variables.

Qualitative Analyses

We applied qualitative textual analysis to identify respondents' main motivations for (RQ3) and challenges of (RQ4) working on national and transnational collaborative projects in Latin America. We used the constant comparative method (Tracy 2013), which applies an iterative analysis that alternates "between emic, or emergent, readings of the data and an etic use of existing models, explanations, and theories" (p. 184). This process looks for what is present in the data in the primary rounds of coding and groups the codes hierarchically on secondary rounds.

Results

A first glance at the numbers indicates journalists who work for investigative units are a minority. Out of the 1,541 reporters who participated in our survey, only 251 conduct investigative journalism on a regular basis, which is 16% of the sample. In this group, 60% have participated in national collaborations, and 45% have been part of transnational collaborative projects. In other words, roughly half of those who make investigative journalism the main focus of their practice has collaborated with teams nationally and internationally.

Investigative reporters show a high usage of expert material (such as official reports published by experts) but their use of savvy investigative techniques varies depending on the technique – reporters seem to use mathematical techniques less often than other techniques (see Table 1).

In terms of gender, males and females are equally likely to participate in collaborations, either nationally or internationally. We found some differences attributable to age—those who have collaborated in national projects are slightly older than those who have not participated in such projects (41 versus 38 years old, respectively, $t = 1.98$, $p < .05$), but this difference does not hold for transnational collaborations.

Table 1. Savvy investigative techniques and expert material usage.

Savvy investigative techniques	Mean	SD
Accessing and downloading data	4.34	0.90
Data analysis (textual analysis, computer-aided analysis)	4.11	0.97
Scholarly database searching	3.80	1.13
Computer Assisted Reporting	3.79	1.26
Web scraping	3.32	1.36
Mathematical techniques (running averages, pivot tables)	2.86	1.29
Expert material		
Databases	4.29	0.93
Official reports published by experts	4.08	0.99
Documents obtained through public access law mechanisms	4.05	1.15
Academic studies	3.90	1.04

As illustrated by Table 2, respondents who collaborate in investigative projects at the national and transnational levels show higher levels of savvy investigative techniques usage. When looking at those who have participated in collaborations nationally, their average usage of savvy techniques is significantly higher than the score of those who do not participate in national collaborations ($t=2.70$, $p<.01$). Similarly, reporters who have participated in joint projects at the transnational level are also significantly savvier than colleagues who have not collaborated in transnational projects ($t=2.22$, $p<.05$). In contrast, results from Table 3 indicate no significant differences in terms of access to expert material. In other words, participating in collaborative projects nationally or internationally is not related to using expert material to write stories.

Table 2. Collaborations and savvy investigative techniques usage.

	Participation in collaborative projects		
	YES	NO	T-test
National	3.8 (0.7)	3.4 (0.8)	2.70**
Transnational	3.9 (0.8)	3.5 (0.7)	2.22*

Note: cell entries represent means (and standard deviations in parentheses) of savvy investigative techniques usage.

Table 3. Collaborations and access to expert material.

	Participation in collaborative projects		
	YES	NO	T-test
National	4.2 (0.7)	4.1 (0.8)	1.33 n.s.
Transnational	4.1 (0.8)	4.1 (0.8)	0.37 n.s.

Note: cell entries represent means (and standard deviations in parentheses) of access to expert material.

To summarize, age and use of savvy investigative techniques make a difference for reporters working for national collaborations, while only savvy techniques usage differentiates investigative journalists who have from those who have not participated in transnational collaborative efforts. **These findings answer both RQ1a and RQ1b.**

Results from Table 4 indicate journalists working for digital-native outlets are more likely to participate on national and transnational collaborative projects than those who work for print and TV, but not more likely than radio reporters. More than 70% of journalists working for digital-native organizations have participated on national collaborations, a significantly larger proportion than reporters working for TV and print. This pattern is also evident when considering transnational projects. Radio journalists are the most likely group to collaborate with other media at both national and transnational levels. As such, **H1a and H1b are partially supported.**

Table 4. Type of news organization.

	National collaborations		Transnational collaborations	
	Yes	No	Yes	No
TV	27.8%	72.2%	27.8%	72.2%
Print	47.2%	52.8%	29.2%	70.8%
Radio	85.7%	14.3%	100%	0%
Digital	71.0%	29.0%	56.1%	43.9%
Total	59.2%	40.8%	44.8%	55.2%
X2	15.524***		11.524**	

Findings from the logistic regressions indicate that age, home region, type of organization, and savvy techniques are significantly related to collaborating in investigative projects at the national level. Results presented in Table 5, Model one suggest that older reporters located in Brazil, the Andean Region, or the Southern Cone, working for digital-native organizations, and using savvy techniques often, have higher odds of collaborating nationally than those who are younger, located in Mexico, working for either print or TV outlets, and not using savvy techniques in their daily work. When looking at transnational collaborations, findings in Table 5, Model two suggest that only home region and type of organization are related to collaborating in transnational projects—those located in Brazil have higher odds of participating in transnational collaborations than Mexican reporters, and those working for print have lower odds than digital-native reporters. **These findings answer both RQ2a and RQ2b.**

Table 5. Logistic regression models to explain national and international collaboration.

	Model 1 National Exp(B)	Model 2 Transnational Exp(B)
Age	1.105*	0.978
Gender (male)	1.127	0.343
Andean Region	6.961*	0.607
Southern Cone	24.431*	0
Brazil	11.351*	29.176*
Central America	5.098	1.245
Savvy investigative techniques	2.227*	2.345
Access to expert material	1.039	1.341
TV	0.075*	0.195
Print	0.178*	0.044**
Radio	1.603	46921880

Notes. $N = 251$. Mexico and Digital-native organizations are the baseline categories for home region and type of news organization, respectively.

Regarding motivations for collaboration, the qualitative textual analysis revealed similarities and differences among motivations to participate in collaborative projects at the national and transnational level. Respondents mentioned the following categories at the national level:

Moved By the Public's Interest
In this category, respondents mentioned the importance of reporting the truth, letting people know about important issues, and presenting a better picture of national context. For instance, "to disseminate the truth among as many news organizations as possible to be able to face the constant censorship from the government" was the main motivation for a Venezuelan digital reporter. Others would simply answer "the truth" or would explain that they would do "everything to help improve journalistic coverage because it benefits the reader," as a print journalist from Peru emphasized.

Keeping Each Other Safe
Most of the respondents in this category were from Venezuela, although journalists from Argentina, Colombia, Honduras, and Mexico also commented on the need to look out for their safety through collaboration. A digital reporter from Venezuela

expressed his main motivation as "to join efforts, to add resources, and to strengthen security measures." Respondents also mentioned "threats to democracy" and "censorship" as motivations to collaborate because the more news outlets were involved in a project, the more they could "disseminate the truth." Journalists in this group used words such as protection and safety very often.

A clear category mentioned exclusively at the transnational level was:

Verification of Information
Respondents were specific about fact-checking sources, "Fact-checking, verification, corroboration, finding diverse sources. To know if it is people creating fake news," was a comment made by an Argentinian reporter.

The following categories were common as motivations to participate in collaborative efforts at the national and transnational levels:

Larger and Broader Impact
In this category, participants wanted to achieve more visibility for important issues; expand the distribution of stories; reach more, newer, and international audiences; reach more distribution platforms; change the focus from local to regional; achieve a larger repercussion; and have better access to sources and information internationally.

A Quality Process and Product
In this category, participants talked about working on in-depth investigations; getting access to better databases; reaching less accessible places and sources; and covering more realities from more and different angles. Basically, journalists wanted to produce more holistic reporting. "To be able to cover a story in a comprehensive way, in the different scenarios where it develops. To count with the support that represents having a journalist that is knowledgeable of another country's realities where the investigation is taking place," said a newspaper reporter from Ecuador.

Learning and Sharing
Journalists considered that collaborative enterprises provided them with opportunities for professional and personal growth. They talked about learning and sharing new skills, new investigative methods, good practices, and new tools. A digital journalist from Mexico summarized this category by saying, "to learn and share knowledge, experiences, and information." **These motivations answer RQ3a and RQ3b.**

In terms of challenges, categories emerging from the qualitative analysis were consistently homogenous across national and transnational spaces. Respondents mentioned the following challenges:

Project Management
The top concerns for journalists were the ability to plan projects carefully, manage channels of communication, meet deadlines, make good use of resources, and distribute labor and responsibilities properly when working with investigative teams from other news outlets.

Leadership and Competitiveness

Journalists worried about having the support of good leadership that would keep a healthy, competitive environment among collaborators; being able to keep egos at bay; and finding ways to fully share sources, resources, and information.

Editorial Line

Journalists commented that not identifying and agreeing on an editorial line for their projects early on could become an obstacle for the collaboration. Journalists talked about the importance of agreeing on topics, routines, local issues, philosophies, and political ideologies, while at the same time trying not to lose their own identity.

Fact-Checking

Reporters worried about finding ways to verify information, as sources were not always reliable. Being rigorous in the treatment and analysis of the information handled by their colleagues emerged as a challenge for our respondents. **These categories answer RQ4a and RQ4b.**

Discussion

This study analyzes responses from more than 250 Latin American journalists who work on investigative units within their news organizations. By using a mixed-methods approach, we observed how several factors relate to reporters' participation in collaborative investigative projects, their motivations to participate in such projects, and the challenges they face when they work in conjunction with other news outlets at the national and transnational levels. Based on our results, we want to reflect upon three concluding remarks that are relevant for the study of digital journalism in general, and the practice of investigative collaboration in Latin America, in particular.

First, the practice of national and transnational collaboration in the region is still scarce. From our initial sample of more than 1,541 reporters, we selected those who work for investigative units (251 respondents), which means they make investigative journalism the main focus of their daily routine. But this group makes up only 16% of the initial sample, and only half of them participate in collaborations. In perspective, these numbers are, in fact, low.

Second, digital matters, and it matters more than other factors we thought would have an impact on collaboration. Yet, we argue that digital is just the tip of the iceberg that fosters collaboration. Reporters with digital knowledge are not necessarily the youngest in the group as it could be expected, considering the idea of new generations of journalists sharing values from a digital culture such as the one theorized by Deuze (2006). In fact, we found that older journalists are more likely to collaborate than their younger peers. Then, digital knowledge is related to—and eventually dependent on—experience and expertise, qualities that are more relevant than the sole application of computer tools. This is a remarkable finding, because it indicates digital savviness requires other reporting skills to be useful for investigative journalism. As such, instead of digital savviness leading to collaborations, it might be the action of collaborating what leads journalists to adopt digital techniques for their reporting.

As our sample considers only those journalists working for investigative units, their use of digital technologies and their access to expert material is already high. But the significant differences we observed between those who do and do not participate in joint projects tell us that digital savviness does play a role in the collaboration trend we currently observe in Latin America. News organizations should provide digital training to their investigative teams if they want to strengthen experienced reporters in their newsrooms.

Third, journalists' motivations to collaborate focused more on societal and individual factors, while the challenges they mentioned focused more on structural factors related to the profession. For instance, journalists want to participate to change social conditions of their countries (i.e. serving the public interest by delivering the truth) that also affect them personally (i.e. keeping each other safe through collaboration). In contrast, the obstacles they identify focus on project management, leadership, and the exercise of rigorous investigative practices.

Journalists also seek to participate in collaborative projects to strengthen investigative journalism. They want to learn new and better investigative techniques, be better professionals, and share what they know with their colleagues. Reporters also want to make sure they are rigorous in their routines to deliver holistic and quality products. And finally, they want to join efforts with colleagues to extend the impact of their work and the recognition it deserves. In summary, journalists that choose to participate in collaborative efforts do so to become stronger professionals. These findings reveal some similarities with their European and American counterparts. In terms on motivations, learning new techniques and sharing knowledge was also present in the European case studies analyzed by Jenkins and Graves (2019). Stonbely's (2017) analysis of U.S. cases also presented the need for leadership and the establishment of a clear editorial line, as was mentioned by the Latin American journalists.

In addition to our conclusions, differences regarding geographic location are important to discuss. According to our results, Mexico is one of the least likely areas to participate on national and transnational collaborative projects, which relates to findings from previous studies indicating a lack of investigative culture in Mexico. González de Bustamante and Relly (2014) found that Mexican reporters have to deal with intimidation and unthinkable crimes committed against them by criminal groups or corrupt government officials. Similarly, Saldaña and Mourão (2018) found investigative journalism is scarce in Mexico precisely because of the violence and organized crime constantly threatening those interested in conducting investigative reporting. The latest reports on violence against the press indicate that half of the journalists killed in 2019 were from Mexico, making this country the second deadliest country for journalists, only after Syria (Beiser 2019). This situation certainly makes Mexican reporters less likely to participate in collaborative projects.

Our qualitative findings related to safety complement the previous finding. It is notable that journalists considered safety an important motivation to collaborate at the national level but it was almost not mentioned at the transnational level. This may confirm that in countries with high levels of violence and other types of attacks to the press, journalists seek collaboration to strengthen their positions against their attackers, be those cartels or authoritarian governments. Future research should look into other countries where the levels of violence, political attacks, and crime against the press are also high.

This study is not without limitations. Our data come from a non-random sample, which does not necessarily represent the entire population of investigative reporters in Latin America accurately. As we worked with a subsample of respondents (journalists working for investigative units), some groups in this subsample are misrepresented. As observed in Table 4, a 100% of the radio reporters have participated in transnational collaborations, which is extremely high. All respondents in this category were from the same country, which implies they all might have worked in the same collaborative project. Consequently, it would be wrong to assume that radio reporters in general are the most likely group to collaborate based solely on this group of radio journalists. Despite these issues, our sample covered 20 countries in the region and respondents worked for different news platforms and organizations. As such, our sample might be more representative than samples used in previous studies.

We echo Mitchelstein and Boczkowski (2009) call to understand digital journalism not as a phenomenon-centered or a theoretically tributary stance, but as a study object that should be observed through "trends that lead to rethinking major building blocks in the understanding of journalism and its role in society" (p. 578). We also want to call attention to the need to analyze Latin American countries separately instead of as a whole, advocated by previous research about journalism in the continent (Saldaña et al. 2017; Waisbord 2000), to understand the nuances and specificities of each region. Finally, as the literature and journalism award circuits show, there is a clear trend among digital journalists to work on national and transnational collaborative investigative enterprises. In this study, we have tried to unpack *the who and why* in the Latin American region. By doing so, this study has made at least three contributions to the field: 1) it shows that digital savviness is not enough to enhance collaboration if experience and expertise are absent; 2) it reveals the motivations and challenges faced by reporters who embark in collaborative enterprises with the goal of strengthening the profession, becoming better professionals, and keep the group safer by staying together; and 3) it tackles collaborations across newsrooms, which is a less studied area in the field. Most of the research on collaboration looks into collaborative efforts among journalists and other social actors, or journalists and professionals from other disciplines. This study, in contrast, observes the pros and cons of working with colleagues from other outlets.

Acknowledgements

The authors would like to thank Rosental Calmon Alves, director of the Knight Center for Journalism in the Americas at the University of Texas at Austin and the Knight Center Research Unit for giving us access to the data that made this article possible. We also thank all the Latin American journalists who took the time to answer our survey and collaborated with our study.

Disclosure statement

No potential conflict of interest was reported by the author(s).

Funding

The authors received no financial support for the research, authorship, and/or publication of this article.

References

Alves, R. C. 2005. "From Lapdog to Watchdog: The Role of the Press in Latin America's Democratization." In *Making Journalists: Diverse Models, Global Issues*, edited by H. de Burgh, 181–200. New York, NY: Routledge.

American Association for Public Opinion Research. 2016. *Standard Definitions: Final Dispositions of Case Codes and Outcome Rates for Surveys*. 9th ed. Washington, DC: AAPOR. https://www.aapor.org/AAPOR_Main/media/publications/Standard-Definitions20169theditionfinal.pdf.

Beiser, E. 2019. *Number of Journalists Killed Falls Sharply as Reprisal Murders Hit Record Low* (CPJ Database of Journalists Killed). New York, NY: Committee to Protect Journalists. https://cpj.org/reports/2019/12/journalists-killed-murdered-syria-mexico-impunity/.

Borger, M., A. Van Hoof, I. Costera Meijer, and J. Sanders. 2013. "Constructing Participatory Journalism as a Scholarly Object: A Genealogical Analysis." *Digital Journalism* 1 (1): 117–134.

Bueno, C., T. Mioli, and S. Higuera. 2016. "96 Latin American Journalists Collaborate on the Panama Papers, a Global Investigative Project." *Journalism in the Americas*, April 4. https://knightcenter.utexas.edu/blog/00-16884-96-latin-american-journalists-collaborate-panama-papers-global-investigative-project.

Carson, A., and K. Farhall. 2018. "Understanding Collaborative Investigative Journalism in a "Post-Truth" Age." *Journalism Studies* 19 (13): 1899–1911.

Coleman, E. G. 2012. *Coding Freedom: The Ethics and Aesthetics of Hacking*. Princeton, NJ: Princeton University Press.

Convoca. 2018. Proyecto "Investiga Lava Jato" gana premio internacional Excelencia Periodística 2018 [Non-profit news organization]. *Convoca.Pe*, September 5. http://www.convoca.pe/agenda-propia/proyecto-investiga-lava-jato-gana-premio-internacional-excelencia-periodistica-2018

de Assis, C. 2019. "Cláudio Weber Abramo Award Celebrates Excellence in Data Journalism Made in Brazil." *Journalism in the Americas*, July 3. https://knightcenter.utexas.edu/blog/00-21017-claudio-weber-abramo-award-celebrates-excellence-data-journalism-made-brazil.

Deuze, M. 2006. "Participation, Remediation, Bricolage: Considering Principal Components of a Digital Culture." *The Information Society* 22 (2): 63–75.

Fernández, P. 2019. "Automation and the Future of Fact Checking: Chequeado, Argentina." In *2019 International Symposium of Online Journalism*, Austin, TX, April 12. https://www.youtube.com/watch?v=miBMJ_ynvN4&feature=youtu.be.

Freedom House. 2007. "Freedom in the world 2007: Peru." https://freedomhouse.org/report/freedom-world/2007/peru

Freedom House. 2019. "Americas." https://freedomhouse.org/regions/americas

González de Bustamante, C., and J. E. Relly. 2014. "Journalism in Times of Violence: Social Media Use by US and Mexican Journalists Working in Northern Mexico." *Digital Journalism* 2 (4): 507–523.

Graves, L., and M. Konieczna. 2015. Sharing the News: Journalistic Collaboration as Field Repair. *International Journal of Communication* 9: 1966–1984. https://ijoc.org/index.php/ijoc/article/viewFile/3381/1412.

Harlow, S., and R. Salaverría. 2016. "Regenerating Journalism: Exploring the "Alternativeness" and "Digital-Ness" of Online-Native Media in Latin America." *Digital Journalism* 4 (8): 1001–1019.

Henrichsen, J. R., M. Betz, and J. M. Lisosky. 2015. *Building Digital Safety for Journalism: A Survey of Selected Issues* (UNESCO Series on Internet Freedom). Paris, France: UNESCO. https://unesdoc.unesco.org/ark:/48223/pf0000232358.

Houston, B. 2010. "The Future of Investigative Journalism." *Daedalus* 139 (2): 45–56.

Hovden, J. F., and N. N. Kristensen. 2018. "The Cultural Journalist around the Globe: A Comparative Study of Characteristics, Role Perceptions, and Perceived Influences." *Journalism*. Advance online publication. doi:10.1177/1464884918791224.

Howe, J., A. Bajak, D. Kraft, and J. Wihbey. 2017. "Collaborative, Open, Mobile: A Thematic Exploration of Best Practices at the Forefront of Digital Journalism." *SSRN Electronic Journal*. doi:10.2139/ssrn.3036984.

International Center for Journalists. 2019. *The 2019 State of Technology in Global Newsrooms*, 82. Washington, DC: International Center for Journalists (ICFJ). https://www.icfj.org/sites/default/files/2019-10/2019%20Final%20Report.pdf.

Iordanidou, S., E. Takas, L. Vatikiotis, and P. García. 2020. "Constructing Silence: Processes of Journalistic (Self-)Censorship during Memoranda in Greece, Cyprus, and Spain." *Media and Communication* 8 (1): 15–26.

Jenkins, J., and L. Graves. 2019. *Case Studies in Collaborative Local Journalism* (Digital News Project), 1–46. Oxford, UK: Reuters Institute for the Study of Journalism.

Konieczna, M. 2020. "The Collaboration Stepladder: How One Organization Built a Solid Foundation for a Community-Focused Cross-Newsroom Collaboration." *Journalism Studies* 21 (6): 802–819.

Konow-Lund, M., A. Gearing, and P. Berglez. 2019. "Transnational Cooperation in Journalism." In *Oxford Research Encyclopedia, Communication*, edited by Jon Nussbaum, 1–19. Oxford, UK; New York, NY: Oxford University Press.

Lewis, C. 2018. "Tear down These Walls: Innovations in Collaborative Accountability Research and Reporting." In *Global Teamwork: The Rise of Collaboration in Investigative Journalism*, edited by Richard Sambrook, 5–25. Oxford, UK: Reuters Institute for the Study of Journalism.

Lewis, S. C., and N. Usher. 2013. "Open Source and Journalism: Toward New Frameworks for Imagining News Innovation." *Media, Culture & Society* 35 (5): 602–619.

Mazote, N. 2017. "How the Argentinian daily La Nación became a data journalism powerhouse in Latin America." *NiemanLab*, April 20. https://www.niemanlab.org/2017/04/how-the-argentinian-daily-la-nacion-became-a-data-journalism-powerhouse-in-latin-america/

Meléndez Yúdico, J. 2016. *Primer Estudio de Medios Digitales y Periodismo en América Latina: Iniciativas, Modelos de Negocios y Buenas Prácticas*. Ciudad de México, México: Factual A.C.

Meneses, M. E. 2016. "#Panama Papers: El Resurgimiento Del Periodismo de Investigación." *Foreign Affairs Latinoamérica* 16 (3): 103–110.

Mioli, T. 2018. "Latin American Has Strong Showing for 2018 Data Journalism Awards." *Journalism in the Americas*, May 31. https://knightcenter.utexas.edu/blog/00-19721-latin-america-has-strong-showing-2018-data-journalism-awards.

Mitchelstein, E., and P. J. Boczkowski. 2009. "Between Tradition and Change: A Review of Recent Research on Online News Production." *Journalism: Theory, Practice & Criticism* 10 (5): 562–586.

Nalvarte, P. 2016. "Media Outlets from Argentina, Bolivia, Brazil, Mexico and Peru Nominated for International Data Journalism Award." *Journalism in the Americas*, May 27. https://knightcenter.utexas.edu/blog/00-17154-media-outlets-argentina-bolivia-brazil-mexico-and-peru-nominated-international-data-jo.

Red Internacional de Periodistas. 2018. *Periodismo Colaborativo*. Washington, DC: Red Internacional de Periodistas. https://ijnet.org/es/toolkit/periodismo-colaborativo.

Relly, J. E., and C. González de Bustamante. 2014. "Silencing Mexico: A Study of Influences on Journalists in Northern States." *The International Journal of Press/Politics* 19 (1): 108–131.

Requejo-Alemán, J. L., and J. Lugo-Ocando. 2014. "Assessing the Sustainability of Latin American Investigative Non-Profit Journalism." *Journalism Studies* 15 (5): 522–532.

Romera, P., and C. S. Gallego. 2018. "How ICIJ Deals with Massive Data Leaks like the Panama Papers and Paradise Papers." *International Consortium of Investigative Journalists*, July 3. https://www.icij.org/blog/2018/07/how-icij-deals-with-massive-data-leaks-like-the-panama-papers-and-paradise-papers/.

Salaverría, R. 2017. "Latin America." In *Digital News Report 2017*, edited by N. Newman, R. Fletcher, A. Kalogeropoulos, D. A. L. Levy, and R. K. Nielsen, 47. Oxford, UK: Reuters Institute for the Study of Journalism.

Salaverría, R., D. Rivera-Rogel, and M. Gonzales-Córdova. 2019. "Taxonomía Del Periodismo Digital en Iberoamérica: Evolución en Las Dos Décadas Digitales." In *La Comunicación en el Escenario Digital: Actualidad, Retos y Prospectivas* edited by Romero-Rodríguez, Luis M. and Rivera-Rogel, 263–285. Lima, Perú: Pearson Education.

Saldaña, M., V. Higgins Joyce, M. de, A. Schmitz Weiss, and R. C. Alves. 2017. "Sharing the Stage: Analysis of Social Media Adoption by Latin American Journalists." *Journalism Practice* 11 (4): 396–416.

Saldaña, M., and R. R. Mourão. 2018. "Reporting in Latin America: Issues and Perspectives on Investigative Journalism in the Region." *The International Journal of Press/Politics* 23 (3): 299–323.

Schmitz Weiss, A., V. de Higgins Joyce, S. Harlow, and R. Calmon Alves. 2018. "Innovación y Sostenibilidad: Una Relación Examinada en Organizaciones Periodísticas Emprendedoras de América Latina." *Cuadernos.Info* 42: 87–100.

SembraMedia. 2017. *Punto de Inflexión. Impacto, Amenazas y Sustentabilidad: Estudio de Emprendedores de Medios Digitales Latinoamericanos*. Los Angeles, CA: SembraMedia. http://data.sembramedia.org/wp-content/uploads/2017/09/Punto-de-Inflexion-SembraMedia-span-7-24.pdf.

Shoemaker, P. J., and S. D. Reese. 2013. *Mediating the Message in the 21st Century: A Media Sociology Perspective*. New York, NY: Routledge.

Sociedad Interamericana de Prensa. 2018. "SIP exalta la labor del periodismo nicaragüense al anunciar los Premios a la Excelencia Periodística 2018." *Sipiapa.Org*, September 5. https://www.sipiapa.org/notas/1212684-sip-exalta-la-labor-del-periodismo-nicaragense-al-anunciar-los-premios-la-excelencia-periodistica-2018

Stonbely, S. 2017. *Comparing Models of Collaborative Journalism*. Montclair, NJ: Center for Cooperative Media.

Tracy, S. J. 2013. *Qualitative Research Methods: Collecting Evidence, Crafting Analysis, Communicating Impact*. Hoboken, NJ: Wiley-Blackwell.

Waisbord, S. 2000. *Watchdog Journalism in South America: News, Accountability, and Democracy*. New York, NY: Columbia University Press.

Waisbord, S. 2013. *Reinventing Professionalism: Journalism and News in Global Perspective*. Cambridge, UK: Polity.

Walulya, G., and G. L. Nassanga. 2020. "Democracy at Stake: Self-Censorship as a Self-Defence Strategy for Journalists." *Media and Communication* 8 (1): 5–14.

Weaver, D. H., and L. Willnat. 2012. *The Global Journalist in the 21st Century*. New York, NY: Routledge.

Westlund, O., and M. Ekström. 2020. "News Organizations and Routines." In *The Handbook of Journalism Studies*. 2nd ed., edited by K. Wahl-Jorgensen and T. Hanitzsch, 73–89. New York, NY: Routledge.

The Mechanisms of "Incidental News Consumption": An Eye Tracking Study of News Interaction on Facebook

Adrián Vergara, Ignacio Siles ⓘ, Ana Claudia Castro, and Alonso Chaves

ABSTRACT
This exploratory study examines how participants incidentally consumed news on social media through an eye tracking analysis of their visual interaction with posts on Facebook. By interaction, we refer to the attention participants gave to news (measured through the time devoted to looking at the content); how they read these news items (measured through ocular movements on the screen); and the way they engaged with this content (measured through forms of participation such as liking, commenting, or sharing news). The data were triangulated through interviews with Facebook users and an analysis of the metrics of posts from Costa Rican news organizations on Facebook from 2017 to 2020. We draw on scholarship in communication studies and multimodal discourse analysis. We argue for a more nuanced approach to what study participants did when they incidentally encountered news on social media that focuses on mechanisms, that is, the specific procedures and operations that shape user interaction with news on Facebook (such as visual fixations on parts of news posts; the visual entry points through which they begin to interact with the news; the sequences that characterize how they navigate content; and the time they spend assessing various multimodal elements).

Introduction

Consuming the news incidentally has grown in importance over the past years. Although encountering news that was not sought out purposefully has been a common practice historically; it is considered to be a defining feature of the digital age (Ahmadi and Wohn 2018; Boczkowski, Mitchelstein, and Matassi 2018). Consequently, researchers have devoted increasing attention to the incidental consumption of news on social media (Fletcher and Nielsen 2018; Kligler-Vilenchik et al. 2020; Yadamsuren and Erdelez 2016).

This article supplements recent approaches to incidental consumption through an analysis of how certain users in Costa Rica consume news on social media. To this end, we implemented an exploratory eye tracking study of the interaction between a group of users with news on their Facebook News Feed. By interaction, we refer to three specific issues: the attention participants in our study gave to news (measured through the time devoted to looking at the content); how they read these news items (measured through ocular movements on the screen); and the way they engaged with this content (measured through forms of participation such as liking, commenting, or sharing news). Scholars have often recommended eye tracking as a promising method to explore incidental news consumption because it "measures selective exposure mechanisms in real time during reception [...] [and] provides more objective indicators about perceived contents because it is less susceptible to biases, such as social desirability" (Sülflow, Schäfer, and Winter 2019, 7) (c.f. Matthes et al. 2020; Yadamsuren and Erdelez 2016). We triangulated these data through interviews with these Facebook users and an analysis of the metrics of posts from Costa Rican news organizations on Facebook from 2017 to 2020.

We combined scholarship in communication studies and multimodal discourse analysis to examine issues of incidental news consumption. This allowed us to understand not only how participants in our study made sense of the news they encountered on Facebook (and why this matters), but also how they interacted with multimodal stimuli.

We argue that incidental news "consumption" can be a problematic term to account for user interaction with content on Facebook. This is because users such as our study participants interacted in various ways with the news they encountered. By examining the specific mechanisms of these users' visual interactions with content on Facebook, we argue for a more nuanced approach to what they actually did when they incidentally encountered news on social media. By mechanisms, we mean the specific procedures and operations that shape user interaction with news on Facebook (such as visual fixations on certain parts of news posts; the visual entry points through which they begin to interact with the news; the sequences that characterize how they navigate content; and the time they spend assessing various multimodal elements, among others).

The focus on Costa Rica allows us to discuss findings from a leader in the use of the Internet in Latin America. Costa Rica typically ranks high in connectivity rates in the region. According to Latinobarómetro (2018), 77% of the Costa Rican population uses Facebook (the highest percentage in Latin America), compared to a regional average of 60%. Costa Rica also leads the use of apps typically employed for sharing news, such as WhatsApp (Latinobarómetro 2018). News consumption online is a widespread practice in the country. The analysis of Costa Rica also enables us to analyze news consumption issues in a part of Latin America that has not received major academic attention.

Bridging Scholarship on Incidental News Consumption and Research on Attention to Multimodal Stimuli

The incidental consumption of news is not an entirely new phenomenon. Researchers have examined incidental exposure to news in relation to print, broadcast, and digital media (Kim, Chen, and de Zuñiga 2013; Lee and Kim 2017; Tewksbury, Weaver, and

Maddex 2001). In the case of digital media, scholars have focused on three particular issues associated with incidental consumption: the phases that characterize it, the practices that shape it, and the political consequences of this phenomenon.

Research has shown that incidental news consumption on social media is typically carried out through a set of specific *phases*. Yadamsuren and Erdelez (2016), for example, argued that it consists of seven steps: noticing, stopping, reading, capturing, sharing, returning, and wandering off. Studies generally reveal the centrality of the subject matter of the news as a trigger of user attention. This body of work has typically resulted in the production of ideal types of news consumption and online news consumers (c.f. Meijer and Kormelink 2015).

The focus on phases has been supplemented through an assessment of the *practices* of incidental consumption. In a study conducted in Argentina, Boczkowski et al. (2018) showed that this form of reading the news is shaped by two groups of practical traits:

> (1) strong connections between technological and content practices, "anywhere and anytime" coordinates of news consumption, derivative information routines, and increasingly mediated sociability and (2) brief and fragmentary reading patterns, re-contextualization and loss of hierarchy of the news report, and the coexistence of editorial, algorithmic, and social filtering. (3524)

Fletcher and Nielsen (2018) also noted that those who are less interested in news tend to experience a greater incidental exposure to this kind of content than those with higher interest. Incidental exposure to news also increases when received through weak ties rather than strong ties (Ahmadi and Wohn 2018).

Another central analytic concern has been the *consequences* of incidental news consumption (Oeldorf-Hirsch 2018; Valeriani and Vaccari 2016). Regarding this issue, findings are "downright contradictory" (Kligler-Vilenchik et al. 2020, 2). Individuals who experience the news incidentally consider to be well informed (Bergström and Jervelycke Belfrage 2018). However, Lee and Kim (2017) concluded that "incidental exposure to news has causal effects on learning about public affairs [...] spending some time on actual news stories is necessary to learn sufficient information about public affairs in order to recall it later" (1013). Drawing on survey data, Zuñiga et al. (2017) similarly noted that "individuals who perceive that news will find them tend to show lower levels of political knowledge" (115 and 116).

Most research on incidental news consumption has relied on self-reported data, primarily from surveys or interviews with social media users. This has made it possible to better understand how reflexive individuals make sense of the information environment they inhabit. However, despite their many contributions, these studies tend to take for granted the descriptions given by users of what catches their attention on social media. To deal with this issue, we studied incidental consumption issues through an eye tracking analysis of how a group of users in Costa Rica visually interacted with news on Facebook.

Multimodal discourse analysis provides a useful approach to better understand how users interact with the news. Studying news and publications on Facebook as multimodal stimuli invites a thorough consideration of semiotic resources and modes (Bateman, Wildfeuer, and Hiipala 2017; Kress 2010; Kress and van Leeuwen 2001). This allows understanding that processing texts is achieved through the attribution of meaning to their distinct components and their interrelation (Schnotz and Bannert 2003; Schnotz and Horz 2010).

The eye-mind hypothesis posits that, when a word or image is looked at, the mind is processing what they eye is watching (Just and Carpenter 1980). Eye tracking methods thus allow observing phenomena such as fixations (a marker of attention when the eye stops to look at something such as an image or word) and saccades (paths or ocular movements between fixations) (King et al. 2019). In this way, it becomes possible to better identify the mechanisms that people employ to process and interact with texts (e.g. whether texts are actually read or not, what components catch the attention of people, or what kind of relationships are established between components).

Few scholars have used eye tracking techniques to study interaction with news on social media. Bode, Vraga, and Troller-Renfree (2017) exposed users to a simulated Facebook News Feed. They concluded that users pay differentiated attention to various formats (such as links, photos, and texts) and to distinct kinds of content (such as politics and social issues). In their experiment, links and images received more attention than texts, and users skipped over political content faster than posts on other issues. In a similar manner, Sülflow and colleagues (2019) designed a laboratory experiment to analyze attitude consistency, source credibility, and attention to and engagement with the news. They showed that users tended to select content that reinforced their attitudes and that they "spend more time looking at news posts from sources with high credibility compared with sources with low credibility" (Sülflow, Schäfer, and Winter 2019, 184).

Eye tracking studies of both digital and print advertising have focused, for the most part, on issues of composition and combinations of texts and images (Grigaliūnaitė, Pilienė, and Bakanauskas 2016; Zantides and Kourdis 2014). Much more research has been devoted to multimodal stimuli from sources other than digital media (Kurzhals et al. 2016). Studies have found that verbal cues tend to receive more attention than images on billboards (Grigaliūnaitė, Pilienė, and Bakanauskas 2016; Zantides and Kourdis 2014), newspapers (Holsanova, Rahm, and Holmqvist 2006), stories in online newspapers (Zambarbieri, Carniglia, and Robino 2008), or when simple images and simple verbal texts are combined (Arndt, Schüler, and Scheiter 2015). All these studies suggest that texts receive more visual fixations, regardless of the size, color, place, and nature of images. However, Holsanova and colleages (2006) indicate that the primacy of images in media such as newspapers is explained by the fact that these are usually a visual entry point to navigate content.

Informed by the scholarship discussed previously, in this article we provide empirical answers to the following research questions:

- How did study participants encounter news on Facebook?
- How many news items did they encounter?
- For how long did participants visually interact with the news?
- How did participants visually interact with the news they encountered?
- What news themes and stories did participants pay attention to?

Table 1. Prevalence of news and non-news on Facebook during the eye tracking session.

	News	Non-news	Total of posts available on users' Facebook News Feed
Total	127	1,286	1,413
Percentage	9%	91%	100%
Average	3	31	34
Median	1	29	31

To this end, we implemented the mixed methods research design described next.

Research Design

We began by conducting an exploratory eye tracking study with 41 Facebook users. Rather than seeking to obtain generalizable findings, the purpose of this exploratory research was to gain new insights into the mechanisms of incidental news consumption, a largely unexplored issue in the literature. Previous exploratory studies using this method have relied on data from a comparable number of individuals (or even fewer) (King et al. 2019). Participants were recruited through a call for participation that circulated on social media platforms associated with the University of Costa Rica. Interested individuals filled out an online questionnaire. Only participants who had a Facebook account were selected. The final sample included a larger representation of women (62%) than men (38%). Participants were either college students at the University of Costa Rica or had recently graduated. They studied majors such as Architecture, Biology, Business, Engineering, English, Communication Studies, Computer Science, Geography, Law, Microbiology, Nursing, Pharmacy, Philology, Physics, Political Science, and Sociology, among others. The average age of participants was 21 years old (ranging from 18 to 33). Participants came primarily from urban backgrounds.

Participants sat in front of a 21-inch screen with a SMI RED500 eye-tracker, which was placed next to the screen where the stimuli were shown. Eye movements were tracked using a sampling rate of 250 Hz. A screen with instructions was shown first to each person. These instructions were also read out loud by a researcher. Calibration was then conducted for each participant. Only participants with a deviation of the *x*- and *y*-axis below 1.0° were included in the final sample. Individuals were asked to open their Facebook profile and interact with their News Feed in a natural way for five minutes without interruptions. After five minutes, the eye tracking session closed automatically. Because the first two minutes included time devoted to logging in to Facebook accounts, this article reports findings from interactions with news during the final three minutes of the session only. This represented a total of 1,413 posts (see Table 1). The use of Facebook for short periods of time is also consistent with the nature of incidental news consumption.

Stimuli came from posts available on users' own Facebook News Feed. Participants could scroll through their News Feed for as long as they wanted or could click on any link they wished to. Eye tracking sessions were recorded upon approval. These videos were then exported and coded by members of the research team using ELAN software. To identify the number of news items that appeared on users' News Feed, we applied Nielsen's Nielsen (2017) typology. First, by "news-as-impressions," we

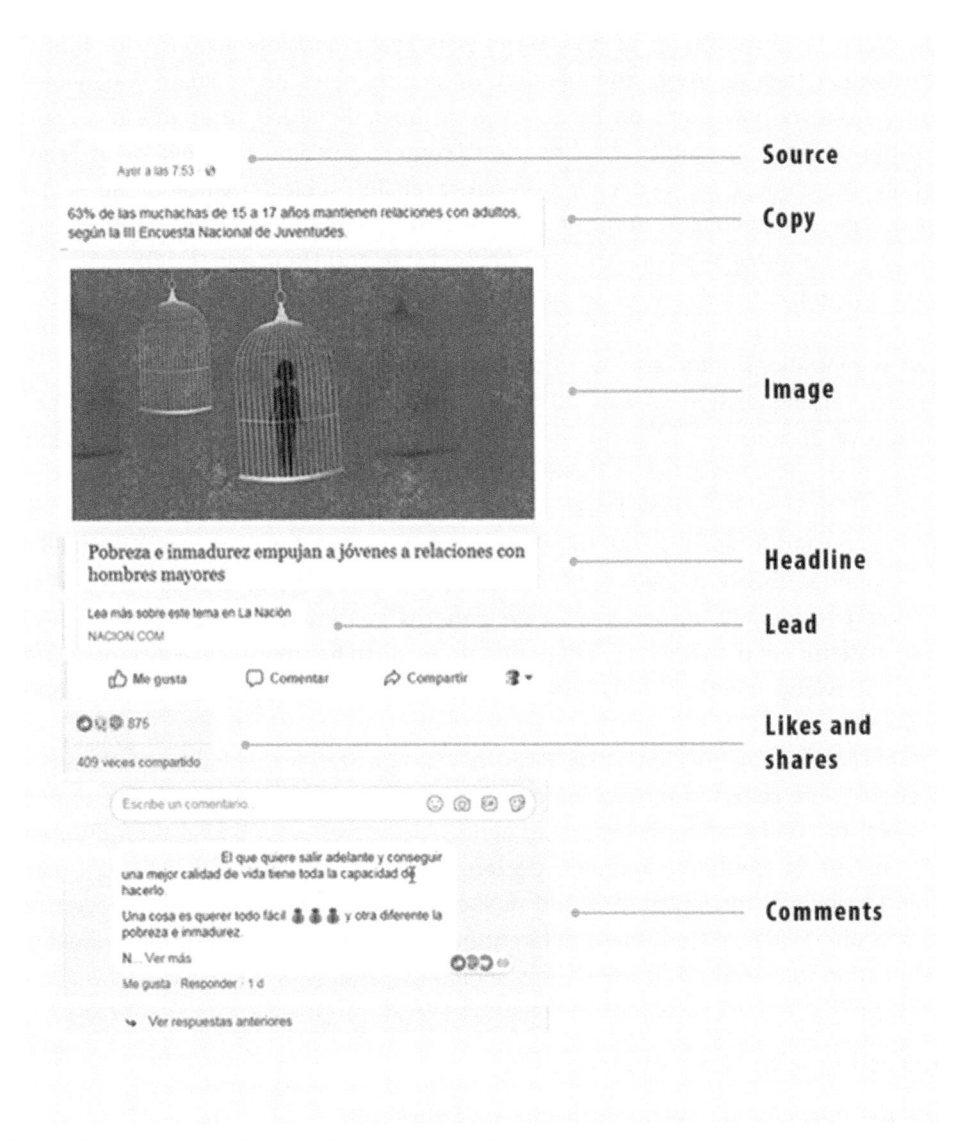

Figure 1. Components of publications on Facebook.

considered "decontextualized snippets of information presented via headline services, news alerts, live tickers, and a variety of new digital intermediaries including search engines, social media, and messaging apps" (Nielsen 2017, 93). Second, "news-as-items" refer to typical, "self-contained, discrete articles and news stories bundled together in a newspaper, a broadcast stream, on a website, or in an app" (Nielsen 2017, 93). And, finally, "news-about-relations" were considered as combinations of "elements of long-form 'contextual' or 'explanatory' forms of journalism [...] with new forms of data journalism, visualization, and interactivity enabled and empowered by digital technologies" (Nielsen 2017, 93).

We coded videos based on three particular issues: the time devoted to looking at different kinds of news (as an indicator of attention); patterns in ocular movements on the screen (as an indicator of how news were read); and interactions with forms of participation such as liking, commenting, or sharing news (to evaluate engagement). Figure 1 shows how posts on Facebook were operationalized to enable this coding. Drawing on previous studies, we also coded content available on users' News Feed to identify preferences for public or non-public affairs, subject matter of news items (main topic and secondary topic; international or national issues), and framing issues (Boczkowski and Mitchelstein 2013; de Vreese, Esser, and Hopmann 2016).

We triangulated these data by interviewing participants and by scraping data on the most-liked, commented, and shared news on Facebook produced by Costa Rican news organizations. Interviews were semi-structured and took place immediately after the eye tracking session (in May 2018). Conversations with participants lasted for an average of 20 min. We asked them about their typical news consumption practices (online and offline) and asked them to discuss specific examples of news posts that appeared on their Facebook News Feed during the eye tracking sessions. Interviews were conducted in Spanish. (All translations are our own.) We analyzed the interviews in a grounded theory manner (Corbin and Strauss 2015). We conducted three rounds of coding to identify, respectively, main patterns in the data, relationships between these patterns, and theoretical categories to account for these relationships. Quotes from interviews cited in this article reflect the main patterns and categories we identified.

Publications from the ten Costa Rican news organizations with most followers on Facebook were collected through an app from 2017 to 2020 (Siles 2020). The top 10% of news that gathered most likes, comments, and shares were coded through a content analysis to identify longitudinal patterns. Data from interviews and social media mining helped to triangulate and add nuance to findings derived from the eye tracking sessions. Evidence from these different methods is thus integrated throughout the next section to provide a clearer understanding of patterns in the data.

Interacting with News on Facebook

How did Participants Encounter News on Facebook?

Participants in our exploratory study recognized the centrality of Facebook in how they consume the news. As an interviewee put it, "News is what I focus on Facebook, that's what I use Facebook for." Interviewees indicated that they follow at least one news outlet on Facebook, usually Costa Rican news organizations (print, pure players, and television news outlets). They also claimed to follow international news organizations (such as CNN or BBC). These users argued that news matter to them for both personal (e.g. they learned about their social importance at some point in their lives) or professional reasons (e.g. news allow them to be updated in their fields of work).

Other study participants were open and straightforward about their relative disinterest in the news (most notably about public affairs) or in following mainstream media outlets on Facebook. These users indicated being primarily interested in what their friends and contacts post, in non-news items (such as memes), or in non-public affair issues (such as soccer and entertainment).

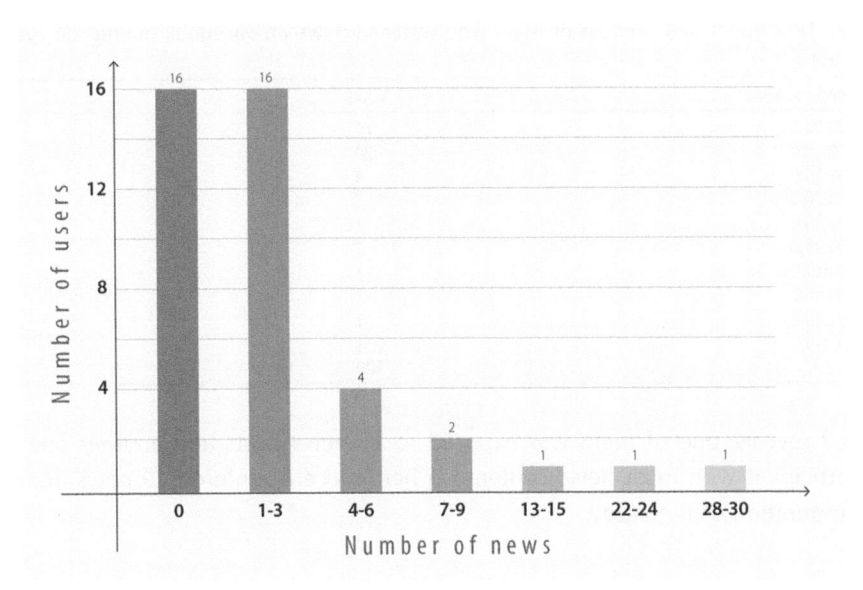

Figure 2. Number of users who received news on Facebook during the eye tracking session.

During the interviews, participants described practices that are consistent with the incidental consumption of news. Both those interested and uninterested in the news admitted to typically encountering them without necessarily looking for them. As a person put it: "[I just] receive them." According to another interviewee, "News show up when I scroll down." Participants indicated to have installed the Facebook app on their cellphones and said they check their News Feed constantly and quickly throughout the day. A person noted, "I check [Facebook] many times a day but for brief periods. It is very hard for me to stay an hour watching content. I'll spend ten minutes now and I'll check it again in fifteen minutes or so." Almost any occasion seems appropriate to check the Facebook app. As one user put it, "[I check it] when I get bored … through small lapses [that add up to] two hours a day." Users also indicated receiving unsolicited news content from others through messaging apps such as WhatsApp.

How Many News Items did Participants Encounter?

To assess how participants interacted with the content they encountered on Facebook, we began by identifying the number of news items that appeared on their News Feed during the eye tracking sessions. As Table 1 shows, 9% of posts ($n = 127$) displayed on users' News Feed could be considered news and 91% were coded as non-news, following Nielsen's (2017) definition. Leaving out of the analysis the two individuals who were exposed to the highest number of news, this percentage of news on Facebook would drop to almost 5% (see Figure 2).

As Table 1 shows, study participants encountered an average of three news items on the News Feed during the study and the median of news exposure was one news item. 78% of users in the sample were exposed to less than three news items. Less than half of participants (39%) did not encounter a single news post on their Facebook feed. Only three people were exposed to more than ten news items. As

Table 2. Time spent and number of users who watched news on Facebook during the eye tracking session.

Time spent on news	News	Users
00:00,5-00:05,0	76	19
00:05,1-00:10,0	20	13
00:10,1-00:15,0	4	4
00:15,1-00:20,0	3	3
00:25,1-00:30,0	1	1
00:30,1-00:35,0	1	1
00:35,1-00:40,0	1	1
00:40,1-00:45,0	1	1
01:05,1-01:10,0	1	1
02:40,1-02:45	1	1
Total	109	41

Figure 2 reveals, one of them was exposed to 15 news posts and another one to 23. The participant with most news content on her feed encountered 29 news items during the duration of the study.

For How Long did Participants Visually Interact with the News?

Encountering news posts on Facebook does not mean that people pay attention to them. To make sense of this difference, we analyzed how participants visually interacted with news on their Facebook News Feed. Building on extant literature, we considered as a visual fixation each time a user looked exclusively at a specific content for at least 500 milliseconds (Liversedge, Gilchrist, and Everling 2011) (see Table 2). This has been proved enough to recognize images and words, but it does not necessarily mean that the person read or understood them.

Table 2 illustrates the time that study participants spent interacting with news items. Participants paid attention to most news items (that is, looked at them for more than 500 milliseconds). They looked at 70% of the news they encountered for less than five seconds. To better understand what this finding means, we compared time of attention to news with the most common kind of non-news content found in our study: memes. In this way, we sought to bring specificity to this comparison, given that the category of "non-news" items integrates a wide variety of content types. The KS Test indicates that there was less than a 2% chance the two samples of content (news and memes) came from the same distribution. We found that 78% of news and 75% of memes were observed under 6 s. There was no major difference in the temporal attention that both news and memes received, χ^2 (1, $N = 331$) $= 0.43, p > .05$.

During the interviews, participants provided various reasons to account for this form of interaction with the news. They emphasized contextual reasons. According to an interviewee, "I have a bunch of components around me that don't let me just watch a [news site] or Facebook." This explanation suggests that news can't receive all the attention because users have to conduct other activities simultaneously. Others explained their practices as a reaction to the nature or the affordances of platforms such as Facebook. As one person put it, "There are so many things [on the screen] that I just have to go through them quickly." In this account, the abundance of information prevents users from devoting more time to specific content items.

Figure 3. Example of a reading sequence during eye tracking study.

How did Participants Visually Interact with the News they Encountered?

We also analyzed eye movements in order to determine reading sequences when participants encountered news on their Facebook News Feed. Specifically, we examined the order of eye fixations when participants looked at elements such as the news copy, images, headlines, source of posts (that is, the person or organization who shared the content), the text of the news post, videos, and participation features (such as likes, shares, or comments) before moving on to another post. Figure 3 presents an example of a reading sequence during the eye tracking sessions.

A sequence can consist of a combination of six possible elements: 1) person or organization that publishes the content; 2) image; 3) lead; 4) headline; 5) copy; and 6) participation features. Table 3 shows how many elements were included in reading sequences of participants.

Participants examined news items on their News Feed through sequences with less than three steps. Participants did not look at every element that makes up news posts. They looked at two elements or less before moving on to another post 61% of the times they encountered news posts and looked at three elements or less 84% of the times. Participants thus processed minimal information when they incidentally encountered news on Facebook, considering the number of visual stimuli that news posts contain. Moreover, they engaged in relatively few integratory movements, that is,

Table 3. Reading sequences of users who interacted with news during the eye tracking session.

Number of elements in the sequence	1	2	3	4	5 or more
Frequency	23	43	25	11	7
Percentage	21%	40%	23%	10%	6%

ocular movements through which a person attempts to relate information contained in different components of a post, considering that two elements in a sequence are required to form one integratory movement. A typical example of this kind of movements—which combines both fixations and saccades—is returning to an element that was previously seen during a sequence. This suggests that reading or interacting with all components of a post is not necessarily relevant to understand a post or a news item.

We further examined what was the entry point (the first fixation) to look at news posts, that is, where participants started visually navigating the news they encountered. Figure 4 demonstrates the centrality of images as a visual entry point. Users looked at an image before anything else on 70% of occasions when they encountered news. Considering videos as a kind of image, iconic elements were the visual privileged entry point to interact with the news. During the interviews, participants recognized the importance of visual stimuli in their use of Facebook. Asked what typically caught her attention on Facebook, an interviewee quickly responded: "Videos and photos. In that order."

The headline of news stories was the second most frequent visual entry point when encountering news on Facebook (13%). Third was the copy that accompanied the news post (11%). Thus, verbal statements were the preferred way to assess news on Facebook 24% of the times. Yet, the difference between iconic and textual elements was significant. Verbal statements didn't account for half of the times an image was the preferred element to start assessing news on Facebook.

As noted previously, studies on incidental news consumption confirm the importance of trust in the source of news published on Facebook (Sülflow, Schäfer, and Winter 2019). During the interviews, participants corroborated the importance of this factor in their attention to Facebook. In a typical statement, one user noted:

> It's [a matter of] trust. You feel like, "Ah! [indicating pleasure]: This person or outlet knows what I like, I will give them an opportunity." If their recommendation is good [si la "pegaron"] the first time and then a second time, then it's like, "Ok. I will always like it."

However, participants rarely began evaluating news based on the source of the post during the eye tracking sessions. On 11% of occasions when users encountered news posts, they looked at who shared it as a visual entry point or the following step.

Participants engaged in diverse combinations of elements when they examined news posts. There were at least 41 sequences that combined these elements differently. The most common sequence was beginning with an image and then looking at the headline, which occurred 28% of the times that users examined news posts. The other 40 element combinations were more much more episodic and did not occur more than 8% of the times each.

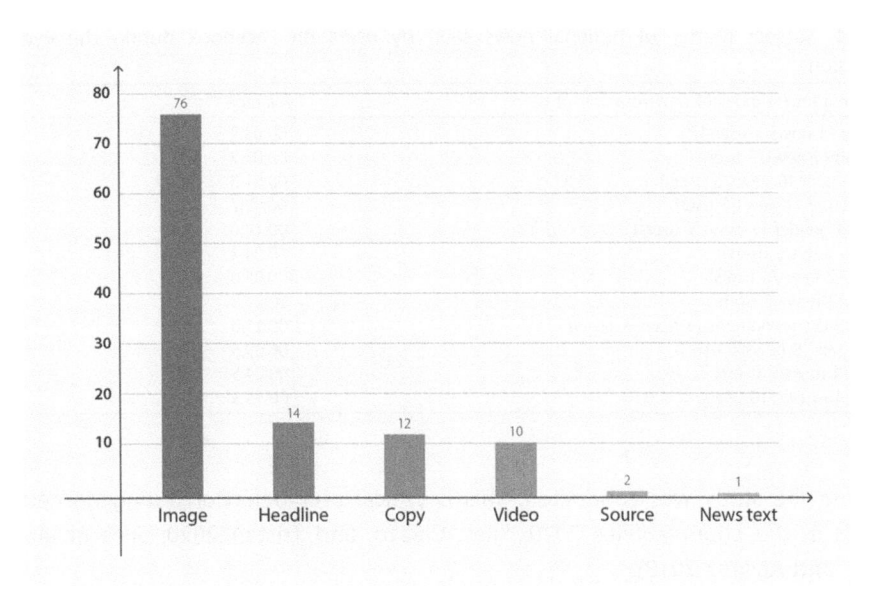

Figure 4. Type of visual entry point into news post during the eye tracking session.

What News Themes and Stories did Participants Pay Attention to?

We also analyzed what was the subject matter of the news that study participants looked at on Facebook. First, we examined attention differences to national and international news. Participants paid attention to more news stories about national issues (73%) than international affairs (27%). During the interviews, participants indicated they preferred news they felt was "closer"—as one person described it—to their lives and interests. An interviewee thus explained the range of national issues that he cared about: "National politics, cultural events, concerts, exhibitions, theater plays, dance presentations, food festivals, and everything that happens in the country."

We then identified patterns of attention to public affairs and non-public affair news, to determine whether this made a difference in how users interacted with news posts. This has been a key concern in literature on online news consumption (Boczkowski and Mitchelstein 2013). Among the news that received some form of user attention, 51% was about public affairs and 49% was about non-public affairs. In the particular case of national news, stories about *sucesos* (crime) (20%), sports (18%), politics (15%), social issues (such as education and migration) (10%), and entertainment (8%) gathered the most attention from participants in terms of frequency. This could also be explained by the notion that users feel these issues are "closer" to their lives than typical public affairs.

The preference for news about crime, sports, and entertainment is consistent with our analysis of metrics of posts from Costa Rican news organizations on Facebook. During non-electoral periods, typically between 65% and 70% of the news published by Costa Rican news organizations on Facebook that receive likes, comments, and shares are about non-public affairs issues (Siles, Campos, and Segura-Castillo, 2018; Tristán, Álvarez, and Siles 2020). As with the eye tracking sessions, news about *sucesos*, politics, and sports also received the highest levels of engagement on Facebook at

Table 4. Subject matter of national news seen by users on Facebook during the eye tracking session.

Subject matter (number of news/number of users)	Average	Median
Economy (3 news/3 users)	00:03,2	00:02,0
Education (2 news/2 user)	00:02,2	00:02,2
Entertainment (6 news/5 users)	00:01,8	00:02,0
Infrastructure (1 news/1 user)	00:01,7	00:01,7
LGBT and gender (5 news/5 users)	00:14,0	00:12,3
Others (6 news/5 users)	00:04,4	00:04,7
Politics (12 news/6 users)	00:05,0	00:04,3
Religion (3 news/2 users)	00:21,8	00:21,8
Science and environment (4 news/4 users)	00:11,0	00:06,9
Social issues (8 news/6 users)	00:09,5	00:02,5
Sports (14 news/9 users)	00:04,5	00:02,8
Sucesos (16 news/10 users)	00:15,3	00:06,0

the time the study was conducted. This is typical user behavior during non-electoral periods in the country (Siles 2020; Siles, Carazo, and Tristán 2020; Siles et al., 2018; Tristán and Álvarez 2018).

As a supplement to the analysis of the subject matter of news, we also examined how much time was spent looking at specific issues and themes. We used Eta correlation to estimate whether the variance of temporal attention to the news was explained by individual participants. We found that 43% of the total variation in temporal attention to the news could be attributed to specific participants. In this sense, attention to news is different to non-news. Eta correlation showed that 18% of the variance of temporal attention to memes is explained by specific participants.

Table 4 shows that temporal attention to the news was relatively distributed among various issues. *Sucesos* was the category that gathered most attention from participants in terms of the time users spent looking at news. Twenty-five percent of users in our study spent time interacting with this category, which also had one of the two highest medians. This result is significant in that, unlike the average, the median is not affected by extreme cases of users who spent more time interacting with one kind of news. In this sense, the median is arguably a more reliable way to assess the time that participants spent watching or reading news posts (Table 4).

Table 4 shows both the average and median time spent interacting with specific subject matters of national news to further illustrate this distinction. Religion and LGBT and gender were the categories with the highest median (21 and 12 s, respectively), although relatively few users encountered news about these topics (2 and five users, respectively). This finding is somewhat inconsistent with user behavior tracked through data scraping. This might be explained contextually. The eye tracking sessions were conducted exactly one month after the presidential election in Costa Rica, which centered largely on the discussion of same-sex marriage (Pignataro and Treminio 2019). Social media was a key space for sharing opinions about this issue for a significant segment of the public (Siles, Carazo, and Tristán 2019, 2020). During an interview, one user described how the context of the election shaped her attention to this kind of news: "I was a very active user during the presidential [election], but that's not common in me. It was really, really because of the context. I mean, if you were to see my Facebook, you'd only find birthday messages!" We thus argue that study participants were still interested in news about these two issues one month after the election.

Science and technology had a median of 12 s, which is also relatively high. This could be explained by the characteristics of our user sample: they were mostly college students who agreed to participate in a scientific study. As noted above, participants were students in science and technology majors (such as Biology, Engineering, Microbiology, or Pharmacy, among others). It is expectable that news about these issues might be of professional interest to them. Some social desirability might also explain this finding. Users spent more than ten seconds interacting with a news post in only 13% of the cases they encountered. Thus, in the case of *sucesos*, only two users exceeded the average of 15 s watching a news post but eight of them were below this average.

Discussion

The incidental consumption of news was widespread in our sample of study participants. They tended to find news on their Facebook News Feed that they did not purposefully seek. However, there was so much variety in the ways these users visually interacted with the news that the use of the term "incidental consumption" warrants further consideration and precaution. We argue that encountering and interacting with news on Facebook is characterized by several mechanisms that help to broaden our understanding of what incidental consumption means.

To begin with, consuming news (incidentally or not) depends on encountering it. 9% of the content to which participants were incidentally exposed was news (and 5% when the two individual users who encountered the most news were left out of the sample). Much has been said about how "algorithmic gatekeepers" tend to show news that exploits the tendency of readers to consume exclusively information with which they agree (Boczkowski, Mitchelstein, and Matassi 2018). But these gatekeepers are central to the incidental consumption of news also because they get to partially decide how many news posts users will encounter in the first place.

Recent research has begun to show empirically how algorithms might be shaping news consumption practices (Diakopoulos 2019). Some authors have argued that platform operators can manipulate the flow of news and information through algorithms to favor certain commercial or political interests (Napoli 2015). As Thorson (2020) notes, "On algorithmically curated platforms like Facebook, content selection is shaped not only by user preferences and news gatekeeping processes but also by the dynamics of platforms themselves" (12). By shaping how news surfaces and who gets to receive it, algorithms thus play a key role in the incidental exposure to news.

The incidental consumption of news is also characterized by differentiated patterns of visual attention. Participants in our study looked at both news and non-news items for similar periods of time. This finding is significant in that it allows understanding incidental consumption as a cognitive issue. In this way, it becomes possible to separate issues such as how people encounter and scan the news from how they actually process it (Matthes et al. 2020). Individuals typically require between 200 and 300 milliseconds to actually process individual words (Liversedge, Gilchrist, and Everling

2011). Complex images require at least 300 milliseconds of processing (or more if individuals are not familiar with the issues portrayed). In light of these patterns, the incidental consumption of news on the Facebook of our participants could be associated with relatively superficial processing of multimodal stimuli. This result is also significant for the production of news. In our study, participants made decisions about which news posts (and memes) they wanted to read in less than 6 s. To be sure, this finding applies only to our sample of participants and requires further investigation.

Our findings also show that, for users in our sample, the consumption of news on Facebook was not exclusively triggered by the relevance of the subject matter of the news—as most studies contend—but that was also significantly conditioned by visual stimuli. Iconic elements were the visual entry point to interact with news 79% of the times. On 28% of occasions, participants immediately look at the headline right after examining an image.

The very same notion of "consumption" can be misleading in that it evokes an image of similarity in user behavior. In many ways, it standardizes how users can interact with the news and the significance of these interactions. To speak of "incidental consumption" thus suggests that, when people encounter news they did not purposefully seek, they behave in the same way. However, participants in our study did different things when they encountered news on social media. For this reason, Mitchelstein et al. (2020) argue for considering incidental consumption "on a continuum, rather than as an either-or phenomenon" (13). In a similar manner, our study participants engaged in differentiated reading sequences (that is, combinations of visual steps where particular elements of news posts are looked at). The only relatively common mechanism in our study was to begin examining news posts by looking at images first and then assessing the headline. But, as noted earlier, there were more than 40 different sequences that characterized interaction with the news. These reading sequences tended to incorporate either two or three steps, but usually not more than that. This provides an important supplement to research on the phases of incidental consumption reviewed earlier. By focusing on mechanisms, our research suggests that attention sequences to news on Facebook are neither linear nor follow any particular order.

By combining different methods, we sought to overcome the perils of self-reported data. Eye tracking sessions helped us identify some of the concrete mechanisms that might shape incidental news consumption. Interviews offered a means to add nuance and detail to these mechanisms. Scraping data from Facebook then provided us with an opportunity to triangulate data sources and situate findings from small groups of participants within aggregate user behavior. They also helped us place findings within longitudinal perspective.

There were several consistencies between the data gathered from these three different methods. For example, participants in eye tracking sessions paid more attention to content that tends to receive more engagement (that is, news about non-public issues, particularly *sucesos* and sports). Data collected at the aggregate level, eye tracking sessions, and interviews also revealed the significance of specific contexts (such as a presidential election) in modifying user behavior. In our results, news articles about LGBT issues—a prominent theme in the Costa Rican 2018 election—received relatively more attention than they typically get. However, triangulating methods also made it possible to identify differences in findings from certain data collection procedures. For example, eye tracking sessions offered a way to counterbalance accounts offered by interviewees about the centrality of their trust in media outlets as a trigger of attention or the prominence of the subject matter of the news.

Conclusion

To conclude, it is important to note some of the limitations of our research. Some limitations are derived from the exploratory nature of this study. Our data came from 41 college students (or graduates) in one specific country (Costa Rica). We examined specifically three minutes of their visual interactions with content on Facebook on a desktop computer, and then interviewed them for an average of twenty minutes. We then compared findings with scraped data about user engagement with content on Facebook. Because of its exploratory nature, this study sought to gain further insight into the mechanisms of incidental news consumption. We privileged a relatively more natural setting to conduct the research (since the content came from the real News Feed of users). Yet, the lack of experimental control limits the potential for the generalization of our findings. Moreover, since Facebook's content changes each time a person logs on, it is reasonable to suspect that the number of news items that participants in our study incidentally encountered could vary.

As noted in the previous paragraph, our eye tracking sessions and interviews focused primarily on college students. This might explain why certain subject matters received more attention from participants than expected (e.g. science and technology). This specific population is appropriate for this kind of studies because the phenomenon of incidental news consumption is particularly relevant for those who are less interested in the news (Fletcher and Nielsen 2018). However, some research suggests that there are significant differences in how people aged 20 to 30 years old use social media (Perrin and Anderson 2019). Although this difference is less substantial in the case of Facebook compared to other social media platforms, it still suggests that more precision might be necessary to analyze how college students encounter certain types of content, such as news. Recent studies also indicate that less educated people "are more likely to be incidentally exposed news users than [...] educated people" (Goyanes 2019, 725). For this reason, college students might be incidentally exposed to fewer news articles than other segments of the public.

Thus, it would be important to conduct similar studies with older users to help confirm some of our findings for people who tend to be more interested in following media organizations on Facebook or who receive different kinds of news. For example, given that a relatively high percentage of the variance in temporal attention to the news was explained by specific participants, it would be relevant to consider groups of Facebook users from different age groups, educational backgrounds, and geographic locations.

Finally, we collected the data (both eye tracking sessions and interviews) exactly one month after the presidential election. It could be argued that this qualifies as a transitional period between moments of unusual interest in public affairs and everyday politics when non-public affairs are more prominent (Boczkowski and Mitchelstein

2013; Siles, Carazo, and Tristán 2020; Tristán, Álvarez, and Siles 2020). We could expect to find different user behaviors if data were collected during either elections or post-electoral contexts (rather than their transition).

Despite the cautions, we believe the results presented in this article open valuable directions for future research. It would be important to determine how many news items do users in other contexts encounter on their News Feeds. This would help to further make sense of the significance of our findings (most notably the specific percentage of news that our study participants encountered). Moreover, further research could assess how patterns of attention and interaction with news posts compare to non-news items, given their prevalence in the content displayed on study participants' News Feed. Our comparison with non-news items, for example, revealed that were no major differences in the time that participants spent looking at news and memes. It would also be appropriate to compare forms of interaction with different kinds of content and to examine what users remember from their interactions with both news and memes at a later time.

An important limitation of this exploratory study comes from investigating news consumption in desktop devices. Recent research has indicated this is a relatively uncommon form of interacting with the news, notably among younger generations (Newman et al. 2019). Comparing these results with similar studies for news consumption on smartphones could provide a more nuanced account of what interacting with incidental news means in practice. This is not only because smartphones represent a relatively more natural setting for receiving news, but also because recommendation algorithms typically adjust to the technological device that users employ to access apps such as Facebook.

Finally, our study began investigating the procedures and operations that shape visual interaction with news on Facebook. To expand the results, research would benefit from a much more thorough investigation of the time that users spend on interacting with the news and, more precisely, of how long it takes to read complex news and actually understand them. This would provide more empirical data to support (or problematize) the recent push for "slower, better news" in the journalistic field (Luo 2019).

Acknowledgements

We also thank Brayan Rodríguez and Larissa Tristán for their help in conducting the research. We thank Carolina Carazo, Amy Ross, the anonymous reviewers, and the journal's editors for their most helpful comments on previous versions of this article.

Disclosure Statement

No potential conflict of interest was reported by the author(s).

Funding

This work was supported by Universidad de Costa Rica's Espacio de Estudios Avanzados (UCREA).

ORCID

Ignacio Siles http://orcid.org/0000-0002-9725-8694

References

Ahmadi, Mousa, and Donghee Y. Wohn. 2018. "The Antecedents of Incidental News Exposure on Social Media." *Social Media + Society* (April–June): 1–8.

Arndt, Jana, Anne Schüler, and Katharina Scheiter. 2015. "Text–Picture Integration: How Delayed Testing Moderates Recognition of Pictorial Information in Multimedia Learning." *Applied Cognitive Psychology* 29 (5): 702–712.

Bateman, John A., Janina Wildfeuer, and Tuomo Hiipala. 2017. *Multimodality: Foundations, Research and Analysis, a Problem-Oriented Introduction*. Berlin: De Gruyter.

Bergström, Annika, and Maria Jervelycke Belfrage. 2018. "News in Social Media: Incidental Consumption and the Role of Opinion Leaders." *Digital Journalism* 6 (5): 583–598.

Boczkowski, Pablo J., and Eugenia Mitchelstein. 2013. *The News Gap: When the Information Preferences of the Media and the Public Diverge*. Cambridge, MA: MIT Press.

Boczkowski, Pablo J., Eugenia Mitchelstein, and Mora Matassi. 2018. "'News Comes across When I'm in a Moment of Leisure': Understanding the Practices of Incidental News Consumption on Social Media." *New Media & Society* 20 (10): 3523–3539.

Bode, Leticia, Emily K. Vraga, and Sonya Troller-Renfree. 2017. "Skipping Politics: Measuring Avoidance of Political Content in Social Media." *Research & Politics* 4 (2): 205316801770297–205316801770299.

Corbin, Juliet, and Anselm Strauss. 2015. *Basics of Qualitative Research: Techniques and Procedures for Developing Grounded Theory* (4th ed.). Los Angeles: Sage.

de Vreese, Claes, Frank Esser, 2016. and, and David N. Hopmann. *Comparing Political Journalism*. London: Routledge.

Diakopoulos, Nicholas. 2019. *Automating the News: How Algorithms Are Rewriting the Media*. Cambridge, MA: Harvard University Press.

Fletcher, Rirchard, and Rasmus K. Nielsen. 2018. "Are People Incidentally Exposed to News on Social Media? a Comparative Analysis." *New Media & Society* 20 (7): 2450–2468.

Goyanes, Manuel. 2020. "Antecedents of Incidental News Exposure: The Role of Media Preference, Use and Trust." *Journalism Practice* 14 (6): 714–729.

Grigaliūnaitė, Viktorija, Lina Pilelienė, and Arvydas P. Bakanauskas. 2016. "The Analysis of the Influence of Internal Factors on Outdoor Advertising Effectiveness." *Research for Rural Development* 2 (2): 166–173.

Holsanova, Jana, Henrik Rahm, and Kenneth Holmqvist. 2006. "Entry Points and Reading Paths on Newspaper Spreads: Comparing a Semiotic Analysis with Eye Tracking Measurements." *Visual Communication* 5 (1): 65–93.

Just, Marcel A., and Patricia A. Carpenter. 1980. "A Theory of Reading: From Eye Fixations of Comprehension." *Psychological Review* 87 (4): 329–354.

Kim, Yonghwan, Hsuan-Ting Chen, and Homero G. de Zuñiga. 2013. "Stumbling upon News on the Internet: Effects of Incidental News Exposure and Relative Entertainment Use on Political Engagement." *Computers in Human Behavior* 29 (6): 2607–2614.

King, Andy J., Nadine Bol, R. Glenn Cummins, and Kevin K. John. 2019. "Improving Visual Behavior Research in Communication Science: An Overview, Review, and Reporting Recommendations for Using Eye-Tracking Methods." *Communication Methods and Measures* 13 (3): 149–177.

Kligler-Vilenchik, Neta, Alfred Hermida, Sebastián Valenzuela, and Mikko Villi. 2020. "Studying Incidental News: Antecedents, Dynamics and Implications." *Journalism* 21 (8): 1025–1030.

Kress, Gunther, and Theo van Leeuwen. 2001. *Multimodal Discourse: The Modes and Media of Contemporary Communication*. London: Hodder Education.

Kress, Gunther. 2010. *Multimodality: A Social Semiotic Approach to Contemporary Communication*. London: Routledge.

Kurzhals, Kuno, Brian D. Fisher, Michael Burch, and Daniel Weiskopf. 2016. "Eye Tracking Evaluation of Visual Analytics." *Information Visualization* 15 (4): 340–358.

Latinobarómetro 2018. *Informe 2018*. Santiago: Corporación Latinobarómetro.

Lee, Jae Kook, and Eunyi Kim. 2017. "Incidental Exposure to News: Predictors in the Social Media Setting and Effects on Information Gain Online." *Computers in Human Behavior* 75: 1008–1015.

Liversedge, Simon P., Iain Gilchrist, and Stefan Everling (Eds.). *The Oxford Handbook of Eye Movements*. Oxford: Oxford University Press.

Luo, Michael. 2019. "The urgent quest for slower, better news." https://www.newyorker.com/culture/annals-of-inquiry/the-urgent-quest-for-slower-better-news

Matthes, Jörg, Andreas Nanz, Marlis Stubenvoll, and Raffael Heiss. 2020. "Processing News on Social Media: The Political Incidental Exposure Model (PINE)." *Journalism* 21 (8): 1031–1048.

Meijer, Irene Costera, and Tim G. Kormelink. 2015. "Checking, Sharing, Clicking and Linking." *Digital Journalism* 3 (5): 664–679.

Mitchelstein, Eugenia, Pablo J. Boczkowski, Keren Tenenboim-Weinblatt, Kaori Hayashi, Mikko Villi, and Neta Kligler-Vilenchik. 2020. "Incidentality on a Continuum: A Comparative Conceptualization of Incidental News Consumption." *Journalism* 21 (8): 1136–1153. in press.

Napoli, Philip M. 2015. "Social Media and the Public Interest: Governance of News Platforms in the Realm of Individual and Algorithmic Gatekeepers." *Telecommunications Policy* 39 (9): 751–760.

Newman, Nic, Richard Fletcher, Antonis Kalogeropoulos, and Rasmus K. Nielsen. 2019. *Reuters Institute Digital News Report 2019*. Oxford: University of Oxford.

Nielsen, Rasmus K. 2017. "Digital News as Forms of Knowledge: A New Chapter in the Sociology of Knowledge." In *Remaking the News: Essays on the Future of Journalism Scholarship in the Digital Age*, edited by Pablo J. Boczkowski and C. W. Anderson, 91–109. Cambridge, MA: MIT Press.

Oeldorf-Hirsch, Anne. 2018. "The Role of Engagement in Learning from Active and Incidental News Exposure on Social Media." *Mass Communication and Society* 21 (2): 225–247.

Perrin, Andrew, and Monica Anderson. 2019. "Share of U.S. Adults Using Social Media, Including Facebook, is Mostly Unchanged Since 2018." Pew Research Center. https://www.pewresearch.org/fact-tank/2019/04/10/share-of-u-s-adults-using-social-media-including-facebook-is-mostly-unchanged-since-2018/

Pignataro, Adrián, and Ilka Treminio. 2019. "Reto económico, valores y religión en las elecciones nacionales de Costa Rica 2018." *Revista de ciencia política (Santiago)* 39 (2): 239–264.

Schnotz, Wolfgang, 2010. and Horz. and H. "Technology and Learning - Supports for Skill Learning: New Media, Learning From." In *International Encyclopedia of Education*, edited by Penelope Peterson, Eva Baker, and Barry McGaw, 140–149. Oxford: Elsevier.

Schnotz, Wolfgang, and Maria Bannert. 2003. "Construction and Interference in Learning from Multiple Representation." *Learning and Instruction* 13 (2): 141–156.

Siles, Ignacio (Ed.). 2020. *Democracia en digital: Facebook, comunicación y política en Costa Rica*. San José: CICOM.

Siles, Ignacio, Carolina Carazo, and Larissa Tristán. 2019. "Comunicación y política en clave digital: Redes sociales y el proceso electoral 2018." In *Tiempos de travesía: Análisis de las elecciones del 2018 en Costa Rica*, edited by Manuel Rojas and Ilka Treminio, 175–196. San José, Costa Rica: FLACSO.

Siles, Ignacio, Carolina Carazo, and Larissa Tristán. 2020. "El "matrimonio gay" como tema electoral en Costa Rica: Eventos mediáticos en sistemas híbridos de comunicación." In *Democracia en digital: Facebook, comunicación y política en Costa Rica*, edited by Ignacio Siles, 207–232. San José: CICOM.

Siles, Ignacio, Pedro, Campos, and Andrés Segura-Castillo 2018. "Sitios costarricenses de noticias en Facebook: ¿Qué "likean", comentan y comparten sus usuarios?" *Revista de Ciencias Sociales* 160 (II): 37–55.

Sülflow, Michael, Svenja Schäfer, and Stephan Winter. 2019. "Selective Attention in the News Feed: An Eye-Tracking Study on the Perception and Selection of Political News Posts on Facebook." *New Media & Society* 21 (1): 168–190.

Tewksbury, David, Andrew J. Weaver, and Brett D. Maddex. 2001. "Accidentally Informed: Incidental News Exposure on the World Wide Web." *Journalism & Mass Communication Quarterly* 78 (3): 533–554.

Thorson, Kjerstin. 2020. "Attracting the News: Algorithms, Platforms, and Reframing Incidental Exposure." *Journalism*, 21 (8): 1067–1082.

Tristán, Larissa, and Mariana Álvarez. 2018. "'¿Brecha de las noticias?'. Una comparación de la oferta y el consumo de contenidos en Nacion.com y CRHoy.com." *Revista de Ciencias Sociales* 160 (II): 57–74.

Tristán, Larissa, Mariana Álvarez, and Ignacio Siles. 2020 "Entre "brechas" y "cuotas" informativas: Tendencias generales del consumo de noticias en Facebook en Costa Rica." In *Democracia en digital: Facebook, comunicación y política en Costa Rica*, edited by Ignacio Siles, 19–36. San José: CICOM.

Valeriani, Augusto, and Cristian Vaccari. 2016. "Accidental Exposure to Politics on Social Media as Online Participation Equalizer in Germany, Italy, and the United Kingdom." *New Media & Society* 18 (9): 1857–1874.

Yadamsuren, Borchuluun, and Sanda Erdelez. 2016. *Incidental Exposure to Online News*. San Rafael, CA: Morgan & Claypool.

Zambarbieri, Daniela, Elena Carniglia, and Carlo Robino. 2008. "Eye Tracking Analysis in Reading Online Newspapers." *Journal of Eye Movement Research* 2 (4): 1–8.

Zantides, Evripides, and Evangelo Kourdis. 2014. "Graphism and Intersemiotic Translation: An Old Idea or a New Trend in Advertising?" *Image* 19 (1): 54–73.

Zuñiga, Homero G. de., Brian Weeks, and Alberto Ardèvol-Abreu. 2017. "Effects of the News-Finds-Me Perception in Communication: Social Media Use Implications for News Seeking and Learning about Politics." *Journal of Computer-Mediated Communication* 22 (3): 105–123.

Between Attack and Resilience: The Ongoing Institutionalization of Independent Digital Journalism in Brazil

Sarah Anne Ganter and Fernando Oliveira Paulino

ABSTRACT
Digital journalism in Brazil is dominated by a few big players and has recently been threatened by the country's challenging political and economic environment. Still, organizational structures promoting independent digital journalism (IDJ) persist. Originally understood as "the blogosphere," independent digital journalism in Brazil (IDJB) quickly evolved into several professionalized initiatives and now consists of dozens of news organizations. This article contributes to the field by (a) adding to scholarly conceptualizations of independent journalism in North America, Europe, and Latin America through the idea of "positive dependence" and (b) refining the understanding of IDJ in times of acute crisis. Based on an analysis of six emblematic cases, we show that IDJB is relational and distinct and that it functions without clearly defined boundaries. We further find that this relationality is necessary for IDJB to survive the attacks it faces. Different support networks shape "models of resilience" that, while not perfect, facilitate the institutionalization of IDJB by allowing for the slow but ongoing creation of new structures within the news ecosystem. Thus, the findings of this study suggest that the continuing institutionalization of IDJB and its particular characteristics contributes to the creation of a more diverse news ecosystem.

Introduction

Independent digital journalism (IDJ) has flourished over the last decade in Brazil, and in doing so, has prompted the diversification of a Brazilian media system historically characterized by high levels of political parallelism and ownership concentration (De Albuquerque 2005, 2013; Matos 2012). Recurring political and economic unrest is nothing new to Brazil, and the country currently faces unstable politics relating to a shift to the extreme right since the 2018 election of President Jair Bolsonaro. This situation coincides with deep political polarization, economic challenges, and an increased distrust of democracy (Sponholz and Christofoletti 2019), which this article will show pose important challenges in terms of safety for independent journalism. Since large media conglomerates dominate public commentaries and reporting on political, economic, and socio-cultural tensions (Matos 2012), attempts to institutionalize journalistic structures that operate outside mainstream media have increased, despite the many threats these independent news organizations face.

Building on new institutionalism and the news literature (Kaplan 2006; Ryfe 2006; Sparrow 2006; Asp 2014), we argue that independent digital journalism in Brazil (IDJB) and its persistence are responses to the various exogenous shocks Brazil is experiencing. The rise of IDJB exemplifies what Ryfe (2006) described as the "interruption of the reproduction of institutional orders" (138). Several scholars have suggested that journalism in other country contexts tends to be homogeneous (Ryfe 2006; Boczkowski and de Santos 2007). In contrast, our findings indicate that the ongoing institutionalization of IDJB counteracts tendencies towards homogenization. In short, in this article, IDJ is viewed as creating change within the news ecosystem by sharing norms, ideas and values with a wider public and creating cultural persistence (see Zucker 1991). Here, institutionalization is an ongoing process, which we understand as the establishment of a set of values, ideas, and rules in society through changes to the news ecosystem. Furthermore, our analysis suggests that IDJB carries important relational aspects that are critical for its persistence. Building on the relational dimensions established in social movement theory (Della Porta and Diani 2006; O'Brien and Evans 2017), we explain how network structures are used to enhance success and longevity. IDJB is, thus, in line with the idea of "networked journalism," which favors the diversification of news structures and contents (Beckett 2010; Ananny 2018; Robinson 2018). Consequently, we argue that IDJB would not persist without what we describe as "positive dependence."

We analyze attempts to institutionalize mechanisms for the production, distribution of, and access to journalistic content outside traditional media. Asp (2014) identified a spectrum of economic, political, and cultural factors that can explain media institutionalization, which we refine based on six case studies emblematic to the ongoing institutionalization of IDJ in Brazil. Specifically, we identify safety for journalism (UNESCO 2007; Henrichsen, Betz, and Lisosky 2015; Orgeret and Tayeebwa 2016; UN 2016; Posetti 2017) as an important dimension of the ongoing institutionalization.

We argue that one of the indicators for this process is that independent digital news organizations in Brazil have adapted models of resilience that, though not perfect, help ensure the survival of the organizations and their journalists in the face of professional, physical, and psychological attacks. We explore this field of tension between attack and resilience that challenges the very understanding of independence. Based on the literature on new institutionalism, independent journalism, resource dependence theory, and safety for journalism, our analysis contributes to the understanding of IDJB and its institutionalization through models of resilience as distinct, relational, and ongoing.

Journalism, the Market, and the State in Brazil

It was only in the 1980s, following the end of the dictatorship, when news organizations began to aggressively commercialize news-making in Brazil (Waisbord 2000; De Albuquerque 2005). Due to the country's history, "commercial" came to mean "opposing the dictatorship," and private media was perceived as democratic (Kucinski 1991). As a consequence, media power was consolidated through the influence of powerful private media companies, such as Globo, which often claim to be more representative than political institutions (De Albuquerque 2013). Additionally, the field lacked clear limitations on levels of foreign ownership and government advertising, making news media susceptible to political manipulation (De Albuquerque 2005; Matos 2012; Rovai 2018), and on policy decisions, such as the privatization of regional wirelines, which stimulated private investments. The result was a market prone to political influence and dominated by ten families until the late 1990s, with Globo being the most powerful player in the media industry (Moreira 2015; Noam and Mutter 2016). Consequently, Brazil now has one of the most commercialized and concentrated media systems in the world (Márquez-Ramírez and Guerrero 2014).

The major media players were the first to take advantage of digitalization, reproducing their offline structures in the online news ecosystem. It was not long before 70% of the online news market was controlled by four large groups: Folhapar through UOL, Telefônica through Terra Noticias, Globopar through globo.com, and Telemar through the iG system. These were the most important founding organizations of digital journalism in Brazil (Moreira 2015; Rovai 2018). Even today, the structural advantages held by these companies determine the country's news ecosystem, and Globo, UOL online, Folha de São Paulo online, and Terra online are still considered Brazil's top news brands (Newman et al. 2018). As in the U.S. (Hindman 2009) digitalization did not lead to democratization in Brazil. On the contrary, the major players gained even more influence as they were better able to reach larger audiences through their digital websites and because of the rise of smartphones as the most popular devices for news consumption in Brazil (Newman et al. 2018; Rovai 2018). With the emergence of new competitors in online news advertising, such as large digital platforms like Google and Facebook, the revenue generated through advertisements was increasingly redistributed (Oliveira Paulino and Gomes 2012; Statista 2019), and news organizations began to depend more and more on digital platforms to reach their audiences and succeed economically (Nielsen and Ganter 2018). Together, these market shifts led to the consolidation of existing structural issues in the Brazilian online news ecosystem, a development that added to smaller news organizations' economic and political struggle to survive (Jenkins and Nielsen 2020).

The Rise of Independent Digital Journalism in Brazil Despite Times of Acute Crisis

New forms of Brazilian news organizations have emerged since 2011 and, most notably, since 2013 (Guazina 2013; Figaro, Nonato, and Kinoshita 2017; Rovai 2018). The urge to create independent journalistic structures is deeply rooted in Brazilian journalism's political, economic, and socio-cultural conditions. Many journalistic entrepreneurs, often journalists trained by the traditional news media, have established media organizations, reshaping the country's news ecosystem. In the early 2000s, digital journalism in Brazil consisted mainly of the online versions of dominant media organizations. However, these traditional forms of journalistic production were challenged by the rise of the Brazilian blogosphere (Guazina 2013; Rovai 2018). The blogosphere developed at a time of significant political unrest and political and economic instability, which frustrated professional journalists (Figaro, Nonato, and Kinoshita 2017) and traditional news organizations, which struggled to adapt to the new playing field (Osvald Ramos and Müller Spinelli 2015). During this time, a new form of independent journalism evolved: a professionalized stream drawn from the uncertainties of the wider news ecosystem. The mandates of these new journalistic organizations ranged broadly from commercial to public interest orientations. The attacks the organizations have experienced constitute far-reaching, acute, and multilayered crises that differ from the financial journalistic crises most referenced in scholarly works exploring Western contexts (e.g. Gasher et al. 2016). Despite these complex crisis situations and their intensification into explicit threats to the safety of digital journalists since the national elections of 2018, independent news organizations in Brazil continue to rise.

Reporters Without Borders has repeatedly warned that Brazil is one of the most violent countries in Latin America for media work, particularly for journalists covering corruption, public policy, and organized crime. The situation has worsened since the 2018 election of President Jair Bolsonaro, which marked "a dark era for democracy and for freedom of the press in Brazil" (Reporters Without Borders 2019). Brazil is also listed on the Index of Impunity 2019, established by the Committee for Protection of Journalists (CPJ), which identifies countries in which crimes against journalists are largely unprosecuted (CPJ 2019). Online journalists are particularly exposed and vulnerable to attacks, and as online tools like social media platforms have begun to play more important roles, threats to journalists have complexified (Henrichsen, Betz, and Lisosky 2015; Orgeret and Tayeebwa 2016; Henrichsen 2019; Ireton and Posetti 2019). Female journalists are particularly affected, as they often experience "double attacks" (Henrichsen, Betz, and Lisosky 2015, 43) for being both journalists and women (Orgeret 2016). Potential consequences include personal intimidation, intimidation of sources, financial costs, and damage to credibility, integrity, and confidence and can result in self-censorship. Henrichsen (2019) emphasized that the need for protection grows particularly important in such circumstances and argued that protection must be three-fold, addressing the self, the story, and the different roles (e.g. watchdog, prosecutor, skeptic) of a journalist. Journalists' safety has historically been handled by either international and national nongovernmental organizations (UNESCO 2007; UN 2016) or journalists themselves (Lisosky and Henrichsen 2009; Henrichsen, Betz, and Lisosky 2015). In its current form, however, IDJB offers individual journalists an organizational structure that can enhance their protection on an organizational level. This protection manifests in what we describe as "models of resilience," which foster financial, psychological, and technical support for independent digital journalists.

We argue that the ongoing institutionalization of independent digital journalism in Brazil is part of a broader development of diverse approaches towards a democratic communication system that supports liberation through participative communication. Brazil's media system has been targeted by various reform initiatives focused on equal access, dialogue, and participation beyond what the international system of media development suggests (Beltrán 2014; Torrico 2016; Cruz Tornay Márquez and Oller

Alonso 2018). The reform is partially politically supported through such programs as "Pontos de Cultura," established by the Ministry of Culture, and the organization of and participation in Free Media Forums held in Rio de Janeiro, Dakar, and Tunis since 2008 (Rovai 2018). Historically, however, structural reforms to the media system have been unsuccessful. Civil society actors have repeatedly attempted to push for a reform of the media system, but since political motivation to do so is low, there has been little change on the macro level (Ganter 2018).

We argue that the various shifts established within the media ecosystem, such as the creation of the blogosphere (Guazina 2013; Rovai 2018) and the subsequent rise of new types of media organizations, have created the slow but continuous institutionalization of IDJ in the traditional Brazilian media system. Brazil's political, socio-cultural, and economic crises, which have increasingly led to a crisis of safety for journalists, have not discouraged repeated efforts to institutionalize the country's IDJ. These democratizing efforts go beyond attempts to reform media through policy change. As Osvald Ramos and Müller Spinelli (2015) pointed out in their assessment of the rise of non-profit and impartial journalism in Brazil, it was during times of economic crisis that journalists began to create multidisciplinary teams that worked together to achieve a more just and equal society through the creation of a "space of possibilities" (Ananny 2018, 116) for reflection. The importance of bringing this mission to the heart of society is a major factor in creating models of resilience that enable the institutionalization of IDJB. As Matos (2012) states, media democratization is capable of supporting the country's ongoing political democratization, which has been a primary driver of the rise of IDJ organizations.

This intrinsic motivation is culturally rooted in the need for a democratic media environment, which dates back to the dictatorship (1964–1985). The desire to create new media environments arose, for example, in 1998, when the socio-cultural desire for independent journalism received sufficient political support to create Law 9.612 for licensing community radio stations (Rovai 2018). This was a political decision that substantially increased the number of independent radio stations across the country (das Graças Targino, Portela de Carvalho, and Dias Gomes 2008). Moreira (2015) interpreted this spread of licensed community radio stations as an indication of a socio-culturally rooted need to create independent structures outside Brazil's traditional media system. More recently, the founder of The Intercept Brasil, Glenn Greenwald, noted that the financial support his organization receives shows "a tremendous hunger for independent journalism that is passionate and impactful" (Glenn Greenwald, newsletter, June 17, 2019). In this article, we show how this socio-cultural desire has supported the ongoing institutionalization of IDJB.

"Positive Dependence" as a Conceptual Dimension of Independent Digital Journalism

In the following, we discuss, juxtapose, and connect scholarly conceptualizations of journalistic independence in the North American, European, and Latin American literature. Drawing from this literature, we develop a conceptual approach that considers the complexity of independence and helps us understand and explain IDJB.

Journalistic independence is a broad concept, and its meaning is highly subjective and dependent on context, existing norms, and day-to-day experiences. North American and European scholars generally define "independence" as being free from control, not dependent, and autonomous to ensure authority for journalistic work (Karppinen and Moe 2016; Carlson 2017). Karppinen and Moe (2016) argued that, from a Scandinavian perspective, the relational nature of independence makes it a problematic normative principle. Asp (2014) saw independence as professional norm, but stated that its character can vary, and Carlson (2017) explored this variety in his relational approach to studying journalistic authority in the U.S. as fundamentally social, reliant on context, and constituted through the ongoing "remaking of these relations through interactions among a fluctuating set of diverse actors" (13). Several Latin American scholars (e.g. Assis et al. 2017; Figaro, Nonato, and Kinoshita 2017; Rovai 2018) have explored notions of independent digital journalism as a relational construct. Similar to Holt, Figenschou, and Frischlich (2019), who published a conceptual work on "alternative news media," these scholars (e.g. Assis et al. 2017; Carvalho and Bronosky 2017; Figaro, Nonato, and Kinoshita 2017; Rovai 2018) have emphasized the relational nature of independent journalism in Latin American contexts by suggesting positions that counter or complement the news ecosystem.

Independent digital journalistic organizations are often described as intrinsically motivated, entrepreneurial (e.g. Carbasse 2015; Osvald Ramos and Müller Spinelli 2015; Carvalho de Magalhães 2018), or innovative (e.g. Flores and Marta 2017). For example, Carvalho and Bronosky (2017) use the term "alternative journalism" to describe a kind of journalism that creates a dialectic relationship with the audience, provides a different perspective on reality, and challenges the inflexibility of conventional journalism. "Alternative journalism" is seen as necessary to shape society's transformation through dialectics created through changes within audience–industry relationships (Carvalho and Bronosky 2017). Figaro, Nonato, and Kinoshita (2017), in their article on journalistic work conditions, analyzed media they considered to be outside the traditional news ecosystem and explored working conditions for journalists from "other" media organizations, which they summarized as alternative, independent, collective, entrepreneurial, and innovative journalism. Their findings suggest, however, that the terms are used discursively and are created by their ideological foundations. Consequently, the terms can be used to refer to being free from the influence of political parties, religion, and large enterprises or to refer to any "counter-hegemonic" journalistic element (Figaro, Nonato, and Kinoshita 2017). In this context, the word "relational" refers to different notions of independent journalism that are "counter-hegemonic" to existing power structures (Peruzzo Krohling 2009; Carvalho and Bronosky 2017; Figaro, Nonato, and Kinoshita 2017; Rovai 2018). The conceptual work deriving from these Latin American scholars is comparable to Holt, Figenschou, and Frischlich (2019) definition of alternative news media as relational, non-binary, and positioned "on a continuum" (864). In this broader approach, the only way to think about IDJ is in relation to hegemony, implying not dependence on but reaction to the traditional news ecosystem. For example, Assis et al. (2017) defined independent media as activist initiatives working together against economic power. Similarly, Rovai (2018) used the term *"jornalismo livre"* (free journalism) (34), which he defined as existing in opposition but also linked to large media organizations. Accordingly, he defined *"medialivrismo"* as a politically motivated strategy: "a tactic and technique, a way to create communication that is independent from traditional structures" (Rovai 2018, 40, our translation), by which he means not organizationally constituted.

On the contrary, in this article, we explore those types of IDJ that are embedded within organizations and, therefore, still adhere to highly professionalized structures. We conceptualize independent digital journalism in a non-monolithic frame, which considers that IDJ is discussed in the literature without any clearly defined boundaries. In the following, we systematize this broad perspective by categorizing the six emblematic cases as counter-hegemonic, niche, community, and entrepreneurial types of independent digital journalism in Brazil. We establish this systematization by analyzing the six cases according to the goals of their particular mandates, their structures, their main actors, the specific types of influence they experience, and the different types of relations they maintain.

We use this broader relational approach to study IDJ by building on the literature on safety for journalism (UNESCO 2007; Orgeret and Tayeebwa 2016; Posseti 2017; Henrichsen 2019) and resource dependence theory as established in social movement theory (see Della Porta and Diani 2006; O'Brien and Evans 2017). Drawing from these different areas of scholarly work and the data analysis, we establish a new notion we refer to as "positive dependence." We argue that, in countries in which attacks on journalism rise in states of crisis, being relational can provide security for IDJ. We establish our argument by enriching the relational understanding employed for example by Carlson (2017) and Holt, Figenschou, and Frischlich (2019) with work from Latin American scholars (e.g. Assis et al. 2017; Carvalho and Bronosky 2017; Figaro, Nonato, and Kinoshita 2017; Rovai 2018) who have described IDJ in a way that considers opportunities of empowerment through this relationality. This understanding is the basis for what we establish as the "positive dependence" of digital independent journalism in Brazil.

Methodology

We based our analysis on a data corpus that combines document analysis, industry data, and interviews with actors involved with the ongoing institutionalization of IDJB, studying the cases of Agência Pública,[1] Brasil 247, Poder360, Nexo, The Intercept Brasil, and Metrópoles. These organizations were selected for their established organizational structures and ability to reach solid audience bases while pursuing different organizational mandates and following different editorial philosophies. All of them self-identify as news organizations that present IDJ and that have survived, so far, Brazil's turbulent political and economic environment. They are what Flyvbjerg (2001) described as "emblematic cases" (78): they are illustrative and informative, rather than average. Comparing them enables us to identify patterns of IDJB and strategies of economic and political survival. In addition to using information available from each organization's websites, reports, and ministry documents, in 2019, we conducted Skype interviews with five high-level representatives, including founders and editors-in-chief of the different journalistic initiatives. We used an interview guideline as the basis for our semi-structured interviews, which were conducted in Portuguese and translated by the authors into English when needed for quotes. The guideline posed questions concerning (a) the organizations' missions and mandates; (b) business models and financial means; (c) forms of access to non-monetary resources; (d) socio-political delimitations and attacks; and (e) strategies of resilience. All interviewees gave their consent for their interviews to be used for this publication. Both authors analyzed the interviews independently. Using thematic analysis, we organized the material according to themes (Herzog, Handke, and Hitters 2019) we identified across the different organizations, then compared and structurally organized the themes into patterns that describe IDJB conceptually. Based on our data, we identified the relevant actors, challenges, and mandates of the selected organizations and inductively generated conclusions regarding Brazil's panorama of digital independent journalism. We triangulated the data by contrasting our analysis and contextualizing documentary information with the data obtained from the interviews (Flick 2011). The draft version of the article was shared with our interviewees to give them the opportunity to comment and provide feedback on our findings to increase the validity of our interpretations (see e.g: Ganter and Ortega 2019).

The Ongoing Institutionalization of Independent Digital Journalism in Brazil

In the following section, we analyze six emblematic cases of organizations that represent different forms of independent digital journalism in Brazil. We show that IDJB is (1) distinct, as it assumes many different forms and mandates; (2) relational and embedded within wider networks, protecting it from attacks; and (3) involved in an ongoing process of institutionalization, as different models of resilience are built out of a socio-cultural desire to diversify Brazil's media landscape and the fundamental need to enhance the safety of digital journalists in the country.

Distinct Mandates of Independent Digital Journalism in Brazil

While IDJ first developed slowly in Brazil, 2013 saw an explosion of related initiatives (Figaro, Nonato, and Kinoshita 2017). We argue that IDJB organizations have different and potentially overlapping motivations (Figure 1). While some IDJ organizations lean towards entrepreneurial motivations, others are driven by political and socio-cultural interests. Consequently, IDJB is distinct and can be represented by more than one type of organization across different dimensions of the spectrum (Figure 1). Among our six emblematic cases, we identified four forms of organizations according to their mandates, structures, main actors, specific types of influence, and different types of relations.

Economic sustainability is an important organizational mandate in the entrepreneurial forms of IDJB. To survive, news organizations can view news primarily as a business, as is the case with Metrópoles (see Figure 1), or understand the economic aspects of IDJ as necessary parts of professional journalism, as in the case of Poder360 and The Intercept Brasil (see Figure 1). Metrópoles follows a concept of "service journalism," meaning that it aims to reach larger audiences by providing quality journalistic coverage that adapts to what audiences want (Interview with Lilian Tahan, director,

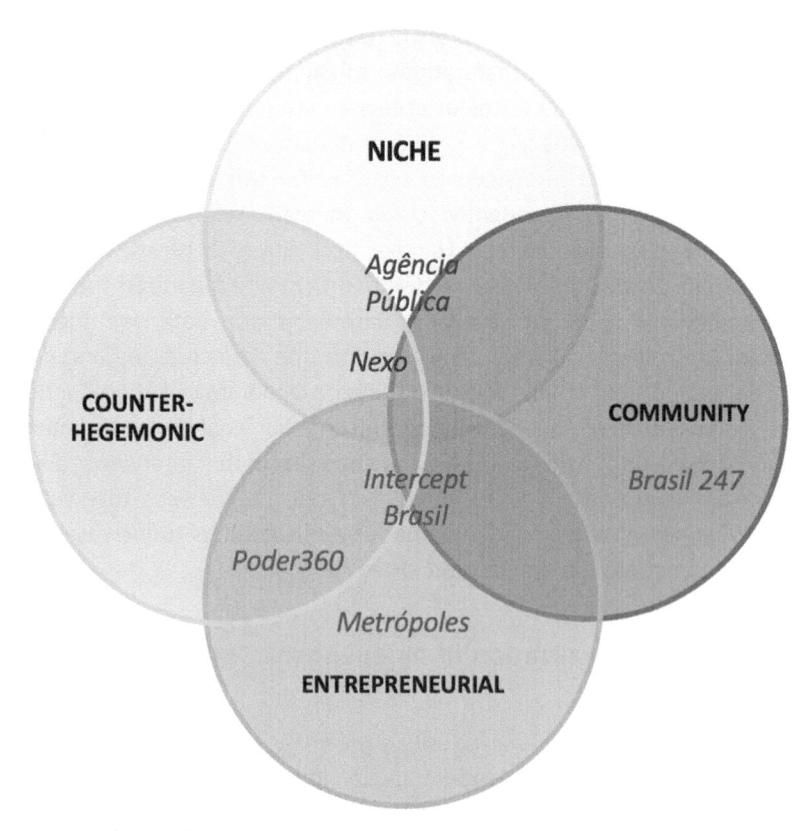

Figure 1. Distinct forms of IDJB and the distribution of emblematic cases.

Metrópoles, 2019). When Metrópoles was founded in 2016, "the managerial leadership of the group reasoned that, in a time of technological transitions, new windows of business opportunities can be identified in the market" (Interview with Lilian Tahan, director, Metrópoles, 2019). Whereas Metrópoles is part of a large group, however, Poder360 lacks external associates and investors and has a much smaller social media presence.

In our interviews, most other organizations presented their primary motivations as socio-political. These cases viewed the diversification of perspectives, angles, and topics to be a necessary response to the country's troubled economic and political situation: "A part of the public has been waiting for decades for more diversity in political news reporting. The founders of Nexo see journalism as a powerful tool to strengthen the overall quality of public debates and democracy in Brazil" (Interview with Paula Miraglia, co-founder and general director, Nexo, 2019). Nexo's editorial principles include balance, clarity, and transparency (Nexo 2019). When they launched Nexo in 2015, during a tumultuous political moment,[2] the founders felt the need to contribute to the public environment by allowing the public to more easily understand what was happening in Brazil. This goal could be achieved through "explanatory journalism," an educational and interactive form of journalism (Interview with Paula Miraglia, co-founder and general director, Nexo, 2019). The founders of Nexo identified the need to establish "explanatory journalism" as a niche in which the organization was able to operate as a non-profit entity.

While Nexo's editorial mission is to enhance democratization through information, other organizations position themselves as more clearly counter-hegemonic, seeking to question those in power (Nexo 2019). The Intercept Brasil, for example, describes itself as "a news agency dedicated to using activist and adventurous journalism to hold those in power responsible" (The Intercept Brasil 2019). Founded in 2016 with private money by Glenn Greenwald and inspired by a U.S. pilot project founded in 2014, The Intercept Brasil was created during the post-Snowden era (Interview with Leandro Demori, executive editor, The Intercept Brasil, 2019). Its work has a strong counter-hegemonic element, as highlighted in the following quote:

> Glenn [Greenwald] was inspired by the frustrations he experienced when trying to distribute journalistic work on the Snowden case in Brazil. As a consequence, he thought that it was necessary to have a network of enough independent media which would be able to distribute materials easier in the future, even though these materials were in opposition to the ruling political and economic interests. (Interview with Leandro Demori, executive editor, The Intercept Brasil, 2019)

Similar to Nexo, The Intercept Brasil seeks to impact citizens' everyday lives. Further, like Agência Pública, The Intercept Brasil advocates investigative journalism that confronts the established system; the organization is known for rigorous fact-checking and a focus on human rights issues (Agência Pública 2019; The Intercept Brasil 2019).

Several of the organizations we studied focus on community engagement (see Figure 1): Brasil 247, The Intercept Brasil, and Agência Pública all involve communities in their work, while other organizations, such as Metrópoles, reach out to their audiences via social media platforms. The motivation behind community engagement is based on the perception that journalism can help achieve much-needed societal change. The collaborative efforts established by some of these organizations are apparent in the roles played by freelancers and volunteers. Brasil 247, for example, explicitly states that it follows a "collaborative philosophy:" the organization employs only 20 staff members, but works with more than 200 volunteers. The organization also actively invites subscribers to weekly meetings to connect the editorial work with the organization's audience (Interview with Leonardo Attuch, founder and editor, Brasil 247, 2019). In a newsletter, Glenn Greenwald emphasized that readers' contributions are fundamental to The Intercept's aim of creating "dense journalism, as done for example during the Brazil election campaign in 2018" (Glenn Greenwald, newsletter, May 17, 2019). This is important to note, since this example shows how communities can be involved and how specific communities may be called upon through crowdfunding initiatives and other forms of private donations.

Recent Attacks on Independent Digital Journalism in Brazil and the Search for Models of Resilience

The current threats to the safety of journalists are central to the work of IDJ organizations in Brazil. We argue that the issue of safety in IDJB triggers ongoing institutionalization, as organizations search for models of resilience to protect their work on various levels (see Henrichsen 2019). Some of the attacks described by our interviewees involved abusive judicial proceedings and the erosion of sources' confidentiality.

Our interviewees' reflections on these attacks highlighted (a) editorial, (b) economic, (c) ideological, (d) psychological, and (e) reputational pressures. Our interviewees also confirmed earlier findings that female journalists are particularly under attack (see Henrichsen, Betz, and Lisosky 2015; Orgeret 2016).

Perceptions of which challenges are the most threatening to IDJB varied among our interviewees. Some believed economic challenges to be the most difficult. For example, in the case of Poder360, "finding a sustainable business model that provides professional journalism" was an important issue because, "without economic independence, there cannot be professional independence" (Interview with Fernando Rodrigues, founder and majority shareholder, Poder360, 2019). Some interviewees described how economic pressure could evolve into editorial pressure. At organizations that emphasize a social media presence, such as The Intercept Brasil, interviewees referred to "a permanent attempt to adapt headlines and texts to the logic of social media (…) And, as a consequence, social media shapes the content" (Interview with Leandro Demori, executive editor, The Intercept Brasil, 2019). While this experience is common to newsrooms around the world, in Brazil, where the need for independent journalism is a socio-cultural factor, these delimitations are seen as particularly harmful, as they create an environment in which it is even more difficult to pursue "reporting which is free from the influence of big corporations" (Interview with Leandro Demori, executive editor, The Intercept Brasil, 2019). In addition to economic pressures and, correspondingly, editorial pressures to work on certain topics and formulate headlines in particular ways, in Brazil, ideological pressures against independent digital news organizations are common and can quickly evolve into physical and psychological violence. Leonardo Attuch explained that:

> (…) while many other news organizations shifted towards the right, we shifted to the left (…) the political environment contributed towards journalists working for Brasil 247, mainly at the end of [President] Dilma's term in government, when [President] Temer was replacing her. During this time, leftist media was seriously discussing the idea of impeachment. (Interview with Leonardo Attuch, founder, Brasil 247, 2019)

The Intercept Brasil has received "public and private threats that are particularly aimed at female journalists." In the current environment, with the rise of the new right, psychological pressure has increased, leading to "collective psychological damage during the elections" (Interview with Leandro Demori, executive editor, The Intercept Brasil, 2019). This environment has also consisted of attacks designed to create reputational damage. Agência Pública, for example, was accused of censorship after a journalist launched an inquiry into Kim Kataguiri, a leader of the *Movimento Brasil Livre* (MBL), to verify information the politician had provided (Agência Brasil 2018; Quadros 2019).

Relational Aspects of Independent Digital Journalism in Brazil and Network Types

We have shown that independent digital journalism in Brazil is distinct, meaning a broad spectrum of news organizations identify as independent digital news organizations. These organizations are sustained through economically, politically, technologically, and socio-culturally enhanced networks. The term "relational" can assume different forms and meanings (see Figure 2) based on context, motive, and network

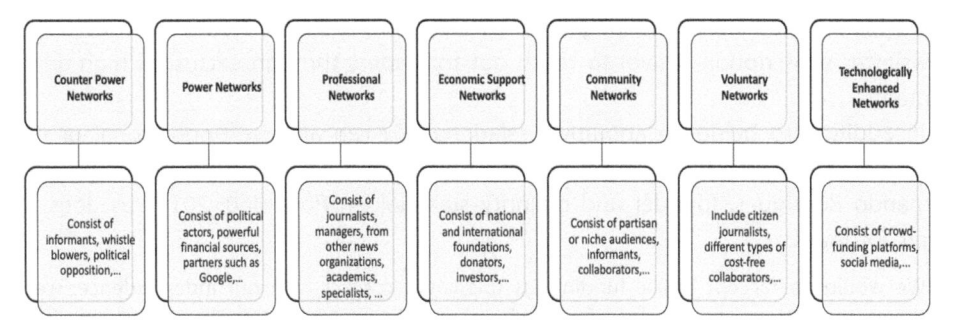

Figure 2. Relational properties and network types of IDJB.

types (Figure 2). Whereas some relationships and interactions are problematic and fluctuating, others are fruitful and help solidify IDJ in the country. Relationality in organizational contexts is often conceptualized using Emerson's (1962) idea of power-dependence relations that establish power asymmetries or, at least, mutual dependence. However, resource dependence theory, as employed in the study of social movements, has described how resource-dependent formation can lead to network organizations that create dense, informal networks critical for goal achievement (Della Porta and Diani 2006; O'Brien and Evans 2017; Segura 2018). These organizational networks that create IDJB embeddedness by relating to multiple and overlapping resource providers enable the emergence of what we describe as "positive dependence:" a situation in which dependence on various collaborators and partners exists, but the diversity of connections distributes dependences and power among different resource holders. IDJB organizations, in particular, accept some degree of dependence because it supports their goals and enables them to push back against the different types of attacks they experience. They achieve this relational power by building what Della Porta and Diani (2006) described as meaningful and engaged relations with networks of supporters of strategic collaborative activities.

The relational character of IDJB is visible in the spaces created for the purpose of interacting. These can be digital spaces, such as social media sites, or physical spaces, such as the Cultural Centre for Journalism, created by the Agência Pública (2019). Brasil 247 organizes meetings with subscribers and invites them to participate in fundamental debates about the organization's philosophy (Interview with Leonardo Attuch, founder, Brasil 247, 2019). Other organizations, such as Nexo, work together with academia to improve their content quality. The Intercept Brasil follows a similar model, as it works in conjunction with other regional news organizations, professors, and researchers to obtain access to information (Interview with Leonardo Demori, executive editor, The Intercept Brasil, 2019). Agência Pública also continually works to extend its professional networks through mentoring programs and training for journalists. Economic support networks include such foundations as The Ford Foundation, Luminate, and Fundação Dom Cabral. However, some of the organizations we studied for this article also collaborate with powerful actors, such as Google Adsense and Outbrain. IDJ organizations are often keen to establish close relations with their audiences. In the case of Nexo, digital forms enhance "the profile and arrangement" by supporting the "establishment of a radical policy of transparency" (Interview with

Paula Miraglia, co-founder and general director, Nexo, 2019). Poder360 uses a daily newsletter subscription (Drive) to reach out to readers through exclusive, high-quality content.

In addition to being collaborative, relational IDJ can also be oppositional or non-relational. Poder360, for example, rejects all governmental funding (Interview with Fernando Rodrigues, founder and majority stakeholder, Poder360, 2019), as does The Intercept Brasil:

> We would not accept public funding, as this could conflict with our independence; we, therefore, distinguish ourselves from other journalistic organizations as based on this decision. Self-censorship is not a problem in our organization. (Interview with Leonardo Demori, executive editor, The Intercept Brasil, 2019)

IDJ news organizations use their networks to build resilience against the different attacks they face. Elements of these strategies vary, but they involve all economic, organizational, legal, political, psychological, technological, and editorial aspects. For all the organizations studied here, strategies to create economic resilience involve the diversification of income sources. In the case of Metrópoles:

> (...) the media group covers 30% of the monthly costs, which creates a huge advantage in comparison with other independent digital news organizations. If the financial side is stable, it is so much easier to produce good quality journalism. (Interview with Lilian Tahan, executive director, Metrópoles, 2019)

The remaining expenses are covered by digital advertisements administered through Google Adsense and Outbrain. Lilian Tahan argued that this cooperation for digital advertising helps "to circumvent that advertisers try to exercise influence on editorial decisions" (Interview, Metrópoles, 2019). However, she also admitted that:

> (...) the model is not ideal, as the hunt for clicks to reach economic sustainability is a problem that can affect journalistic quality, and, therefore, it is important to seek income sources other than advertising, for example through collaborations with foundations. (Interview with Lilian Tahan, executive director, Metrópoles, 2019)

At Metrópoles, the aim is "to reach economic sustainability within the next five years" (Interview with Lilian Tahan, executive director, Metrópoles, 2019). Similarly, Brasil 247 has established a strategic relationship with Google that increases its independence from governmental advertisements. According to its founder, Brasil 247 has been economically stable since 2014 and is "able to think financially in the long term and independently from political and economic interests" (Interview with Leonardo Attuch, founder, Brasil 247, 2019). Poder360 sources a large share of its income from newsletters, advertisements, and sponsored content in the digital journal, as well as from opinion polls (Poder360 2019). In contrast, other organizations collect much of their funding through foundations. Nexo, for example, generates some of its resources through subscriptions, but is also supported through specific investments by Luminate, a philanthropic organization owned by eBay founder Pierre Omidyar.[3] This donated money is "mainly used for the marketing, particularly of the new platform Nexo Edu, which specializes in preparing educational materials to be used in classrooms: content that Nexo has started to sell to schools" (Interview with Paula Miraglia, co-founder, Nexo, 2019).

Other IDJ organizations in Brazil take a broader approach by involving their communities in the pursuit of economic sustainability. In the case of Agência Pública, crowdfunding and other types of reader support make up 35% of financial resources. Other income sources include donations from private national and international foundations (67%), sponsorships (9%), and specific projects (21%) (Agência Pública 2019). The Intercept Brasil combines donations from foundations and crowdfunding activities. It uses the platform Catarse for some of its crowdfunded projects and has reached, at the time of this writing, more than 9,500 contributors.[4]

In addition to using different economic models, some IDJB organizations try to create legal resilience by incorporating protection through legal counselling as a permanent aspect of their work (Interview with Leonardo Attuch, founder, Brasil 247, 2019; Interview with Leonardo Demori, executive editor, The Intercept Brasil, 2019). Legal counselling is important for creating resilience against online threats, hate speech, and other forms of psychological pressure. It is particularly relevant for organizations using social media platforms, which increase exposure to verbal attacks and threats. As Leonardo Demori stated concerning The Intercept Brasil, "when we left our Twitter account unattended for 48 hours, we had to block 2000 people" (Interview with Leonardo Demori, executive editor, The Intercept Brasil, 2019).

In the context of Brazil's current political moment, psychological support systems are created both formally and informally. At The Intercept Brasil, after the last elections, staff members felt the need "to talk, unload, offer tips, and provide compassion" (Interview with Leandro Demori, executive editor, The Intercept Brasil, 2019). Paula Miraglia emphasized that "regardless of the physical attacks, it is necessary to promote debate in a critical context that fosters dialogue in the country" (Interview with Paula Miraglia, co-founder, Nexo, 2019). Brasil 247 is promoting permanent dialogue with other news organizations, such as DCM (Diário do Centro do Mundo), Revista Fórum, and GGN (Jornal GGN), with whom they occasionally produce content (Interview with Leonardo Attuch, founder, Brasil 247, 2019).

Organizational ways of creating resilience include "the facilitation of flat hierarchies, particularly around editorial decisions to foster identification with Metrópoles" (Interview with Lilian Tahan, director, Metrópoles, 2019). Other attempts to create resilience through editorial decisions have been implemented by The Intercept Brasil and Nexo. The Intercept Brasil "seeks to use simple language to reach readers outside of the intellectual bubble" by "develop[ing] a journalism without jargon, without buzzwords, without clichés, without technical language, avoiding political–business bureaucracy," which, according to Demori, is often used "to hide information and avoid debate in sensitive issues, such as the current proposal of pension reform" (Interview with Leonardo Demori, executive editor, The Intercept Brasil, 2019).

Nexo aims for "balance, clarity, and transparency" and attempts to be amenable to its readers' interests. Its decision to offer advertisement-free content is based on the understanding that "advertisements harm the readers' experience" and provide the "wrong incentives when thinking about content types" because, "when revenue is generated by clicks, quality matters less;" thus, Nexo needs to provide "quality content to convince the public to pay for it" (Interview with Paula Miraglia, co-founder, Nexo, 2019). Another important element in the creation of resilience is the training of staff members. Metrópoles, for example, offers courses for its 200 employees through Fundação Dom Cabral, one of its main supporters:

> Nexo offers training to employees, which is also open to the general public in an annual course at Escola N, an initiative that was founded by Nexo as part of the qualification policies established by human resources. (Interview with Paula Miraglia, co-founder, Nexo, 2019)

Nexo has also produced a series of editorial and technological handbooks "to make sure everyone is on the same page and to create clarity with regards to our project" (Interview with Paula Miraglia, co-founder, Nexo, 2019).

Conclusion

Brazil is one of the most violent countries in Latin America for journalists to work in, particularly online and female journalists. Given these conditions, it is surprising that IDJB has continued to develop in Brazil over the last few years. However, we have argued that IDJ network organization structures are needed to enhance journalists' safety by establishing strategies of resilience, which also contribute to the cultural persistence of independent journalism in Brazil's digital sphere. Ensuring journalists' safety has historically been the responsibility of either international and national non-governmental organizations or journalists themselves (Lisosky and Henrichsen 2009; Henrichsen, Betz, and Lisosky 2015). IDJB, however, offers individual journalists organizational structures designed to enhance their protection. This protection manifests in what we call "models of resilience," which increase financial, psychological, and technical support for independent digital journalists through different types of networks. Our data indicate that the relational character of IDJB and its ongoing institutionalization are enhanced by what is known as the "networked society" (Castells 2000): a society that favors the establishment of "networked journalism" (Beckett 2010; Ananny 2018; Robinson 2018). Our understanding of "networked journalism" is not limited to digital networks, but inclusive of socio-cultural networks that transport and shape journalistic practices.

Our analysis shows that IDJB is relational in many different ways and thrives in a variety of network types: professional, economic, counter-hegemonic, community, voluntary, and technological. Looking at social movement theory, we can point to Della Porta and Diani (2006), who have argued that building and using network structures can enhance the success and longevity of causes over time. We have explained that, unlike social movements, IDJB organizations are formalized entities that do not follow one common cause, but still use strategies similar to social movements to enable resilience through entanglements in broad and diverse networks. This enables what we conceptualize as a "positive dependence" on supporters that allows IDJB to remain independent from powerful state and media owner interests. In this study, we have emphasized the role "positive dependence" plays in the ongoing construction of resilience models to show that, even when under attack, IDJ is still institutionalizing in Brazil. Our study, thus, identifies safety for journalism (Henrichsen, Betz, and Lisosky 2015; Orgeret and Tayeebwa 2016; Posetti 2017) as an important dimension of the ongoing institutionalization of IDJB. However, further studies should explore the moral, ethical, and professional dilemmas (e.g. Konieczna and Robinson 2014) "positive dependence" may pose in the future for independent digital journalism in Brazil.

Based on our data, we have shown that IDJB is distinct by identifying different types of independent digital journalism on the broader IDJ spectrum (entrepreneurial, community, niche, and counter-hegemonic). Hence, our findings indicate that IDJB counters tendencies of homogenization in online journalism. The pursuit of independent journalism is about democratizing the media; developing more diverse, more easily accessible media structures and content (Pickard 2006); and supporting a more independent press in a "space of possibilities" (Ananny 2018, 118). The IDJB organizations analyzed here aim at an audience that is otherwise underrepresented in Brazil's highly concentrated media system. The process of establishing independent journalistic structures in the online news ecosystem, like any act of media democratization, may be described as a messy, "contradictory and uneven process involving different groups and strategies" (Freedman and Obar 2016, 12). In the end, creating a network of independent journalistic organizations in a highly concentrated market may be one of many "tiny acts" (Margetts 2019, 108) that can add up to support a more distinct and diversified media system. Together, specific actors, such as journalists, editors, and journalistic entrepreneurs, create a standard of structures, actions, and functions through which distinct forms of IDJ can be institutionalized.

Finally, we have explained that, in Brazil, there is a socio-cultural desire for independent journalism that dates back to the dictatorship experience and has developed further as the news ecosystem increasingly became commercialized and concentrated. As news organizations test different models of resilience, they establish in the short- and mid-term a sense of economic, political, and cultural sustainability, success, and protection. In this way, IDJ organizations in Brazil are able to create cultural persistence by continuing to share their values, ideas, and norms, particularly in times of acute and multilayered crises.

Notes

1. Agência Pública was one of the first IDJB organizations. We reached out to the organization for an interview; however, the organization currently does not grant any interviews for research purposes. Thus, we used data retrieved through desk research.
2. Between 2015 and 2016, a series of protests shook Brazil in relation to "Operation Car Wash," which consisted of a number of investigations into cases of corruption inside the government of President Dilma Rousseff. Hundreds of state officials and politicians were arrested, and the conflict finally led to the impeachment of Rousseff.
3. Nexo received USD $920,000 from the foundation in February 2019.
4. Current numbers can be seen at https://www.catarse.me/users/958285-the-intercept-Brasil

Disclosure Statement

No potential conflict of interest was reported by the author(s).

Funding

This article is funded by Simon Fraser University Presidential Start-up Fund, and by the Editorial Support Fund for Faculty Members with English as additional language granted by the Faculty of Communication, Art and Technology at Simon Fraser University.

References

Agência Brasil. 2018. "Facebook condena ataques a agências Brasileiras de checagem de dados." https://valor.globo.com/empresas/noticia/2018/05/19/facebook-condena-ataques-a-agencias-Brazileiras-de-checagem-de-dados.ghtml

Ananny, Mike. 2018. *Networked Press Freedom: Creating Infrastructures for a Public Right to Hear*. Cambridge, MA: MIT.

Asp, Kent. 2014. "News Media Logic in a New Institutional Perspective." *Journalism Studies* 15 (3): 256–270.

Assis, Evandro D. E., Leonel Camasão, M. R. Silva, and R. Christofoletti. 2017. "Autonomia, ativismo e colaboração: contribuições para o debate sobre a mídia independente contemporânea." *Pauta Geral - Estudos em Jornalismo* 4 (1): 3–20.

Beckett, Charlie. 2010. *The Value of Networked Journalism*. POLIS. Journalism and Society. http://www.lse.ac.uk/media@lse/POLIS/documents/Polis%20papers/ValueofnetworkedJournalism.pdf

Beltrán, Luis R. 2014. "Premisas, objetivos y métodos foráneos en la investigación." In *Communicalogía de la liberación, desarrollismo y políticas públicas*, edited by Manuel Chaparro. Málaga, España: Luces de Gálibo.

Boczkowski, Pablo J., and Martin de Santos. 2007. "When More Media Equals Less News: Patterns of Content Homogenization in Argentina's Leading Print and Online Newspapers." *Political Communication* 24 (2): 167–190.

Carbasse, Renaud. 2015. "Tino, Para Os Negócios E Bom Jornalismo? A figura do jornalista empreendedor nos debates sobre o future da profissão." *Brazilian Journalism Research* 11 (1): 262–283.

Carlson, Matt. 2017. *Journalistic Authority. Legitimating News in the Digital Era*. Columbia: Columbia University Press.

Committee to Protect Journalists (CPJ). 2019. "Getting Away with Murder. Global Impunity Index 2019." https://cpj.org/reports/2019/10/getting-away-with-murder-killed-justice.php

Carvalho, Guilherme, and Marcelo Bronosky. 2017. "Jornalismo alternativo no Brazil: do impresso ao digital." *Pauta Geral - Estudos em Jornalismo* 4 (1): 21–29.

Carvalho de Magalhães, Eleonora. 2018. "Jornalistas empreendedores: o segmento progressista-como nicho de mercadona web." *Aurora: Revista de Arte, Mídia e Política* 18 (32): 110–127.

Castells, Manuel. 2000. *The Rise of the Network Society. The Information Age*. Oxford, UK, Malden, USA: Blackwell Publishers, Inc.

Cruz Tornay Márquez, María, and Martín Oller Alonso. 2018. "Hacia un periodismo-otro: una propuesta de cultura periodistica desde y para América Latina." *Journal of Latin American Communication Research* 6 (1–2): 34–48.

das Graças Targino, Maria, Cristiane Portela de Carvalho, and Alisson Dias Gomes. 2008. "Centro de Mídia Independente Brazil: jornalismo cidadão e democracia representativa." *Artigos. Comunicaçao & Inovaçao* 9 (16): 50–66.

De Albuquerque, Alfonso. 2005. "Another 'Fourth Branch'. Press and Political Culture in Brazil." *Journalism: Theory, Practice & Criticism* 6 (4): 486–504.

De Albuquerque, Alfonso. 2013. "Media/Politics Connections: Beyond Political Parallelism." *Media, Culture & Society* 35 (6): 742–758.

Della Porta, Donnatella, and Mario Diani. 2006. *Social Movements. An Introduction*. Malden, Oxford, Carlton: Blackwell Publishing.

Figaro, Roseli Cláudia, Nonato, and Jamir Kinoshita. 2017. "Jornalistas em arranjos econômicos independentes de corporações de mídia: métodos e análises iniciais." Intercom—Sociedade Brasileira de Estudos Interdisciplinares da Comunicação. 40° Congresso Brazileiro de Ciências de Comunicação Curitiba PR-04 a 09/09/2017.

Flick, Uwe. 2011. *Triangulation. Eine Einführung*. Wiesbaden: Springer Verlag.

Flores, Ana, and M. Marta. 2017. "Innovation Journalism: A Multiple Concept." *Associação Brazileira de Pesquisadores em Jornalismo* 13 (2): 156–179.

Flyvbjerg, Bent. 2001. *Making Social Science Matter: Why Social Inquiry Fails and How It Can Succeed Again*. Cambridge, UK: Cambridge University Press.

Freedman, Des, and Jonathan A. Obar. 2016. "Strategies for Media Reform: International Perspectives Media Reform: An Overview." In *Strategies for Media Reform: International Perspectives*, edited by Des Freedman, Jonathan A. Obar, Cheryl Martens, and Robert W. McChesney. New York, NY: Fordham University Press.

Ganter, Sarah A. 2018. "International Development Aid beyond Money: The Push and Pull of Media Democracy Promotion in Three MERCOSUR Countries." *Latin American Journal of Communication Research – ALAIC* 6 (1-2): 116–134.

Ganter, Sarah A., and Félix Ortega. 2019. "The Invisibility of Latin American Scholarship in European Media and Communication Studies: Challenges and Opportunities of De-Westernization and Academic Cosmopolitanism." *International Journal of Communication* 13 (2019): 68–91.

Gasher, Mike, Collete Brin, Christine Crowther, Gretchen King, Errol Salamon, and Simon Thibault, eds. 2016. *Journalism in Crisis: Bridging Theory and Practice for Democratic Media Strategies in Canada*. Toronto, ON: University of Toronto Press.

Guazina, Liziane. 2013. "Jornalismo que tem lado: o caso dos blogueiros Brazileiros progressistas." *Brazilian Journalism Research* 9 (2): 68–87.

Henrichsen, Jennifer R., Michelle Betz, and Joanne M. Lisosky. 2015. *Building Digital Safety for Journalism. A Survey of Selected Issues*. Paris, France: UNESCO Publishing.

Henrichsen, Jennifer R. 2019. "Breaking through the Ambivalence: Journalistic Responses to Information Security Technologies." *Digital Journalism*: 1–19. Online First.

Herzog, Christian, Christian Handke, and Erik Hitters. 2019. "Analyzing Talk and Text II: Thematic Analysis." In *The Palgrave Handbook of Methods for Media Policy Research*, edited by Hilde Van den Bulck, Manuel Puppis, Karen Donders, and Leo Van Audenhove. Basingstoke: Palgrave Macmillan.

Holt, Kristoffer, Tine U. Figenschou, and Lena Frischlich. 2019. "Key Dimensions of Alternative News Media." *Digital Journalism* 7 (7): 860–869.

Hindman, Matthew. 2009. *The Myth of Digital Democracy*. Princeton, Oxford: Princeton University Press.

Ireton, Cherilyn, and Julie Posetti. 2019. *Journalism, 'Fake News' & Disinformation. Handbook for Journalism Education and Training*. Paris: UNESCO.

Jenkins, Joy, and Rasmus K. Nielsen. 2020. "Preservation and Evolution: Local Newspapers as Ambidextrous Organizations." *Journalism* 21 (4): 472–488.

Kaplan, Richard L. 2006. "The News about New Institutionalism: Journalism's Ethic of Objectivity and Its Political Origins." *Political Communication* 23 (2): 173–185.

Karppinen, Kari, and Hallvard Moe. 2016. "What We Talk about When We Talk about 'Media Independence." *Javnost - The Public* 23 (2): 105–1019.

Konieczna, Magda, and Sue Robinson. 2014. "Emerging News Non-Profits: A Case Study for Rebuilding Community Trust?" *Journalism: Theory, Practice & Criticism* 15 (8): 968–986.

Kucinski, Bernado. 1991. *O que são Multinacionais*. São Paulo: Editora Braziliense.

Lisosky, Joanne M., and Jennifer Henrichsen. 2009. "Don't Shoot the Messenger: Prospects for Protecting Journalists in Conflict Situations." *Media, War & Conflict* 2 (2): 129–148.

Margetts, Helen. 2019. "Rethinking Democracy with Social Media." *The Political Quarterly* 90 (S1): 107–123.

Márquez-Ramírez, Mireya, and Manuel A. Guerrero, eds. 2014. "Introduction: Media Systems in the Age of (anti) Neoliberal Politics." In *Media Systems and Communication Policies in Latin America*. Basingstoke, UK, New York, USA: Palgrave Macmillan.

Matos, Carolina. 2012. "Media Democratization in Brazil: Achievements and Future Challenges." *Critical Sociology* 38 (6): 863–876.

Moreira, Sonia V. 2015. "Media Ownership and Concentration in Brazil." In *The International Media Concentration. Who Owns the World's Media?*, edited by Eli Noam. New York, USA: Oxford University Press.

Nielsen, Rasmus, K., and Sarah A. Ganter. 2018. "Dealing with Digital Intermediaries: A Case Study of the Relations between Publishers and Platforms." *New Media & Society* 20 (4): 1600–1617.

Noam, Eli, and Paul Mutter. 2016. "Brazil-Data Summaries." In *Who Owns the World's Media? Media Concentration and Ownership Around the World*, edited by Eli Noam. New York, USA: Oxford University Press.

Newman, Nic, Richard Fletcher, Antonis Kalogeropoulos, David Levy, and Rasmus K. Nielsen. 2018. *Reuters Institute Digital News Report*. https://papers.ssrn.com/sol3/papers.cfm?abstract_id=3026082.

Oliveira Paulino, Fernando, and Pedro Gomes. 2012. "Lei e direito à comunicação. Padrões normativos e judiciais no Brazil." *Mídia e cidadania: conexoes emergentes*, edited by Cesar Suares Murilo, Martin Vicente Maximiliano, Carlo José Napolitano and Rothberg Danilo. São Paulo, Brazil: Cultura Acadêmica.

O'Brien, Nina F., and Sandra K. Evans. 2017. "Civil Society Partnerships: Power Imbalance and Mutual Dependence in NGO Partnerships." *VOLUNTAS: International Journal of Voluntary and Nonprofit Organizations* 28 (4): 1399–1421.

Orgeret, Kristin S. 2016. "Women Making News. Conflict and Post-Conflict in the Field." In Journalism in Conflict and Post – Conflict Conditions. Worldwide Perspectives, edited by Kristin S. Orgeret and William Tayeebwa. Göteburg: Nordicom.

Orgeret, Kristin S., and William Tayeebwa, eds. 2016. *Journalism in Conflict and Post-Conflict Conditions. Worldwide Perspectives*. Göteburg: Nordicom.

Osvald Ramos, Daniela, and Egle Müller Spinelli. 2015. "Iniciativas de Jornalismo Independente no Brazil e Argentina." *Revista Extraprensa* 9 (1): 114–123.

Peruzzo Krohling, Cicilia M. 2009. "Aproximações entre a comunicação popular e comunitária e a imprensa alternativa no Brazilna era do ciberespaço." *Revista Galáxia* 17: 131–146.

Posetti, Julie. 2017. *Protecting Journalism Sources in the Digital Age*. Paris: UNESCO.

Pickard, Victor. 2006. "United yet Autonomous: Indymedia and the Struggle to Sustain a Radical Democratic Network." *Media, Culture & Society* 28 (3): 315–336.

Quadros, Vasconcelo. 2019. *Kataguiri admite pressão ruralista e de governo em substitutivo contra controle ambiental*. https://apublica.org/2019/08/kataguiri-admite-pressao-ruralista-e-de-governo-em-substitutivo-contra-controle-ambiental/

Reporters Without Borders (RSF). 2019. Country Report Brazil. https://rsf.org/en/Brazil.

Robinson, Su. 2018. *Privilege Shape Public Discourse in Progressive Communities*. Cambridge, UK, New York, USA, Melbourne, Australia, New Delhi, India: Cambridge University Press.

Rovai, Renato. 2018. *Um Novo Ecossistema Midiático*. Ciudad Autónoma de Buenos Aires: CLACSO.

Ryfe, David M. 2006. "Guest Editor's Introduction: New Institutionalism and the News." *Political Communication* 23 (2): 135–144.

Segura, María S. 2018. *De la Resistencia a la incidencia. Sociedad civil y derecho a la comunicación en la Argentina*. Buenos Aires, Argentina: Ediciones UNGS.

Sparrow, Bartholomew H. 2006. "A Research Agenda for an Institutional Media." *Political Communication* 23 (2): 145–157.

Sponholz, Liriam, and Rogério Christofoletti. 2019. "From Preachers to Comedians: Ideal Types of Hate Speakers in Brazil." *Global Media and Communication15* 15 (1): 67–84.

Statista. 2019. *Advertising Revenue of News Corp. Worldwide from 2015-2019 (in Billion U.S. Dollars)*. www.statista.com.

Torrico, Erick. 2016. *La comunicación pensada desde América Latina*. Salamanca, España: Comunicación Social Ediciones y Publicaciones.

United Nations Educational, Scientific and Cultural Organization (UNESCO). 2007. "Press Freedom: Safety of Journalists and Impunity." International Conference on Press Freedom: Safety of Journalists and Impunity. Colombia, Medellín. https://unesdoc.unesco.org/ark:/48223/pf0000156773.

United Nations (UN). 2016. *UN Plan of Action on the Safety of Journalists and the Issue of Impunity*. CI-2016/WS/10. https://unesdoc.unesco.org.

Waisbord, Silvio. 2000. *Watchdog Journalism in South America: News, Accountability, and Democracy*. New York, USA: Columbia University Press.

Zucker, Lynne G. 1991. "The Role of Institutionalization in Cultural Persistence." In *The New Institutionalism in Organizational Analysis*, edited by Walter W. Powell and Paul J. Di Maggio. Chicago, USA, London, UK: University of Chicago Press.

Websites

https://apublica.org
https://cpj.org
https://www.nexojornal.com.br
http://www.poder360.com
https://rsf.org/index.php
https://theintercept.com

Interviews Conducted

Leonardo Attuch, Founder of Brasil 247 (March 25, 2019).
Fernando Rodrigues, Founder and Majority Stakeholder of Poder360 (April 1, 2019).
Lilian Tahan, Director, Metrópoles (April 4, 2019).
Leandro Demori, Executive Editor, The Intercept Brasil (April 30, 2019).
Paula Miraglia, Co-Founder, Nexo (May 7, 2019).

Index

Note: Page numbers followed by "n" denote endnotes.

Aakhus, Mark 26
actors 5, 22, 112, 117, 121
Agência Pública 112, 115, 117, 119, 121n1
algorithms 5, 16, 99
artefacts 5, 22
Asp, Kent 107, 111
assessments 16, 62, 88, 110
attacks 16, 106, 107, 109, 112, 113, 115–118, 120
audiences 4, 5, 7, 8, 10, 11, 16, 17, 19, 21, 22, 49, 108, 111, 113; interaction 5, 49

Bachmann, I. 5, 49
Bargsted, M. 5
Bennett, L. V. 52
Berglez, P. 72
Betz, M. 72
Bloom, T. 63
Boczkowski, P. J. 8, 9, 13, 17, 20, 40, 82, 88
Bode, Leticia 89
Bodrunova, S. 10, 21
Borger, M. 69
Bossio, D. 51
Boulianne, Shelley 41
Bradshaw, Samantha 31
Brady, S. R. 53
Brazil 14, 31, 78, 106–110, 112–121; independent digital journalism in 4–6, 107, 108, 112, 113, 115, 116, 121
Brazilian blogosphere 109
Bretschneider, S. I. 51, 60
Broersma, Marcel 30
Bruns, A. 49

Caracol TV 12–17, 21
Carlson, Matt 111
causality 32, 41
Chile 2, 4, 6, 26, 27, 31–32, 34, 36, 39–41
CityTV 5, 8, 12–19, 21, 22
Cleary, J. 63
Coddington, M. 11

collaborative/collaborations 67, 68, 72–78, 80–82; efforts 68, 73, 77, 79, 81, 82, 115; enterprises 73, 74, 79, 82; journalism 68, 72, 75; projects 4, 68, 69, 73–78, 81, 82
Colombian TV news organizations 8, 20
communities 9, 10, 18, 19, 21, 71, 75, 112, 115, 119–121
competing values framework (CVF) 51–53, 55, 56, 58, 61–63
Costa Rica 5, 58, 60, 75, 86–88, 90, 98, 101
Cremedas, M. 51
Cueva Chacon, L. M. 4

Della Porta, Donnatella 117, 120
demographics 73, 75
dependent variables 35, 37, 54, 55, 76
Deuze, M. 80
D'Haenens, L. 51
Diani, Mario 117, 120
digital culture 15, 69, 80
digitalization 108
digital journalists 14, 69, 79, 82, 109, 113
digital-native organizations 71, 77, 78
digital-native outlets 71, 74, 75, 77
digital platforms 5, 8, 15, 17, 21, 22, 41, 108
digital savviness 80–82
digital technologies 7–11, 13, 14, 17, 20, 73, 81
Dorfman, A. 2

economic sustainability 20, 113, 118, 119
editorial line 59, 73, 80
Ekström, M. 22, 50, 72
Emerson 117
Erdelez, Sanda 88
expert material 73–77, 81
eye tracking sessions 90, 92, 93, 95–98, 100, 101

Facebook 4, 5, 18, 30, 87, 88, 92–94, 96, 97, 99–102; Costa Rican news organizations on 87, 97; news interaction on 86–102; users 87, 90, 101

fact-checking 10, 50, 58, 59, 68, 74, 79, 80, 115; policies 59; sources 79
Fernández, P. 69
Figaro, Roseli Cláudia 111
Figenschou, Tine U. 111
Fletcher, Richard 88
Flyvbjerg, Bent 112
Frischlich, Lena 111
Fuduric, M. 52, 61

Garcia de Torres, E. 49
Garcia-Perdomo, V. 5
Gearing, A. 72
geographic scope 54, 56, 60
Global North 2–6
Global South 3
Goh, Debbie 30
Gonzales-Cordova, M. 71
Gonzalez de Bustamante, C. 70, 81
government funding 54, 58
Graves, L. 68, 72–73, 81
Griffin, J. 49
Gutsche, R. E. 10, 21

Habermas, Jürgen 28
Harlow, S. 4, 49, 71
Henrichsen, J. R. 72, 109
Herscovitz, H. 50
Hess, K. 10, 21
Holsanova, Jana 89
Holt, Kristoffer 111
Howard, Philip 31
Howe, J. 72

Ihlebaek, K. A. 51, 60, 63
incidental consumption, news 86, 87, 93, 99, 100
independent digital journalism (IDJ) 6, 106, 107, 109–113, 117, 120–121; ongoing institutionalization of 113–115
independent digital journalism in Brazil (IDJB) 107, 109, 110, 112, 113, 115–117, 120, 121
independent digital journalistic organizations 111
independent digital news organizations 107, 116, 118
independent journalism 6, 69, 71, 106, 107, 109–111, 116, 120, 121
investigative journalism 68–71, 76, 80, 81, 115; projects 74, 75
investigative journalists 68, 70, 71, 77
investigative reporting 67

Jenkins, J. 73, 81

Karppinen, Kari 111
Katz, James E. 26

Kim, Eunyi 88
Kinoshita, Jamir 111
knowledge 3, 26–29, 31, 33, 37, 39, 41
Konieczna, M. 68, 72
Konow-Lund, M. 72, 73

Larsson, O. 51, 60, 63
Latinobarómetro 87
leadership 80, 81
learning 16, 41, 79, 81, 88
Lee, Changjun 41
Lee, J. 51, 60
Lee, Jae Kook 88
legacy media outlets 75
legitimacy 10, 11, 21
Lewis, S. C. 22, 48
Lisosky, J. M. 72
local communities 5, 16–18, 21
Lysak, S. 51

mainstream media 11, 21, 69, 71, 107
Mandelli, A. 52, 61
Manoharan, A. P. 52
Matassi, Mora 40
Matos, Carolina 110
McLeod, D. A. 53
media 3, 10, 11, 13, 14, 16, 17, 19, 28, 49, 54; companies 4, 13–15; outlets 17, 19, 21, 58, 60, 101; players 108
Meléndez Yúdico, J. 71
memes 92, 94, 98, 100, 102
Meneses, M. E. 70
Mergel, I. 51, 60
messaging apps 31, 36, 37, 39, 91, 93
metropoles 112–115, 118–120
Mitchelstein, E. 40, 82, 100
mobile instant messaging services (MIMs) 27, 29, 31, 32, 39, 40, 42
Moe, Hallvard 111
Molyneux, L. 48
Moreira, Sonia V. 110
motivations 28, 40, 67, 68, 75, 78–82, 115
Mourão, R. R. 70, 81
Müller 29
Müller Spinelli, Egle 110
multimodality 30, 40
multimodal stimuli 87, 89, 100
Muscat, T. 10, 21

Nelson, J. L. 10, 21
networks 6, 10, 17, 113, 115–118, 120, 121
news: feed 90, 92, 93, 95, 102; items 87, 89, 90, 92–94, 96, 101, 102; knowledge 26; media 8, 13, 22, 28, 108; organizations 22, 50, 51, 70–76, 80, 81, 107, 108, 116; posts 87, 89, 92, 95–97, 99, 100, 102; themes 56, 89, 97

INDEX

newsrooms 10–12, 47, 48, 52, 53, 56, 58–60, 62, 63, 71, 72; characteristics 53
Nielsen, Rasmus Kleis 88, 90, 93
Nonato 111
normalization 47–49, 51, 61
North, M. 63

ongoing institutionalization 107, 109, 115, 120
online audiences 12, 21
online journalists 14, 15, 17, 109
online media 5, 7, 8, 12–15, 17–22
online news: ecosystem 108, 121; teams 4, 8, 14
online operations 5, 8, 9, 13, 14
online platforms 8, 13, 15, 20
online spaces 9, 49
online teams 8, 14, 15, 17, 19, 20, 22
online users 9, 11, 15–17, 39
open-ended responses 55, 58, 61
Opgenhaffen, M. 51
Osvald Ramos, Daniela 110
ownership 54, 56, 58, 61

personal/private domains 27–28
Peters, Chris 30
polarization 5, 26, 29, 34, 41, 106
policies 4, 28, 48–53, 56, 58–63
political involvement 27–30, 32
political outcomes 27, 28, 32, 33, 37, 40
political participation 26, 28, 31, 34, 35, 41
political/public domains 27–28
politics 3, 5, 28, 35, 37, 40, 89, 97
privacy theme 59
project management 79, 81
ProPublica 73
public affairs 27–33, 35, 37, 39–41, 88, 97
public sphere 28

qualitative textual analysis 76, 78
quality process 79
Quinn, R. E. 52, 53, 62, 63

radio reporters 77, 82
Relly, J. E. 70, 81
research design 90–92
Resende, Gustavo 31
resilience 6, 106, 107, 110, 113, 115, 118–121; models of 107, 109, 110, 113, 115, 120, 121
Rivera-Rogel, D. 71
Rovai, Renato 111
Ryfe, David M. 107

Sacco, V. 51
safety 6, 78, 79, 81, 106, 107, 110, 112, 115, 120
Salaverría, R. 49, 71
Saldaña, M. 4, 50, 70, 75, 81
savvy digital investigative techniques 74

Scheerlinck, H. 51
Schmitz Weiss, A. 50, 68
scholarship 2, 3, 30, 48, 63, 89
Shahin, S. 55
sharing new skills 79
SMI RED500 eye-tracker 90
social filtering 5, 88
social media 5, 9, 15–19, 21, 22, 29, 47–51, 58–61, 63; analysts 16, 17; audience on 16, 17; guidelines 50–52, 60, 62; platforms 11, 18, 19, 22, 29, 37, 49, 50, 109, 115, 119; practices 48, 49, 60; teams 5, 19; use 4, 28, 47–51, 53, 61–63
social media policies 4, 47–51, 53–56, 58–63; content analysis of 51, 61, 62; perceptions of 58, 59; role of 47, 48
Stonbely, S. 72, 73, 75, 81
Sülflow, Michael 89
Swart, Joëlle 30

technological innovations 8, 11, 12, 14
technology 8, 9, 12, 13, 17, 19–22, 69, 71, 99, 101; adoption of 8, 9, 12, 13, 19, 21
television 5, 6, 8, 9, 12–21, 58
television news, re-digitizing 7–22
temporal attention 94, 98, 101
themes 12, 55, 56, 98, 100, 113
Thorson, Kjerstin 99
togetherness 30
topic modeling 55, 56, 58
transnational levels 74, 77–81
Troller-Renfree, Sonya 89
TV 7–17, 19–22, 53, 77
TV media's transition 9–11

Vaccari, Cristian 30, 31
Valenzuela, S. 5
Valeriani, Augusto 30, 31
variables 33–36, 41, 74, 75
Vergara, A. 5
verification 9, 58, 79
visual fixations 87, 89, 94
Vraga, Emily K. 89

Waisbord, S. 69
Westlund, O. 22, 50, 72
WhatsApp 5, 18, 27, 29–33, 35–37, 39–42; usage 27, 32, 33, 37, 41; variables 36, 37
Wolf, J. 51

Yadamsuren, Borchuluun 88
Yamamoto, Masahiro 31
Young, J. A. 53
young audiences 15, 20, 21

Zelizer, B. 22
Zuñiga, Homero G. de 88